CHANGING CONTOURS OF DOMESTIC LIFE, FAMILY AND LAW

Drawing from a wide range of material and sociolegal methods, this collection brings together original essays, written by internationally renowned scholars, investigating emerging patterns in the shape and form of the legal regulation of domestic relations. Taking as a focus the theme of 'caring and sharing', the collection includes chapters which reflect on the changing contours of what we think of as 'domestic relations'; the impact which legal recognition carries in making visible some relationships rather than others; the potential for normative values carried within patterns of legal recognition and regulation; intersections between private law and public policy; the role of private law in the allocation of responsibility and privilege; the differential impact of seemingly progressive policies on economically vulnerable or socially marginal groupings; tensions between family law models and models carried within other fields of private law; and, unusually, architectures in law and the built environment designed to fac[illegible] ul, pro[illegible] ne, wh[illegible] nd pot[illegible] tic rela[illegible]

Oñati International Series in Law and Society

A SERIES PUBLISHED FOR
THE OÑATI INSTITUTE FOR THE SOCIOLOGY OF LAW

Titles in this Series

Social Dynamics of Crime and Control: New Theories for a World in Transition edited by Susanne Karstedt and Kai Bussmann

Criminal Policy in Transition edited by Andrew Rutherford and Penny Green

Making Law for Families edited by Mavis Maclean

Poverty and the Law edited by Peter Robson and Asbjørn Kjønstad

Adapting Legal Cultures edited by Johannes Feest and David Nelken

Rethinking Law, Society and Governance: Foucault's Bequest edited by Gary Wickham and George Pavlich

Rules and Networks edited by Richard Appelbaum, Bill Felstiner and Volkmar Gessner

Women in the World's Legal Professions edited by Ulrike Schultz and Gisela Shaw

Healing the Wounds edited by Marie-Claire Foblets and Trutz von Trotha

Imaginary Boundaries of Justice edited by Ronnie Lippens

Family Law and Family Values edited by Mavis Maclean

Contemporary Issues in the Semiotics of Law edited by Anne Wagner, Tracey Summerfield and Farid Benavides Vanegas

The Geography of Law: Landscapes, Identity and Regulation edited by Bill Taylor

Theory and Method in Socio-Legal Research edited by Reza Banakar and Max Travers

Luhmann on Law and Politics edited by Michael King and Chris Thornhill

Precarious Work, Women and the New Economy: The Challenge to Legal Norms edited by Judy Fudge and Rosemary Owens

Juvenile Law Violators, Human Rights, and the Development of New Juvenile Justice Systems edited by Eric L Jensen and Jørgen Jepsen

The Language Question in Europe and Diverse Societies: Political, Legal and Social Perspectives edited by Dario Castiglione and Chris Longman

European Ways of Law: Towards A European Sociology of Law edited by Volkmar Gessner and David Nelken

Crafting Transnational Policing: Police Capacity-Building and Global Policing Reform edited by Andrew Goldsmith and James Sheptycki

Constitutional Politics in the Middle East: With special reference to Turkey, Iraq, Iran and Afghanistan edited by Saïd Amir Arjomand

Parenting after Partnering: Containing Conflict after Separation edited by Mavis Maclean

Responsible Business: Self-Governance and Law in Transnational Economic Transactions edited by Olaf Dilling, Martin Herberg and Gerd Winter

Rethinking Equality Projects in Law edited by Rosemary Hunter

Regulating Deviance: The Redirection of Criminalisation and the Futures of Criminal Law edited by Bernadette McSherry, Alan Norrie and Simon Bronitt

Living Law: Reconsidering Eugen Ehrlich edited by Marc Hertogh

Multicultural Jurisprudence: Comparative Perspectives on the Cultural Defense edited Marie-Claire Foblets and Alison Dundes Renteln

Changing Contours of Domestic Life, Family and Law

Caring and Sharing

Edited by
Anne Bottomley and Simone Wong

Oñati International Series in Law and Society

A SERIES PUBLISHED FOR
THE OÑATI INSTITUTE FOR THE SOCIOLOGY OF LAW

OXFORD AND PORTLAND OREGON
2009

Published in North America (US and Canada)
by Hart Publishing
c/o International Specialized Book Services
920 NE 58th Avenue, Suite 300
Portland, OR 97213-3786
USA
Tel: +1 503 287 3093 or toll-free: (1) 800 944 6190
Fax: +1 503 280 8832
E-mail: orders@isbs.com
Website: www.isbs.com

Hart Publishing Ltd, 16c Worcester Place, Oxford, OX1 2JW
Telephone: +44 (0)1865 517530 Fax: +44 (0)1865 510710
E-mail: mail@hartpub.co.uk
Website: http://www.hartpub.co.uk

British Library Cataloguing in Publication Data
Data Available

ISBN: 978-1-84113-904-3 (hardback)
ISBN: 978-1-84113-903-6 (paperback)

Typeset by Forewords, Oxon
Printed in the UK by
CPI Antony Rowe, Chippenham, Wiltshire

Contents

List of Contributors

Cindy L Baldassi is a PhD student at the University of British Columbia, Faculty of Law, working mainly on the definition of family, including immigration and the legal consequences of genetic ties. After finishing her LLB at Osgoode Hall, she clerked at the Federal Court of Canada, and then completed an LLM at UBC, where her thesis focused on the question of treating embryo donations as if they were adoptions.

Anne Barlow is Professor of Family Law and Policy at the University of Exeter. The main focus of her sociolegal research has been on cohabitation law and comparative family law, although she also has an interest in housing, property and welfare law. She has led and co-directed a number of funded interdisciplinary empirical projects in these fields. Her recent publications include *Community of Property—A Regime for England and Wales?* (with Elizabeth Cooke and Therese Callus) (Bristol, Policy Press, 2006), and *Cohabitation, Marriage and the Law: Social Change and Legal Reform in 21st Century Britain* (with Simon Duncan, Grace James and Alison Park) (Oxford, Hart Publishing, 2005).

Anne Bottomley is a faculty member of Kent Law School, University of Canterbury. She has published extensively in the areas of feminist theory, and property and trusts; recently editing (with Hilary Lim) *Feminist Perspectives on Land Law*, to which she contributed a chapter entitled 'A Trip to the Mall: Rethinking the Public/Private Divide'. She is now working on two projects, one focused on community aspects to land holding (a portion of which is represented in this collection), and completing a book (with Nathan Moore) entitled *Cities, Cinema, Control.*

Susan B Boyd is Professor of Law and holds the Chair in Feminist Legal Studies at the University of British Columbia in Canada. She has published extensively on family law reform, the privatisation of economic responsibilities, parenthood law, and feminist legal theory. She recently co-edited *Reaction and Resistance: Feminism, Law, and Social Change* (2007), *Poverty: Rights, Social Citizenship, and Legal Activism* (2007) and *Law and Families* (2006). Her book *Child Custody, Law, and Women's Work* was published in

2003. She held a British Academy Visiting Professorship in 2005. She is Director of the UBC Centre for Feminist Legal Studies.

Alison Diduck researches and teaches in the Faculty of Laws at University College London. Her current research interest in family law and feminist legal theory is in the public and private regulation of intimacies and other personal relationships. Her publications include *Law's Families* (LexisNexis, 2003), *Family Law, Gender and the State* (with Felicity Kaganas) (Hart Publishing, 2006) and *Feminist Perspectives on Family Law* (with Katherine O'Donovan) (Routledge-Cavendish, 2006).

Susan Scott Hunt, Attorney (US), Solicitor (UK), is a Principal Lecturer in Law at Middlesex University in North London. She teaches Equity & Trusts and Contract Law and is the programme leader for the CPE/GDL. Her research interests include Equity & Trusts and feminist legal scholarship. Publications include 'Understanding Equity's Secret Understandings', in Scott Hunt and Lim (eds), *Feminist Perspectives on Equity and Trusts* (Cavendish, 2001), and 'To Pay Suspicious Attention: Following the Weave of "Mixed Logics" in Women's Ethical Decision Making' (2005) 13 *Feminist Legal Studies* 205–37.

Nan Seuffert teaches at the University of Waikato, School of Law, in Hamilton, New Zealand. She publishes in critical legal and race and gender studies as well as in securities regulation. She has recently published *Jurisprudence of National Identity* (Ashgate, 2006) and 'Jurisdiction and Nation-building: Tall Tales in Nineteenth-century Aotearoa/New Zealand', in S McVeigh (ed), *Jurisprudence of Jurisdiction* (Routledge, 2007). She is on the editorial and advisory boards of *Law and Literature* (University of California Press), *Law Text Culture* (University of Sydney) and *Sexualis Lex* (Federation Press, Australia). She teaches Contracts, Corporate Securities and Finance Law and Intersectionalities: Race, Gender, Sexuality and the Law.

Carol Smart is Professor of Sociology at the University of Manchester where she is also Co-Director of the Morgan Centre for the Study of Relationships and Personal Life. She is the author of *Personal Life* (Polity, 2007) and she has also published widely on same-sex relationships, divorce, childhood, cohabitation and feminist sociolegal theory. She is currently working on a number of research projects including on 'family secrets' and on 'family resemblances'.

Simone Wong is a Senior Lecturer in Law at the University of Kent. She teaches Equity & Trusts as well as Banking Law. Her particular research interests include cohabitation and equitable doctrines, especially in relation to home-sharing. Her latest publications include: 'Cohabitation and the Law Commission's Project' (2006) 14(2) *Feminist Legal Studies* 145; 'Would You

Care to Share Your Home?' (2007) 58(3) *Northern Ireland Legal Quarterly* 268; and (co-authored with Anne Bottomley) 'Shared Households: A New Paradigm for Thinking about Reform of Domestic Property Relations', in A Diduck and K O'Donovan (eds), *Feminist Perspectives on Family Law* (London, Glasshouse Press, 2006).

Claire Young is Senior Associate Dean, Academic Affairs and a Professor of Law at the Faculty of Law, University of British Columbia, Canada. She teaches, researches and writes on tax law and policy issues, and is currently engaged in work that focuses on women and tax. Her other research interests include feminist legal theory and sexuality and the law. In 2004 she was awarded the Therese Casgrain Fellowship in recognition of her work on women and economic issues.

1

Introduction
Changing Contours of Domestic Life, Family and Law: Caring and Sharing

ANNE BOTTOMLEY AND SIMONE WONG

CHANGING CONTOURS

WHY DOES, AND why should, the law recognise some domestic relationships and not others, and what is the effect of such recognition or lack of it?

When the contours of family law, in jurisdictions derived from European jurisprudence, were limited to the recognition of (opposite-sex) marriage and legitimate children, the policy issues involved in law were quite simple: the status of marriage, predicated on religious teaching, was the defining factor in carrying a cluster of familial rights and responsibilities. Not only were all other forms of partnership or living arrangements 'external' to the law, but 'why' the status of marriage should be the defining factor was unquestionable.

Three trends, however, have challenged this simplicity. The first was a concern to extend the contours of family law so as to 'recognise' all children, whether born of a marriage relationship or not. The extent to which this has been accomplished (the rights, for instance, all children have in relation to inheritance or nationality) has been uneven both within and between jurisdictions—but the general trend has been one of incorporation. This, of itself, challenges the presumption that it is the status of marriage which remains the core of family law, as legal regimes have moved towards a focus on the parent/child nexus rather than on the legal status of their parents. The second trend has underlined this movement: many jurisdictions, in the context of both a weakening of religious ties and the rise in unmarried cohabitation, have designed statutory forms which recognise what many now refer to as de facto marriage, ie a recognition of 'marriage-like relationships' between opposite-sex partners that simply lack the formal status of marriage. However, despite the general movement across jurisdictions in this direction, this extension of family law has remained controversial for many reasons, and indeed, England remains one of the jurisdictions that has not yet taken this step, despite a recent Law Commission report recommending that it should do so.[1] The third trend has been towards the recognition of same-sex partners in 'marriage-like relationships'. This has taken two forms: firstly, the development of forms of status registration, either (but rarely) marriage per se, or a similar, but crucially not the same, form such as (in the United Kingdom) 'civil partnerships'. Second, in jurisdictions which have developed statutes that recognise opposite-sex cohabitation, the extension of these statutes to include same-sex partners.[2] This trend has also been, unsurprisingly, controversial. One factor stands out at this point: if we think of these extensions of the contours of family law as 'stretching the marriage model',[3] how far can it be stretched? How inclusive can family law be(come)?

As with all 'big' questions, it will become obvious that we can only begin to address this issue by breaking it down into smaller questions. But consider this: in a recent application to the European Court of Human Rights two cohabiting sisters argued that their family rights had been prejudiced by the British government in that, when one of them dies, the inheritance tax which will be due on that estate will be such that the remaining sister will be forced to sell the home which they have shared together.[4] This could be simply seen as an argument about how the British government levies inheritance tax on shared homes, but it is much more than that. The sisters' argument was couched around a challenge to the extension of family law, or rather the marriage (like) element of family law, to same-sex couples under the Civil Partnership Act 2004. Registration of a civil partnership allows the privilege of exemption from inheritance tax, once limited to married couples, to be extended to civil partners.[5] The

[1] Law Commission, *Cohabitation: The Financial Consequences of Relationships Breakdown* (Law Com 307 Cm 7182, 2007).

[2] See eg Australia where subnational statutes have been extended from opposite-sex de facto partners to same-sex partners, and in some cases, even domestic partners in relationships of care and support; see Property (Relationships) Act 1984 (New South Wales); Domestic Relationships Act 1994 (Australian Capital Territory); Relationships Act 2003 (Tasmania). See further S Wong, 'Cohabitation and the Law Commission's Project' (2006) 14(2) *Feminist Legal Studies* 145.

[3] A Bottomley and S Wong, 'Shared Households: A New Paradigm for Reform of Domestic Property Relations', in A Diduck and K O'Donovan (eds), *Feminist Perspectives on Family Law* (Abingdon, Routledge-Cavendish, 2006).

[4] *Burden and Burden v UK* (No 13378/05) (12 December 2006).

[5] All estates are subject to taxation (at 40%) above the exempted level, which for each estate currently stands at £360,000. Between spouses and registered partners, estates can pass free of tax, which often operates so as to protect the family home for the remaining partner. Thereafter, on the death of the remaining partner, the estate becomes subject to tax. In October 2007, the government announced a further privilege for spouses and registered partners: each spouse/partner will be allowed the exemption level of (at present) £360,000, thus on the death of the

sisters argued that to allow same-sex couples such a privilege, and not themselves, was contrary to their human rights.

This argument echoes one that was made during the passage of the Civil Partnership Bill. Why should a sexual relationship[6] be the nexus that allows for (some) privileges to be extended to domestic partnerships whilst other equally socially compelling domestic arrangements are ignored? This argument had been, in fact, mounted primarily by opponents to the Bill, who were looking for ways to jeopardise its passage and were, predominantly, anti-gay. But, despite its providence, as an argument it raises some very interesting issues which were also being voiced by feminists: why limit the privileges of family law to sexual partners, whether opposite or same sex? What is, or should be, the policy grounds for allowing a relationship to be recognised?

It is here that the title for our Oñati workshop, and the starting point for this collection, takes shape. If we leave aside, for the moment, the historical record of marriage as a sexual union, then there seem, to us, to be two reasons why many 'marriage-like' relationships require some recognition in law: recognition which carries a cluster of rights and responsibilities, as well as access to the adjudication of law, and remedies, when things go wrong (most obviously separation), or at particularly vulnerable periods (eg death or insolvency). They are: first, economic vulnerability which has arisen from 'caring' within a relationship and, second, unravelling the consequences of bringing to an end a lifestyle predicated on a commitment to 'sharing'. (Recognising that the latter may be the very reason for taking the risk of becoming vulnerable through the former, or that the former may give rise to the need to engage in the latter.)

As feminists, we recognise that it is 'caring and sharing' which have proven to be particularly problematic for women, both historically and contemporaneously, within marriage and 'marriage-like' relationships. Many women, because of social, cultural, biological and economic factors that remain, tenaciously, central in our society, are still made economically,

second partner the exempted level will be doubled to (at present) £720,000, to the benefit of those inheriting the estate. Obviously limiting such privileges is also contentious in relation to non-married or not registered cohabitants; but both groups can 'opt into' the privilege by marriage/registration. The sisters' point was that they had no means by which to access the privilege.

6 Interestingly the Civil Partnership Act does not, as marriage law does, require a sexual act in order to consummate the status of the relationship in law: thus allowing the possibility of two same-sex platonic friends becoming registered partners. This detail was picked up by some progressive commentators to argue for an extension of civil partnership to opposite-sex partners (platonic or not), who might wish to register a relationship, but did not want to enter into marriage. The government was robust in both pointing out that civil partnership is *not* the same as marriage (which remains in the UK a heterosexual union), and that opposite-sex partners do not require another form of registration other than marriage per se (in contrast to, for instance, the regime in France which allows both same-sex and opposite-sex partners to use the Pacte Civile de Solidarité (PACS), whilst continuing to limit marriage to heterosexuals).

emotionally and socially vulnerable through their relationships with male partners, especially when they have children. This is not to ignore the many advances that have been made by and for women, especially in relation to paid employment, or to ignore the fact that many women are empowered through, and enriched by, their domestic relationships, their marriages and their children. But it is to recognise that women too often remain, within marriage and marriage-like relationships, the economically vulnerable partners whose economic vulnerability is the consequence of those relationships, both in terms of what they have given up to secure them, and in terms of what they have invested through 'caring and sharing'. Although some of us may think that the figure of the 'vulnerable' woman is sometimes too overdrawn (especially when that figure is called upon as a rationale for extending the protection of the law[7]), we cannot ignore the reality of economic vulnerability which so many divorced, separated and widowed women face.

If we recognise that it is not simply the history of marriage status which justifies 'recognition', but such factors as the reality of the consequences of 'caring and sharing'; why should the protection of marriage law be limited to only those who have the status of marriage? But if protection is extended, how should the law recognise those who have need of its remit? To date, protection has been extended through two trajectories: first, an extension of a marriage model to those who seem to conform to being 'marriage-like' (opposite-sex couples living together in a sexual relationship), on the basis of potential 'vulnerability'. The second trajectory operates very differently: the extension of 'marriage-like models' to opposite-sex partners through an 'equal treatment' argument.[8] Both carry problematic issues for feminists. For instance, by extending aspects of 'marriage law' to opposite-sex partners through de facto recognition, it becomes very difficult for women to 'opt out' of marriage law should they wish to. Equally, some feminists have argued that extending 'marriage law' to same-sex partners is to replicate a pattern of patriarchal providence that is neither welcome nor relevant to same-sex partners.[9] Both arguments tap into an ambivalence which feminists have historically held towards the status and practice of marriage, and a concern that law not only 'protects' but also 'regulates'. But recognising that many women remain vulnerable in opposite-sex relationships, whether married or not, and that many same-sex partners demand the privileges of recognition which have been limited to heterosexual relationships (even to the extent of wanting

[7] See eg A Bottomley, 'From Mrs Burns to Mrs Oxley: Do Co-Habiting Women (Still) Need Marriage Law' (2006) 14(2) *Feminist Legal Studies* 181.

[8] See further Bottomley and Wong, above n 3.

[9] See eg R Auchmuty, 'Same-sex Marriage Revived: Feminist Critique and Legal Strategy' (2004) 14(1) *Feminism & Psychology* 101.

'marriage' per se[10]), requires us to think, cogently, about shifts in the contours of marriage, family and domestic relationships. In this context, one way to try and begin to re-engage with the politics of family law is to focus on 'caring and sharing' as the key features of intimate domestic relationships which may justify or require some form of legal recognition. Such an approach allows us to move through a wide gamut of domestic scenarios: from those which, through cultural practices, might involve little active 'choice' in 'caring', through to those in which individuals have proactively chosen to 'share'. It does not need to be limited to sexual partners, or indeed dyadic relations.[11] And it allows us to begin to think about not only 'why' and 'when' some people 'care and share', and with what consequences, but also what the potential role is for law, in its many aspects. We can begin to disaggregate aspects which have been associated with the privileges of marriage law and consider relocating them—for instance, considering the sisters who challenged the limitation of privileges given in relation to inheritance tax might make us think of schemes associated with protecting continued occupation of shared homes, rather than of extending privileges associated with the status of partners. And, meanwhile, we need to be cognisant of the many ways in which, by extending the contours of family law through 'recognition', there has been both an increase in regulation of domestic relationships (a pattern which exerts 'responsibilities' as much as conferring 'privileges'), and trace those aspects of the law which continue to privilege marriage as a heterosexual union, especially when dealing with such crucial issues as inheritance, nationality and immigration.[12] In this sense, changing the contours of family law raises crucial questions not only about who is brought into its remit and with what effect, but the extent to which 'marriage' remains the core. There is, therefore, a tension which runs throughout this collection: on the one hand, we have taken the opportunity to think positively about the potential in rethinking contours through 'caring and sharing', and, on the other hand, we remain, necessarily, very aware of the ways in which present changes in those contours carry elements we have to be very cautious of.

[10] Eg the recent case of the two women, Sue Wilkinson and Celia Kitzinger, who married in Canada, taking their case before the English court for their marriage to be legally recognised in the UK. See *Wilkinson v Kitzinger* [2006] EWHC 2022 (Fam). See also C Kitzinger and S Wilkinson, 'The Re-branding of Marriage: Why We Got Married Instead of Registering a Civil Partnership' (2004) 14 *Feminism and Psychology* 127.

[11] Thus the Australian statutes, above n 2, that have extended legal protection to 'carers', have remained limited to a dyadic model. See further Bottomley and Wong, above n 3.

[12] See further, eg, R Graycar and J Millbank, 'From Functional Family to Spinster Sisters: Australia's Distinctive Path to Relationship Recognition' (2007) 24 *Washington University Journal of Law & Policy* 121. And for an interesting account of the continued privileging of (and support for) heterosexual parenting in France, see V Duverger, 'Who's afraid of Gay Parents?' [Nov/Dec 2007] *Radical Philosophy* 2.

CARING AND SHARING

This collection begins with a chapter by Carol Smart who, drawing from empirical evidence, reminds us that 'families' are formed through the everyday practices of people coming together to share their domestic lives, to share with each other and care for each other, rather than derived from definitions deployed by law. From this perspective 'who' or 'what' a family is, is constituted from social practices rather than a legal formula; such an approach recognises a wide range of 'family practices' which are not easily fixed through a simple definition predicated on status. But Smart also draws from her interviews evidence of concerns that 'family members' have when their relationships are not given some recognition in law: recognition which can facilitate and strengthen their 'family ties', as well as allowing them to access certain benefits. In a sense, approaching the issue of recognition from this perspective suggests that law becomes an issue when it seems to block or impede the development of a sense of family and the full potential of familial practices.

Following on from Smart's chapter, the subsequent chapters are divided into four sections, with each section containing two chapters and prefaced by a short introduction written by the editors. The first, 'Property Division in Couple Relationships', examines alternative possibilities for approaching property distribution between partners at the end of a relationship. The second, 'What Is Fair and To Whom?', contextualises the issue of relationship recognition within broader social policy issues. The third, 'Heteronormativity and Marriage Fundamentalism', examines the ways in which neoliberal politics of governance engender the heteronormalisation of intimate couple relationships, both opposite and same sex. The final section pushes at the contours of domestic relationships through examining forms, or settings, for households which move beyond the conventions of a (private) familial model.

2

Making Kin: Relationality and Law

CAROL SMART

INTRODUCTION

THE MAIN THEME of this chapter will be the way(s) in which English family law seeks to create recognised links between individuals and across generations in order to constitute a family that can be recognised as a legal entity. While the general or popular assumption tends to be that law simply maps itself onto pre-given biological relationships, I argue that the relationship between biological connectedness (now usually referred to as genetic ties) and legal recognition of kin has always been more ambiguous and less straightforward than this. What is more the already complex task of recognising and creating legal relationships has become more difficult as the actual and potential shape of modern kinship continues to change. So it is my argument that we should now resist a continued emphasis on how family law seeks to pin down and normalise kinship (in particular to mould new forms of kinship into pre-ordained patriarchal and heterosexual shapes), and instead focus on how contemporary practices of kinship require law to keep up with rapid changes, thus requiring law itself to be more flexible and fluid. I shall argue in a way that is reminiscent of the early work of Michel Foucault[1] that contemporary law does not (any longer) say 'no' to diversity; rather law is becoming more and more willing to embrace difference. But, unlike Foucault, I do not argue that this is a device for the better regulation of families and populations; instead I suggest law is hurrying along in the wake of changes brought about by people themselves because family law has become a popular site for the cultural recognition of social and affective relationships between adults and children. Put more simply, I shall argue that changes in the ways in which people organise their personal lives and relationships, combined with their desire to achieve legal recognition, is driving the liberalisation of

[1] M Foucault, *The History of Sexuality*, vol 1 (London, Allen Lane, 1979).

family law. It is not, contra Foucault, that family law is casting its net wider and wider to normalise potential diversities.

In this chapter I shall explore these themes in a number of ways. First I shall look at ways of thinking about families through the concept of relationality which has become the cornerstone of important new perspectives on contemporary kinship. Then I shall briefly discuss aspects of the history of family law in relation to parenthood and paternity, and it is here that I shall lay the foundations of my argument that law is a kinning practice rather than a regulatory device. Then I shall ground these issues through a discussion of a recent study on same-sex partnerships and will conclude with a discussion of a significant case concerning the recognition of lesbian motherhood.

RELATIONALITY AS A WAY OF THINKING

In the field of anthropology Janet Carsten[2] has mapped the shift in thinking away from traditional approaches to kinship towards what has become known as the 'new' kinship studies. This shift has entailed the adoption of different terminology: Carsten argues that anthropology is now concerned with 'relatedness' rather than formal structures of kinship.[3] Relatedness, as a term, is a different way of expressing two main themes. The first theme argues that individuals are constituted through their close kin ties. That is to say, without both formative and ongoing relationships we do not develop our own sense of personhood or individuality. This is, as Carsten acknowledges, not a new insight but it is one which keeps being submerged in the Western intellectual tradition with its emphasis on the unattached individual who can exist independently of others. The second and particularly important theme is that the kin to whom we relate in this process no longer need to be understood as literal blood relatives. Although the 'new' kinship in anthropology preserves the cultural and personal significance of blood ties, the new approach gives equal significance to people who may not be strictly 'kin' at all, but who occupy the same place in emotional, cultural, locational and personal senses. This conceptual shift has expanded the range of significant others that both anthropology and sociology can grasp as important and formative in the lives of ordinary people. The concept of relatedness takes what matters to people, and how their lives unfold in specific contexts and places, as its starting point. It demotes the importance of traditional ways of understanding either 'family' or key relationships by always enquiring into who matters, rather than assuming that this is known a priori.

2 J Carsten, *After Kinship* (Cambridge University Press, 2004).
3 Ibid, 109.

In sociology Janet Finch[4] and Jennifer Mason[5] have also developed different ways of thinking about families and kin—creating a conceptual shift akin to that accomplished by Carsten in anthropology. Their emphasis on 'kin' was unusual in sociology in the late 20th century and this terminology appears to have been used deliberately to stretch sociological thinking beyond its (then) fixation on the nuclear married couple. The term kin was, at first, used more or less as another word for relatives, and thus it occupied a largely descriptive function. But over time it became the conceptual tool through which Finch and Mason fashioned new ways of understanding complex relationships between people who defined themselves as related. Finch's initial concerns were to challenge the rigid and unrealistic model of family life held in the minds of policymakers, as well as to problematise the notion of duty between kin. On the one hand she argued that kinship (in England) was more fluid and dynamic than the usual static model of fixed relationships allowed. On the other hand (and putting it rather simply) she argued that family obligations and exchanges were based on 'persons' not 'positions', by which she meant that people did not behave in supportive ways towards each other because of a biological link, but because they felt an affection or obligation towards others that had developed as a consequence of a history of interaction and mutuality. More recently these ideas have coalesced into a kind of sociological version of anthropology's 'new kinship'. Finch and Mason argue:

> First, we think that kinship operates at, or is to found at, the level of negotiated relationships more than structures or systems. . . . Essentially, this is why we wish to jettison both the idea of kinship as a structure and the concept of individualism in favour of one of *relationism*. Second, we want to suggest that kinship is constituted in *relational practices*, with the privilege that this concept gives to actors' reasoning, actions and experiences.[6]

Relationality is therefore an important concept because it transcends the conceptual limitations of the older concept of kinship. Significantly the term acknowledges that people relate to others who are not necessarily kin by blood or marriage and so it allows for a much more fluid way of thinking and, of course, can include such ideas as families of choice.[7] But perhaps even more importantly, it captures a way of thinking and also expresses motivations that ordinary people may have. The term conjures up the image of people existing within intentional, thoughtful networks that they actively sustain, maintain or allow to atrophy. Indeed, the combination

[4] J Finch, *Family Obligations and Social Change* (Cambridge, Polity, 1989).

[5] J Finch and J Mason, *Negotiating Family Responsibilities* (London, Tavistock/Routledge, 1993).

[6] J Finch and J Mason, *Passing On: Kinship and inheritance in England* (London, Routledge, 2000) 164.

[7] K Weston, *Families We Choose: Lesbians, Gays, Kinship* (New York, Columbia University Press, 2nd edn, 1997).

of the term relationality with the concept of family practices[8] emphasises the active and to some extent voluntaristic nature of relating.[9] In this way it is possible to challenge the idea that relationships are given simply as a consequence of one's position in a family genealogy or through marriage. Relationality is then a mode of thinking which influences decisions, actions and choices, and which also forms a context for the unfolding of everyday life. Relationality requires action and is not just a state of mind and this means that in order to understand how relations are sustained we need to be attentive to everyday practices and the meanings that people give to them.[10]

More recently these shifts in thinking about families and kinship have been complemented by studies on friendship. As Pahl and Spencer[11] have suggested, it may now be more appropriate to think in terms of a complex continuum of relationships rather than discrete categories such as family or friends. They have therefore developed the concept of suffusion in order to conceptualise types of relationships, and nuances of closeness, can take different forms and shapes.[12] This concept introduces the idea of relationships as more or less 'friend-like' and more or less 'family-like' and allows them to slide between the two depending on various interacting qualities such as affection or responsibility or choice. This suffusion between the content of chosen and given relationships means that it is problematic to focus 'solely on one side or other of the equation'.[13] In order to avoid the predetermining (even overdetermining) categories of friends and family Pahl and Spencer have developed the concept of 'personal communities' which are not pinned down or conceptually restricted by place (physical locality), type (eg work colleague) or affinity (mother, acquaintance, etc). They go on to produce a complex and detailed typology of relationships which still uses the concepts of friends and family as descriptors but which succeeds in revealing the complex mix of different relationships (with their different meanings, purposes and degrees of closeness) that constitute personal communities. Pahl and Spencer are thus seeking to achieve a different form of sociological conceptualisation of relationships while recognising that terms such as family and friends continue to have cultural significance and meaning in everyday life. So it is not that they aspire to expunge terms such as family or friends from the sociological lexicon, rather they argue that these should not be conceptually determining. Moreover, they recognise that for some people interactions with family

[8] D Morgan, *Family Connections* (Cambridge, Polity, 1996).

[9] C Smart, *Personal Life: New Directions in Sociological Thinking* (Cambridge, Polity, 2007).

[10] J Mason, 'Tangible Affinities and the Real Life Fascination of Kinship' (2008) 42(1) *Sociology* 29.

[11] R Pahl and L Spencer, 'Personal Communities: Not Simply Families of "Fate" or "Choice"' (2004) 52(2) *Current Sociology* 199.

[12] L Spencer and R Pahl, *Rethinking Friendship: Hidden Solidarities Today* (Oxford, Princeton University Press, 2006).

remain more important than with friends, and vice versa, so they do not seek to 'flatten out' all relationship types and make general statements about the respective fortunes of either families or friends in modern times.

The question that now needs to be raised is where law might fit into these different ways of thinking about relationality. This is especially important given that law has frequently been depicted as seeking to shore up or give priority to particular kinds of family structures and to prioritise some relationships over others. Typically law has been seen to bolster patriarchal families, nuclear families, heteronormative families and so on.[14] More recently there has been debate about whether law supports and bolsters the genetic family and blood ties or whether it gives succour to social parenting. While not dismissing these arguments, since there is evidence to support the cases on both sides of these debates, I prefer to add a different perspective rather than trying to resolve the dispute. I seek to insert additional layers into the picture because it is my view that law operates in rather complex and sometimes quite contradictory fashions, in other words it does not have one 'mind' or policy goal. Moreover, as will be well known, shifts in law (legislation, case-law or simply practice) can produce unplanned and unintended consequences. So even where law reforms are initially introduced with clear political agendas, their consequences cannot be guaranteed in advance. Borrowing from John Law's[15] ideas on methodology, I suggest that law—at least English family law—is a mess but this condition is not necessarily a problem because the real life it seeks to address is a mess too.[16]

This complex body of law therefore seeks to engage with families that are not clearly demarcated as married, heterosexual and nuclear, but are made up of the kinds of diverse relationships outlined above. Where once it might have been clear that the intent of family law (combined with related jurisdictions such as the Poor Law) did seek to impose order and clear moral boundaries between respectable families and others, this is now far less clear. Indeed gradually law has become more and more engaged in a game of 'catch up' with social reality as it seeks to reformulate itself in line with contemporary fluidity. I suggest that law (case-law and legislation) often seeks to make elective affinities (or chosen kin) into legally recognised relationships, and in so doing law *may* regulate and normalise, but its primary intent is to protect and recognise those affinities that ordinary people themselves wish to recognise, safeguard and respect. I would go

[13] Pahl and Spencer, above n 11, 203.

[14] C Smart, *The Ties That Bind: Law, Marriage and the Reproduction of Patriarchal Relations* (London, Routledge and Kegan Paul, 1984); R Auchmuty, 'Same-sex Marriage Revived: Feminist Critique and Legal Strategy' (2004) 14(1) *Feminism & Psychology* 101; C Stychin, *Governing Sexuality* (Oxford, Hart Publishing, 2003); S Jeffreys, 'The Need to Abolish Marriage' (2004) 14(2) *Feminism and Psychology* 327.

[15] J Law, *After Method: Mess in Social Science Research* (London, Routledge, 2004).

[16] J Dewar, 'The Normal Chaos of Family Law' (1998) 61(4) *Modern Law Review* 467.

even further to suggest that there are outcomes to this kind of intervention which cannot be predicted because the field in which law operates is never static. Every step in the direction of acknowledging new forms of associations takes place within an already complex web of legal relationships and social/personal affinities which means that new measures or decisions are never straightforward or uncomplicated in their outcomes.

LAW AS A PRACTICE OF 'KIN MAKING'

So we arrive at my proposition that it is useful to see law as a practice of kin making or 'kinning', by which I mean that in various ways law operates to create recognised and recognisable forms of kinship. While once these practices of kinning may have been largely imposed, in late modern times they are more likely to be attempts to keep abreast of changing social and cultural practices. Historical examples of this past practice would be the way in which state-formalised marriages (made compulsory in England in 1753[17]) became the means of properly recording marital relationships and ensuring that spouses enjoined a public contract rather than engaging in more private, or clandestine nuptials. In this way the state ensured it knew who was married to whom; from which knowledge the duties and obligations of kinship could ensue. Marriage was also the mechanism for creating recognised and enforceable legal kinship between men and children. Thus marriage performed a number of functions, and a primary one concerned establishing paternity. It is significant that English law also tended to insist—against credibility in some cases—that any child born to a married woman was the legitimate child of her husband. Thus it was marriage rather than biology that determined paternity. In this way we can see that English law has long been about making fictive kinship into legal kinship, or at least it has actively patrolled the boundaries between the two, allowing some incursions but not others. We also know that law sustained marital relationships through the control of economic factors (eg giving ownership and control of women's property to husbands) and through requirements over domicile and desertion.[18] These mechanisms of acknowledging who was and who was not kin (and in turn the duties and obligations of kinship) relied heavily on negative sanctions against those who transgressed the legally constituted boundaries. Following Foucault again, we can see that these mechanisms are the complete antithesis of more modern, permissive measures which developed in the 20th century.

One notable turning point in this strictly regulatory approach to the practice of kinning occurs with the introduction of legal adoption in 1926

[17] CS Gibson, *Dissolving Wedlock* (London, Routledge, 1994) 45.
[18] Smart, above n 14.

(The Adoption of Children Act). It signals the start of a more responsive mode of recognising changing family practices which were already happening informally. Barton and Douglas[19] quote from one of the committees which was looking into the desirability of legal adoption in England after the First World War. The Child Adoption Committee defined adoption as:

> A legal method of creating between a child and one who is not the natural parent of the child an *artificial family relationship* analogous to that of parent and child.[20]

The idea of the artificial family relationship[21] gaining legal recognition was troubling at the time and so this was not an overnight or smooth transition towards a permissive, inclusive kinning strategy. But factors such as the welfare of the child prevailed over older notions of naturalness. This meant that through this piece of legislation it was formally acknowledged that relationships thought to be 'artificial' could become 'real' for all practical and legal purposes.

This malleability of English family law is an interesting quality. It is not uniformly malleable because this law often has its sticking points, yet at other times it seems to yield very easily to slight pressure. Having given up imposing a rigid model of kinship supported by severe measures such as the imposition of the status of bastardy or punitive fault-based divorce, family law began to assume the appearance of an uneven patchwork of measures which gradually took the conditions of everyday life as the basis for legislation. This signalled a rather pragmatic response to changing family practices. An example of this kind of pragmatism can be found in the shifting responses to assisted reproduction which make the 1925 Committee on Child Adoption's queasiness over the artificiality of legal adoption outlined above seem positively mild when compared with some contemporary responses to the consequences of in vitro fertilisation (IVF) and other methods. Martin Richards[22] has traced the complex relationships between law and paternity in England from AID (originally termed *artificial* insemination by donor) to the rise of DNA testing in the late 1990s. In so doing he outlines the ways in which law and policy has dealt with various 'fictions', turning those fictions which were defined as in the public interest into legal facts, while rejecting others. Thus, for example, he

[19] C Barton and G Douglas, *Law and Parenthood* (London, Butterworths, 1995).

[20] First Report, Cmd 2401, para 4 (1924–5) quoted in Barton and Douglas, above n 19, 75 (emphasis added).

[21] This concept of the artificial family resonates with the later concept of 'pretended family relationship' which was introduced in England and Wales in the 1988 Local Government Act, s 28. In this case the then Conservative government sought to deny the family links of same-sex couples.

[22] M Richards, 'Genes, Genealogies and Paternity: Making Babies in the Twenty-first Century' in JR Spencer and A du Bois-Pedain (eds), *Freedom and Responsibility in Reproductive Choice* (Oxford, Hart Publishing, 2006).

quotes from the Warnock Committee Report in its recommendation that a child conceived by a woman of AID should be treated legally as the offspring of her husband, thus conferring legitimacy on the infant. The Committee stated:

> We are fully aware that this can be criticised as *legislating for a fiction* since the husband of a woman who has conceived by AID will not be the genetic father of the child and the register of births has always been envisaged as a true genetic record. Nonetheless, it would in our view be consistent with the husband's assuming all parental rights and duties with regard to the child.[23]

Richards is sceptical that the register of births was ever regarded as 'a true genetic record' of paternity.[24] He points to the presumption of legitimacy discussed above, and also to the fact that illegitimate children often had no father at all named in the register. Moreover he indicates that there is evidence of 'informal' practices (such as Marie Stopes's recommendations to women in the 1920s who could not conceive with their husbands to try do-it-yourself AID) which would suggest that it is unwise to rely on the register of births as a reliable record of genetic links. Fictions therefore, by implication, abound in this field and what becomes interesting is when and why some are embraced and legitimated while others remain unacceptable.

Sally Sheldon[25] has traced some of these shifts in relation to case-law and fatherhood. She discusses in detail the case of *In Re D (A Child Appearing by Her Guardian Ad Litem) (Respondent)*.[26] It is necessary to outline briefly the history of this case to understand just how far case-law in England is moving in its accommodation to changing claims to elective affinity in everyday family life. In this case an unmarried couple, Mr B and Ms D, who had lived together for four years began a course of IVF treatment together, arising from the Mr B's infertility. After undergoing one cycle of treatment Ms D failed to conceive and the couple split up. But later Ms D returned to the clinic for another cycle of treatment (with her new partner Mr S) and succeeded in becoming pregnant without, however, the knowledge of Mr B. The daughter she gave birth to (R) had no genetic relationship to Mr B, but on hearing of her birth, he applied to the courts be acknowledged as R's legal father and to have contact with the baby. Ms D did not want her former partner to be a 'parent' to the child because she

[23] Ibid, 57 quoting from the *Report of the Committee of Inquiry into Human Fertilisation and Embryology* 1984, 26 (emphasis added).

[24] Although it is interesting to note that as late as 1987 Stephen Cretney observed 'The entry of a man's name as the father of a child under the Births and Deaths Registration Act 1953 constitutes prima facie evidence that that man is the father . . . , and registration can thus be a useful way of establishing paternity'. S Cretney, *Elements of Family Law* (London, Sweet & Maxwell, 1987) 238.

[25] S Sheldon, 'Reproductive Technologies and the Legal Determination of Fatherhood' (2005) 13 *Feminist Legal Studies* 349.

[26] [2005] UKHL 33.

had a new partner, she was no longer in a relationship with Mr B and because the child was not genetically related to him. The case was rather complex, moving between the family court and Court of Appeal, but basically the lower court found in Mr B's favour granting him parental responsibility and indirect contact with R, but the Court of Appeal later rejected his claim for paternity. Mr B then appealed to the House of Lords on the issue of paternity but in a unanimous judgment the Law Lords dismissed his appeal. The order for indirect contact with the child, however, remained in place.

Although the Law Lords did not ultimately allow that Mr B should be acknowledged as the legal father to R, the arguments and debates aired at all levels of this case reveal how attentive to claims to elective affinity the family courts have become. Moreover Mr B retained his right to exercise indirect contact which would enable him to form a relationship (if distant) with the child. The Law Lords also left open the possibility that he could return to court later to apply for the granting of parental responsibility. Sheldon argues that in their judgment the judges accepted that a number of adults could play an important role in the child's life and that it was not necessary to restrict her range of concerned adults to just two. She argues that the House of Lords accepted that what matters in terms of the welfare of the child is the 'doing' of family practices rather than 'being' a particular type of family (ie nuclear and heterosexual). Sheldon notes:

> *In Re D* recognises a man who has no genetic links with a child, no existing social relationship with her, and no ongoing relationship with her mother as having paternal rights and interests which merit legal protection.[27]

Mr B's attempt to forge a relationship with R is a particular example of an attempt to create and give legal recognition to elective affinity. In its response Sheldon argues that the law responded flexibly and sympathetically. This suggests that there has been a very rapid movement towards embracing contemporary relationality in legal practice, or put another way we can see clear evidence of kinning practices in legal decisions.

I shall return to this point in my conclusion, but at this stage I shall turn to a discussion of how same-sex couples experience shifts in the legal recognition of their chosen relationships. I am introducing empirical data here because I want to explore the link between everyday desires for recognition and respect for relationships and legal reforms. I have implied above that we should no longer think in terms of law imposing a pre-designed model of heterosexual marriage on same-sex couples but rather we should be open to the idea of relationships in the real world changing and that this gives rise to demands made on law for recognition. This is part of my argument for redefining law as a kinning practice which is to say that family law

[27] Sheldon, above n 25, 360.

has become receptive to demands to legitimate new forms of kinship—even those which were quite recently denigrated as pretended family relationships.

THE STUDY OF SAME-SEX COUPLES

The study[28] from which the empirical section of this chapter draws was based on in-depth qualitative interviews with same-sex couples in 2004 and 2005. We conducted 54 interviews in total, 37 with couples and 17 with individuals. Of these 61 were women and 30 were men. For the sake of simplicity I shall speak mainly of the sample as comprising information about the relationships of 54 same-sex couples. The majority of our interviewees were between 30 and 49 years of age and some couples had been together as long as 30 years. All except one respondent described him or herself as white (mainly White British, White English, White Scottish, etc) and our sample was disproportionately 'middle class' (a ratio of 8:1) taking into account factors of education level, the nature of employment and housing tenure. We contacted our respondents mainly through the gay media (eg *Gay Times*, *Diva*) and websites (eg Pink Wedding Waiting List, Stonewall) and through leaflets distributed at Gay Pride marches, bookshops, local groups and religious groups. When the interviews started in 2004 all the respondents had held some form of commitment ceremony/partnership registration or were planning one in the near future, although later in the project we found that they were planning a civil partnership[29] rather than an informal ceremony. This means that our sample is unique because these couples were in something of a vanguard movement, pressing ahead with their own forms of marriage before the availability of civil partnership proper. The sample is sandwiched between a moment in time when the idea of same-sex marriage may have been desired but was hardly ever achieved (at least in the UK) and the moment when same-sex couples were granted (virtually) the same rights to marry as heterosexual couples. This historical moment is particularly significant for the arguments I make in this chapter because there is evidence that same-sex couples were already forming 'informal' marriages and were adding new dimensions to their families of choice by creating their own 'kinning' rituals. The fact that these

[28] This study was funded by the ESRC ref R 000 23 0418. The research team included Carol Smart, Jennifer Mason and Beccy Shipman. Further information from this study can be found in: B Shipman and C Smart, '"It's Made a Huge Difference": Recognition, Rights and the Personal Significance of Civil Partnership' (2007) 22(1) *Sociological Research Online*, January; and C Smart, 'Same Sex Couples and Marriage: Negotiating Relational Landscapes with Families and Friends' (2007) 55(4) *Sociological Review* 687.

[29] Civil partnership was not available until December 2005 and when we started the interviews in 2004 it was not at all certain that Parliament would pass the civil partnership legislation which was only then being drafted.

may have had no legal consequences did not prevent couples finding the informal procedures highly significant. Finally, all the names used in this paper are pseudonyms, and although ages are included, any references which might compromise anonymity have been removed.

FICTIONS AND FAMILIES OF CHOICE

I suggest that the tendency to redefine important relationships (away from being 'fictions' towards being both 'real') has been at work in the area of same-sex relationships as much as in the field of assisted reproduction. It is possible to see continuity between the legal management of matters such as the presumption of legitimacy, adoption and assisted reproduction, and the recent decision to include same-sex couples in legally recognised webs of elective affinities. This process has had its sticking points too, the most obvious being the decision to reserve the term 'marriage' solely for heterosexual couples, but the rapidity with which the policy recommendation in favour of civil partnership was passed into law, the speed with which registrars of marriages accommodated the new ceremonies, and the growing taken-for-grantedness of such ceremonies suggests that the new legislation was doing little more than endorsing existing ways of forming kinship bonds and affinities.

Weeks, Heaphy and Donovan[30] have argued that social research in Britain was somewhat slow to recognise that homosexuality did not denote a field of sexuality alone. They point out that there was a gradual recognition that gay men and lesbians were forming relationships, many of them enduring over many years, sometimes involving inclusion into wider family networks and also involving the raising of children. The emergence of the term 'families of choice'[31] was highly contested but it did allow for a greater recognition of the creation, and subsequent merging and blurring, of friends and kin. It also established that same-sex couples were not outside the imaginary of 'family'. The concept of families of choice denotes a very fluid set of relationships because such families are made rather than given and even relationships with blood kin may be seen to be fluid in this context because they are not automatically invited into families of choice. So decisions about who should be regarded as being within the compass of one's family has been an issue for same-sex and heterosexual partnerships alike and, even if the exact focus of decisions has been different, the process is potentially understood by all.

The question is, of course, whether the malleability of law in recognising these bonds and seeking to secure them in some ways changes the nature of

[30] J Weeks, B Heaphy and C Donovan, *Same Sex Intimacies: Families of Choice and Other Life Experiments* (London, Routledge, 2001).

[31] Weston, above n 7; Weeks et al, above n 30.

these relationships. As I have noted above, some critics of the reforms see these measures as a way of imposing heteronormative values and structures onto what would otherwise be transgressive relationship forms. Carl Stychin,[32] for example, sees this as a process of normalisation in which the radical potential of same-sex relationships is curtailed and controlled. But others see the legal measures as protective of same-sex relationships in as much as the law provides safeguards for the more vulnerable partners and also protects the relationship itself from incursions from other kin or even some aspects of bureaucracy and officialdom. Same-sex couples themselves are not ignorant of the potential consequences of this recognition,[33] and it seems unwise to imagine that they will not seek to create new meanings in relation to civil partnership and to continue to shape their relationships in diverse ways. Take this quotation from Fran as an example of the awareness of these complex issues and politics that same-sex couples in our study demonstrate:

> **Fran:** I think it was, it was important to us that it was kind of self aware of how, how can I put it, yes it was very important that it was aware, that it was very queer really, and it was very queer. And being both clearly a wedding at the same time. Neither of us really wanted to sit round in a circle in a wood holding flowers and having poems read out which would have been quite sickly. And at the same time we did not want to do something that was entirely traditional and just aping an un-self-aware copy of something. So we had something that was a mixed event. And it started off like I said it did start off as a joke but by the time it came it was not at all. And a few friends said that was really moving. . . . I did not expect to be quite so choked up by that. And it really gelled into a very important and very symbolic activity of exchanges of love in front of all friends. It was cool.

What is often overlooked in discussions about normalisation versus the extension of citizenship is the potential for extending emotional links and resources through the legitimation of forms of elective affinities. In other words civil partnership does not only link couples together in a socially recognised way, it also provides for a range of additional relationships which come into formal existence. This means that a civil partner becomes the 'in-law' or relative of their partner's parents and sibling. Whether these formal links are taken up and become meaningful depends on circumstances, but additional kin do become potentially available and the reach of relationships is extended. In many ways this is precisely what the legal process of adoption has done in relation to children, and equally, moves to recognise paternity and other relationships created through methods of assisted reproduction have given rise to the same possibilities. Put briefly, the scope of meaningful relationships recognised by law is extended. The

32 Above n 14.
33 Smart, above n 28.

ontological significance of acknowledging these relationships in adoption and elsewhere is now recognised and so it may be equally important to recognise them in the context of same-sex relationships. In the quotations below it is possible to see precisely this extension at work:

> **Chris**: Yes it has sort of brought Sarah's family and my family more sort of like knitted together over the last couple of years; since we have been married we are really close.

> **Sarah**: I mean when we go out and everything they always introduce me as a sister in law. And it is like your mother and dad they always introduce me as their daughter and they are perfectly, you could not really expect more than that could you?

> **Sally** *(addressing her partner Judy)*: And I said to your dad 'Shall I call you father now?' and he said in all seriousness 'Oh yes you should do'. I was only joking, so I don't know whether they see us any differently or whether or not it has given them permission to acknowledge us more—your mum and dad at least—to acknowledge us more.

These remarks may sound as if these two couples are being conventional but this surface reading may miss the underlying meanings that are at play when a wider circle of family or friends is invited to witness a same-sex marriage. The desire to place one's relationships within a relational context, witnessed by others, generates a level of significance that goes beyond the relationship itself. The three quotations below show the slightly different nuances that people can put on the significance of a ceremony with witnesses but what they have in common is an understanding that the ceremony turned the relationship into something beyond a form of personal intimacy and into a form of reflexive, self- and other-aware, bond.

> **Eva:** And also it was I think in our vows and that commitment, it was so obvious, our love for each other, in that ceremony, wasn't it? So people were really witnessing that. So that can then be reflected back to you and remind you, when you are hating each other! [Being] horrible to each other!

> **Amy:** I think a lot of it was to do with commitment with each other and we both saw it as an expression really, of our commitment and love and making vows to each other. . . . I suppose I thought if we had a ceremony people would view it on a higher level, people would respect it more—family, friends. But between the two of us the main reason was to demonstrate a commitment . . . really.

> **Steph:** It is about the complexity and the diversity of relationships now. . . . You have complex relationships . . . and you know that should be welcome. I think people's relationships should be welcome and if you show a commitment to somebody and you love somebody and you want to be with them and help look after them and they want to look after you and they want to be part of each other's family and you want to be part of the community, then that should be welcomed. And I think it makes the country richer and I think it makes the world richer.

The potential for acknowledgement and recognition through both a ceremony and through legal status was a strong theme in many of the interviews we carried out. It is this practice that I would argue is a grass-roots kinning practice. These elements may have been less important for couples who had been together for many years since they had established their own ontological security and kinship identity through their long-term relational practices. However, even in these cases, a marriage could express something additional to the personal relationship.

> **Ronny:** Yes we are just doing things for one another. I will not say that it is all rosy, we do have rows from time to time and I am slightly difficult to live with and I know that and he knows that. And when I had my breakdown he really should have left then, so it is to his great credit that he did not. So that is love isn't it, through the hard times. (Relationship of 33 years)

In this quotation Ronny is talking about the creation of meaning between the couple rather than between a couple and a network of significant others, or with a community. However, the point is still clear that they felt that their relationship merited a particular kind of acknowledgement because of its bonded qualities.

It could then be argued that the introduction of civil partnership recognised a process of change which was already occurring, and this practice of kinning through legal process seems, at least in our study, to be regarded in a very positive light by same-sex couples. At the very least these shifts in law do seem to support Sheldon's claim that what might matter more and more in law is the doing of family practices (or as I would say kinning practices) rather than an adherence to a particular model of the heterosexual, nuclear family.

CONCLUDING REMARKS

There is a risk that my emphasis on law as a kinning practice which responds to or reflects the desires and demands of new family formations depicts an overly harmonious and smooth social processes. I have indicated above that family law does not respond automatically to all demands, but of equal importance is the recognition that the demands themselves may be quite contradictory or even arise as a consequence of conflict. In deciding which relationships to recognise and give legal standing to, law is also empowering different parties in relation to each other. Thus civil partnership has empowered partners when compared with parents. Civil partnership creates the partner as next of kin rather than the parent; it also gives the partner rights of inheritance as opposed to parents or blood kin. So this kinning practice also realigns certain expectations and empowers some at the expense of others. This changing landscape creates new opportunities for conflict rather than an harmonious sea of tranquillity.

One example of precisely this sort of new conflict arises where the parents of a child are a same-sex couple but where a progenitor (usually sperm-donating father) also wishes to be an involved parent. The introduction of civil partnership created legally recognised kinship between a co-mother and the child of her civil partner. This means that a co-mother can no longer be ignored in cases of contested parental responsibility. Civil partnership has strengthened her legal visibility considerably and the Human Fertilisation and Embryology Act 2008 refers to the co-mother as a female parent (reserving the term mother for the birth mother). The idea that children can have two recognised female parents is thus a further example of the extension of law as a kinning practice (even if only one can in law be called mother). But this leaves open the issue of whether the male sperm donor should be recognised as a father in cases where he seeks to be a parent. The case of *Re D (Contact and PR: Lesbian mothers and known father)*[34] reveals the desire by courts to be both flexible and accommodating towards such complex kinship arrangements. In this case a lesbian couple, Ms A and Ms C, planned to become parents through the co-operation of Mr B. The original plan was that Mr B should be informally acknowledged as the child's (D) father but that he would play a somewhat distant role akin to a fond uncle while the couple would be left to raise the child as her immediate parents. Unfortunately Mr B came to want more contact and involvement than this and he became rather interfering and demanding. It appears that he wanted an arrangement akin to that of a divorced father where he would have approximately 50 per cent of D's time and an equal parenting role to the birth mother, Ms A. He wished to consign Ms C to a subsidiary role. Mr B therefore applied for a parental responsibility order which he felt was the only way to secure legitimacy for his status as father to D. This order would have allowed him to make joint decisions with Ms A over matters of education and health; it would also have re-created a typical heterosexual hierarchy of parenthood notwithstanding the existence of the long-term relationship between Ms C and Ms A. The High Court judge (The Honourable Mrs Justice Black) was not at all inclined to demote the significance of the relationship between Ms C and Ms A, nor to dismiss the important parenting role of Ms C in favour of the fathering role of Mr B. Rather she sought to give primacy to the lesbian mothers while allowing Mr B some component parts of a parental responsibility order. This creative law-making, in which Mr B was recognised as an important adult in D's life but his ability to interfere in her day-to-day upbringing reduced, managed to square a difficult circle. Mrs Justice Black stated:

[34] [2006] EWHC 2 (Fam).

> As I said in my last judgment, D's home is with Ms A and Ms C. They, together with her sister, are her immediate family. That is where she will derive her primary security throughout her childhood. As Mr B expressly recognises, Ms A and Ms C are her day to day parents and he has no role in her day to day care, whether in relation to decision making or otherwise. He will, however, be kept informed of all major decisions taken by Ms A and Ms C in relation to her. He will thus be recognised as a parent by the grant of parental responsibility but it will be a parent of a very different sort—no less important, just very different. It would be helpful, in my view, if a form of words could be included in the order as part of the pre-amble reflecting this paramount position to the family comprising the two mothers and the two children.[35]

The case of *Re D* is a paramount example of how the courts can respond to the ways in which people enact kinship rather than seeking simply to ratify either heterosexual norms or an apparent biological imperative. Mrs Justice Black did not ignore biology completely, but she saw it in relational terms. That is to say she argued that D would want to know about her biological father and might wish to have a relationship with him. Moreover Mr B's experience of fathering a child was recognised to have changed him at an emotional level and he was acknowledged to be acting towards D in a positive and caring way—even though he was causing problems for D's mothers. All the parents in this case were acknowledged for the ways in which they were acting as parents and not simply because they could claim the status of a parent. It could therefore be said that Mrs Justice Black was applying Morgan's[36] concept of family practices, combined with Carsten's and Finch and Mason's concept of relationality, within the context of a feminist ethic of care,[37] as a way of resolving the conflict!

Re D returns us to the starting point of this chapter, namely the idea of law as a practice of kinning. This case is an example of a refined kinning exercise since it sets out degrees of involvement deemed to be appropriate in specific instances of kinship. It takes little heed of formal structures of kinship (which once would have seen the complete exclusion of Ms C) and it restrains the (excessive) ambitions of genetic fatherhood because in this case these claims were seen as damaging to the core relationships of the mothers and their daughter. Moreover the published judgment provides clear evidence that all the different understandings of kinship held by the parties were given due consideration. Most striking of all was the fact that there were no allusions, no matter how subtle, to the idea that lesbian mothers did not constitute a 'real' family or that there was anything 'fictional' or 'artificial' in their circumstances. No doubt there will be other comparable cases which will not incorporate these insights and values and

[35] *Re D (Contact and PR: Lesbian mothers and known father)* [2006] EWHC 2 (Fam) 19.

[36] Above n 8.

[37] J Tronto, *Moral Boundaries* (London, Routledge, 1993); C Smart and B Neale, *Family Fragments?* (Cambridge, Polity, 1999).

which will (once again) give greater primacy to genetic links and the position of fatherhood. But this to be expected because nowhere in family law has there ever been a straightforward, linear progression of ideas to which all judges (and law-makers) subscribe. The field is always contested. The point is that the terrain of contested kinship is expanding and changing, and outcomes are not easily predicted in advance because the quality of relationships and everyday practices of kinship are now so much a part of the equation. A case like *Re D* suggests that family law can in practice accommodate the 'mess' of everyday kinship while rapidly recognising new forms of kinship as entirely legitimate. Read in this way it seems unduly restrictive to theorise law as always confining and regulating diversity according to a specific set of overarching preferences for a normative family. As Sheldon argued in relation to *In Re D*, the courts seem now to be capable of understanding that children can have more than two parents, so in *Re D* they seem able to acknowledge this multiplicity in the context of same-sex relationships as well. And although the courts are engaged to recognise kinship mostly in the context of interpersonal conflicts, the pressure for family law to be responsive to the new kinship does not only come from the conflicted as our study on gay and lesbian marriage suggests.[38] This may mean that the construction of legally recognised bonds of kinship may be emerging as one of the most critical functions of family law and also that acknowledging family law as a particularly significant kinning practice may be a more adequate way of theorising contemporary legal policy.

[38] See also E Lewin, *Recognizing Ourselves: Ceremonies of Lesbian and Gay Commitment* (New York, Columbia University Press, 1998); and K Hull, *Same-Sex Marriage: The Cultural Politics of Love and Law* (Cambridge University Press, 2006).

Part I

PROPERTY DIVISION IN COUPLE RELATIONSHIPS

INTRODUCTION

THE CHAPTERS IN this section examine the issue of property division in emerging family forms, particularly couple-based cohabitation. Property ownership under English law continues to be governed by the principle of 'separate property', which remains unaffected by couples entering marriage or a same-sex civil partnership. While the courts have been given powers to redistribute property when a marriage[1] or a civil partnership[2] comes to an end, there is at present no statutory regime in England and Wales that provides courts with similar powers on the breakdown of other couple-based relationships. The issue of who owns what will nonetheless surface for such couples. The division of property is often closely aligned with issues of (inter)dependency and economic vulnerability. With cohabitation on the rise, there is the pressing question of how and when property division is to be effected in couple relationships as a result of (inter)dependency and economic vulnerability.

The chapters in this section seek to examine two very different but, to some extent, related questions. First, the chapter by Anne Barlow explores the utility of having some system of community of property in England and Wales to resolve issues relating to the family home and other property during and on termination of couple relationships. Barlow considers the differences between an automatic joint ownership and a deferred community of property regime, and the extent to which either of these approaches were viewed as acceptable to people's sense of how couple relationships should affect property.

The chapter draws on empirical research funded by the Nuffield Foundation on whether some form of European-style community of property regime is suitable for England and Wales. The research findings reveal very mixed views about community of property among the couples interviewed:

[1] Matrimonial Causes Act 1973.
[2] Civil Partnership Act 2004.

a majority prioritised meeting needs rather than asset sharing on the breakdown of their relationships, whether marriage or cohabitation, especially where there were children. More importantly, Barlow's chapter suggests that a form of deferred community of property is probably a more appropriate regime for England and Wales—one that has some means of combining the 'entitlement' principle of sharing that underpins community of property with elements of need or compensation-based discretion. This modified form of community of property appears to fit in better with most couples' views on what should happen on relationship breakdown.

The second chapter by Wong addresses the issue of the normative underpinnings of legal intervention in intimate couple relationships. She investigates the various normative arguments, such as equality and economic vulnerability, which have often been made to justify legal intervention and to bring a wider range of intimate relationships within the fold of the law. There is also, to some extent, an interface between these arguments and the functional similarity (to marriage) argument to push for the extension of legal protection to these intimate relationships. The chapter seeks to explore the use of the economic vulnerability argument as a justification for introducing legal reform and, more specifically, to interrogate the way in which law reformers as well as the courts interpret 'economical vulnerability'. The concern here is that the economic vulnerability argument tends to lend itself to perpetuating images of female dependency and reinforcing patriarchal models of close intimate relationships.

The chapter explores the extent to which 'interdependency', as used in psychology, might provide a more appropriate normative basis for property redistribution than 'economic vulnerability'. The chapter argues, though, that 'interdependency', as a concept, has to date been under-interrogated and under-developed in legal discourse. Given the diversity of intimate couple relationships, Wong asks whether elements such as caring and complementarity, which have been recognised within psychology as crucial elements of an interdependent and committed relationship, ought to be given greater consideration within law, and whether a shift in focus from 'vulnerability' to 'interdependency' might be better at achieving substantive equality and fairness for couples in the division of property.

3

Property and Couple Relationships: What Does Community of Property Have to Offer English Law?

ANNE BARLOW

INTRODUCTION

COUPLE RELATIONSHIPS, PARTICULARLY where a home is shared, are most often economic as well as emotional relationships involving financial dependency or interdependency. Among the traditional functions of family law, at its interface with property law, has been the need to protect the more dependent, weaker economic spouse, typically the wife. This has been done in different ways in different jurisdictions with changes over time. Yet there is a particular division of approach between common law jurisdictions and European civil law jurisdictions which it is now timely to re-examine given the changing face of families and their financial dynamics in the 21st century and the challenge this represents for family law across Europe and beyond.

Marriage in its traditional breadwinner/homemaker model has the economic dependency of women upon men embedded deep within it. The European civil law approach to address this issue has been one of an entitlement on marriage to share equally in specified matrimonial assets under a 'community of property regime'.[1] The essence of such a regime is

[1] These regimes may take different forms, notably an immediate community (the traditional form such a regime took), where all specified matrimonial assets are shared equally from the point of marriage onwards; or a deferred community, where during the marriage the spouses retain their separate property but where the specified matrimonial assets must be shared at the point of divorce, as discussed below. In different jurisdictions the scope of the community varies enormously from those where all assets owned by both spouses before and after marriage are encompassed, to those where only assets acquired after the marriage and excluding gifts, inheritance and personal insurance proceeds fall into the community. Similarly, different jurisdictions specify different assets as 'matrimonial assets' which must form part of the 'community

the legal prescription that entering marriage (or other specified couple relationship) should normally have a direct effect on a couple's property rights. Unless and until a couple have specifically and formally agreed otherwise, community property (as defined by law in each jurisdiction) must be shared (almost always equally) between them.[2] Community of property rules are strictly applied on divorce, and any post-separation needs can only be met through periodic maintenance payments from income, never from capital assets.

The common law approach has rather been to entitle wives to retain their own property following marriage, releasing them in the late 19th century from the doctrine of unity under which husbands alone could own property.

In England and Wales, couple relationships, including entering a marriage or registering a same-sex civil partnership, have no direct or immediate effect on either partner's property which during the relationship continues to be owned separately unless specifically purchased jointly. However, at the point of divorce (or civil partnership dissolution), the court now has wide discretionary powers to redistribute both income and capital assets to achieve a 'fair' outcome between the parties to an equal partnership. This is individually judged at the point of separation and, following recent decisions in the House of Lords and Court of Appeal, is stated to be based on the three strands of fairness—needs, a principle of equal sharing and compensation–the exact juxtaposition of which remains uncertain.[3]

The radical nature of these recent developments in the divorce context is reflected in the suggestion by as eminent a commentator as Stephen Cretney that England and Wales has adopted a judicially created system of deferred community of property.[4] Add to this the fact that the European Commission is very keen to harmonise matrimonial property regimes across the European Union,[5] and it becomes critical to consider what, if anything, the adoption of a statutory community of property regime has to offer English law.

of property' and thus must be shared. See further, E Cooke, A Barlow and T Callus, *Community of Property: A Regime for England and Wales?* (Bristol, Policy Press, 2006) ch 1.

[2] For a comparative overview of the different European matrimonial property regimes, see K Boele-Woelki et al, *Matrimonial Property Law from a Comparative Law Perspective (Huwelijksvermogensrecht in Rechtsvergelijkend Perspectief)* (2000), *Stichting ter Bevordering der Notariële Wetenschap,* in the Series Ars Notariatus C111 (Deventer, Kluwer, 2000). A translation into English by Mr Hans Warendorf, Amsterdam is available at http://www.reading.ac.uk/nmsruntime/saveasdialog.asp?lID=7018&sID=34870

[3] S 25 Matrimonial Causes Act 1973, paras 20–21 to Sch 5 Civil Partnership Act 2004 and see also *White v White* [2001] 1 AC 596 (HL), *Miller v Miller; McFarlane v McFarlane* [2006] UKHL 24, *Charman v Charman (no 4)* [2007] EWCA Civ 503.

[4] S Cretney, 'Community of Property Imposed by Judicial Decision' (2003) 119 *Law Quarterly Review R* 349.

[5] *Green Paper on Matrimonial Property Regimes,* COM (2006) 400.

Pursuing this aim and drawing on the findings of a Nuffield Foundation-funded empirical study focusing on the law in England and Wales, France, the Netherlands and Sweden,[6] this chapter will first critique the different conceptual approaches of the civil law and common law in this area from an historical feminist perspective. It will then consider the difficulties within the current law of financial provision[7] on relationship breakdown in England and Wales. Finally it will explore what might be gained or lost by formally adopting a statutory community of property regime within marriage, civil partnership and indeed other couple relationships, where partnering and parenting are increasingly sited[8] and law reform is proposed.[9]

COMMUNITY OF PROPERTY VERSUS SEPARATE PROPERTY—AN HISTORICAL FEMINIST PERSPECTIVE

Historically, community of property regimes were seen as better recognising the realities of the economic relationship within most breadwinner/homemaker marriages and as offering greater financial protection for the weaker economic spouse, most often the wife, in the form of entitlement to property by virtue of marriage. The 19th-century approach in European jurisdictions such as France and the Netherlands was to create a default matrimonial regime which imposed on marriage an 'immediate community of property'. Indeed both jurisdictions still retain this model of immediate community which automatically applies unless the parties contract differently.[10] Put simply, this means that all of the husband and wife's separately owned property (in the case of the Netherlands) or at least some of it (as is the case in France where only assets acquired post-marriage, excluding inherited or gifted property, are affected), as well as their post-marriage debts, become jointly owned during the marriage and can only be dealt

[6] The project was directed by Elizabeth Cooke and Therese Callus of Reading University and Anne Barlow of University of Exeter between 2004 and 2006. The findings are published in Cooke et al, above n 1.

[7] The term 'financial provision' is used in the general (rather than a technical) sense referring to the range of orders the court can make on divorce, civil partnership dissolution or parental separation for the benefit of a child, and is intended to include rather than exclude property adjustment orders as well as lump sum and periodical maintenance orders.

[8] National Statistics, *Living in Britain: The 2002 General Household Survey* (London, TSO, 2004) shows that whereas the number of married women in Britain has declined from 74 per cent in 1979 to 49 per cent in 2002, the number of single women cohabiting has increased from 8 per cent to 31 per cent over the same period. 26 per cent of all births in England and Wales in 2001 were to cohabiting couples (National Statistics, *Birth Statistics: Review of the Registrar General on Births and Patterns of Family Building in England and Wales, 2002*. Series FM1, no 31 (London, TSO, 2004)).

[9] See Law Commission for England and Wales, *Cohabitation: The Financial Consequences of Relationship Breakdown* (Law Com No 307, Cm 7182, 2007).

[10] See French Civil Code, Title V and Dutch Civil Code, Title 7, respectively.

with by them acting together. Both during and at the end of the marriage, unless specifically agreed otherwise, each spouse would be credited with an equal share in the community assets.

In contrast, separate property was seen as the 19th-century 'feminist' solution in England and Wales. When wives were the chattels of their husbands, all their property and income became owned by their husbands on marriage under the doctrine of unity of husband and wife.[11] English legislative reform in the Married Women's Property Acts of 1870 and 1882 opted to allow married women to own their property as *separate property*. This allowed them to retain control over their own income and capital assets and become liable for their own debts to the extent of their separate property.[12] Given that most married women at that time did not earn or have their own income, had few assets and were financially dependent on their husbands, this, in contrast to what had happened in France, was a reform that only served the interests of middle- and upper-class women.

Writing in the 1950s, Otto Kahn-Freund, a German legal academic working in England, saw the married family as an economic entity with funds of money and property dedicated to common use. He expressed his concern with the English stance:

> The fact that they are husband and wife has no effect on their property. Nothing is by law 'theirs'; everything . . . is in the absence to the contrary, either 'his' or 'hers'. Sociologists must decide whether this rule reflects the *mores* and the ideas of the people.[13]

Yet by this time, the emancipation of women had prompted some community of property jurisdictions to modify their default matrimonial regimes to allow separate ownership of property during marriage but impose a community regime requiring (unless the parties agreed otherwise) an equal division of community assets between the spouses on divorce or death.[14] This concept is known as *deferred community of property* and is a system that aims to strike a good balance between autonomy of the spouses during the marriage and protection for the weaker economic spouse at the end. It is a model now widely used throughout Scandinavia.[15]

Until 1970, divorce law in England and Wales only allowed claims by wives for periodic maintenance payments, with each spouse retaining their own separate property. No transfer of capital or assets was possible on

[11] S Cretney, *Family Law in the Twentieth Century* (Oxford, Oxford University Press, 2003) 91.

[12] Ibid, 99.

[13] O Kahn-Freund, 'Inconsistencies and Injustices in the Law of Husband and Wife' (1952) 15 *Modern Law Review* 133.

[14] See eg The Swedish Marriage Code 1920.

[15] See Boele-Woelki et al, above n 2, and D Martiny, 'A Matrimonial Property System for the European Union?', paper presented to the UK–German Judicial Family Law Conference, 8–11 September 2004, Cardiff.

divorce other than by agreement, no matter how deserving the case. Yet, rises in divorce, owner-occupation, property prices combined with shortages of rented accommodation in the second half of the 20th century brought the harsh effects of the doctrine of separate property into the political limelight.[16] As Professor McGregor summarised it in a parliamentary debate in 1979, the separate property regime had:

> unintentionally institutionalised inequality in the economic relations of husbands and wives. By preventing husbands getting their hands on their wives' money, the statute denied wives rights in their husbands' money. And in the real world it was mostly husbands who had the money.[17]

Between 1956 and 1979 the introduction of a system of community of property or at least of statutory co-ownership of the matrimonial home in England had some powerful supporters. Both were seriously considered by the Law Commission, although in the event neither was to materialise.[18] Rather than interfere with separate property rights within marriage, English law adopted a needs-driven system of discretionary redistribution of assets as well as income according to a list of statutory criteria that it still retains today.[19] By the end of the 1970s, it had also become common practice for husbands and wives to purchase the matrimonial home in their joint names and so the community of property debate became a dead letter. That is until the case of *White v White*.[20]

In 2001 the House of Lords in this case swept away the 'reasonable requirements' ceiling for financial provision awards in favour of the weaker economic spouse which case-law had developed. It replaced it with a 'yardstick of equality', against which all awards have to be measured, at least where there has been a long marriage and the assets available exceed the parties' needs. It is this move towards equal division of assets that gives rise to the claim that we have a judicially created community of property regime. Reasons must be given for departing from equality and the rationale for this is that non-financial contributions to the welfare of the family, such as caring for children, are of equal weight to financial contributions and equal division should not be departed from on this ground.[21] As Lord Nicholls indicated in *White v White*:[22]

16 See further Cretney, above n 11, 118ff.

17 Official Report (House of Lords) 18 July 1979, vol 401, col 1437. For an example of how harshly this operated, see *Gissing v Gissing* [1971] AC 886.

18 See Law Commission, *Financial Provision in Matrimonial Proceedings* (Law Com No 25, 1969); Law Commission, *Family Property Law Working Paper No 42* (London, HMSO, 1971); Law Commission, *First Report on Family Property: A New Approach* (Law Com No 52, 1973); Law Commission, *Third Report on Family Property: The Matrimonial Home Co-ownership and Occupation Rights and Household Goods* (Law Com No 86, 1978).

19 See Matrimonial Causes Act 1973, s 25.

20 [2001] 1 AC 596 (HL).

21 See *White v White* [2001] 1 AC 596, *Lambert v Lambert* [2002] EWCA Civ 1685.

22 [2001] 1 AC 596, 605.

> If, in their different spheres, each contributed equally to the family then in principle it matters not which of them earned the money and built up the assets. There should be no bias in favour of the money earner as against the home-maker and the child-carer.

More recently still, the House of Lords has confirmed that the weaker economic spouse can also be compensated for what is termed 'relationship-generated disadvantage'.[23] This would include disadvantage generated by undertaking child or elder care for a family member rather than paid work, reducing a carer's labour market value, and permits payment of a sum additional to any needs that have been identified.

These decisions are a clear attempt by the House of Lords to strike a blow for gender equality within marriage and acknowledge the different, but in its view equal, roles played by spouses within family life. Its approach is addressing the reality of the situation of many women but can be criticised for doing this in a way that reinforces the patriarchal financial dependence of women childcarers upon breadwinning men,[24] although some have interpreted this and other developments as embodying an egalitarian discourse of partnership.[25]

Thus both community of property systems and the English separate property system have tried to adjust to the changing position of married women (and men) within society. Both claim to have replaced patriarchy with formal equality in the financial frameworks governing marriage and divorce. So confident are they of this, that they have now almost all extended their matrimonial financial provision regimes to same-sex couples. However, very few (Sweden and Scotland are rare examples) have extended even a less extensive version to informally cohabiting couples, although the Law Commission have recently recommended this approach for England and Wales.[26]

Before considering the suitability of a community of property regime for England and Wales, let us first identify the issues we may want such a scheme to address.

PROPERTY AND COUPLE RELATIONSHIPS IN ENGLAND AND WALES

From a legal perspective, there are currently two major problems with financial provision on relationship breakdown which the introduction of

[23] See *Miller v Miller; McFarlane v McFarlane* [2006] UKHL 24, para 140.

[24] See eg A Diduck, 'Fairness and Justice for All? The House of Lords in White v White', (2001) 9 *Feminist Legal Studies* 173

[25] A Bottomley and S Wong, 'Shared Households: A New Paradigm for Thinking about the Reform of Domestic Property Relations', in A Diduck and K O'Donovan (eds), *Feminist Perspectives on Family Law* (Abingdon, Routledge-Cavendish, 2006) 52.

[26] Law Commission, above n 9.

any new system would want to address. First is the current lack of clarity in English law of financial provision on divorce (and consequently civil partnership dissolution). The second relates to the very different legal treatment of cohabiting couples (including those with children) seeking financial provision on relationship breakdown as compared with functionally similar married couples or civil partners.

Lack of Clarity on Divorce and Dissolution

Whereas in Europe, the division of the capital assets on relationship breakdown should always be certain, if not fair, in England and Wales, the pursuit of fairness within a discretionary system has arguably removed all certainty.[27] The statutory framework lacks a clear guiding principle, other than indicating that children are the first consideration,[28] and making it the court's duty to consider a clean break.[29] When deciding on financial provision orders it has been left to case-law to decide the weight to be given to the various criteria[30] to which the court must have regard. Fairness, non-discrimination and the 'yardstick of equality' were principles identified in *White* and developed further in *Miller; McFarlane* with reference to the three strands of fairness, namely need, (equal) sharing and compensation. A distinction was also made for the first time between 'matrimonial/family assets' and 'non-matrimonial/family assets'.[31] However, where assets do not exceed needs, it seems that only needs will be met and the process goes no further. It seems here that both family and non-family assets may be used to this end. Yet, where assets do exceed needs, the principle of equal sharing of the family assets applies regardless of the length of the marriage and sharing (although not equal sharing) may also arise in respect of the non-family assets (depending on the length of the marriage and perhaps other circumstances). Lastly, the element of compensation may be applicable. Although it is not certain how this will work in practice, it seems it may be added to the needs of the party eligible

[27] For further discussion of this as a contrast to community of property regimes, see J Scherpe, 'Matrimonial Causes for Concern: A Comparative Analysis of Miller v Miller; McFarlane v McFarlane' (2007) 18 *King's Law Journal* 348 and E Cooke, 'Miller/McFarlane: Law in search of discrimination' (2007) 19 *Child and Family Law Quarterly* 98.

[28] S 25(1) Matrimonial Causes Act 1973.

[29] S 25A(1) Matrimonial Causes Act 1973.

[30] S 25(2) Matrimonial Causes Act 1973. The criteria include all the circumstances of the case, the standard of living during the marriage, the age of the parties and duration of the marriage, the parties' respective current and future income and assets, needs and resources as well as financial and (critically) non-financial contributions made and likely to be made to the welfare of the family by each of the parties and conduct it would be inequitable to ignore. The welfare of the children is the court's first consideration.

[31] See *Miller v Miller*; *McFarlane v McFarlane* [2006] UKHL 24. Lord Nicholls refers to matrimonial and non-matrimonial assets, whereas confusingly Baroness Hale refers to family assets and non-family assets.

for compensation and may in some cases be payable from non-family assets or from income as was the case in *McFarlane*, where the wife had given up a successful career as a city solicitor to care for the three children.

While we may be inclining towards a deferred community of property approach through an equal sharing principle in 'big money' cases, even here the law has yet to decide a number of issues that would be made clear in or not be relevant to property division under a true community of property regime:

- Should the parties' needs be deducted before or after an equal division of assets? In *Miller; McFarlane*, the House of Lords indicated this would depend on the circumstances of the case, although this may make a great difference to the outcome of an individual case.
- How exactly should we define which 'family assets' must be shared equally? Although there is some common ground, such as the matrimonial home and the household goods, Lord Nicholls and Baroness Hale are not at one on whether business assets or their increase in value over the course of the marriage, or indeed inherited assets, should or could over time become 'family assets'. Recent case-law prior to *Miller; McFarlane* had indicated that inherited assets or farmland could escape the principle of equal sharing[32] and this seems to have been endorsed.
- Which factors will justify a departure from equality? These are still not entirely clear. In particular:

'Special' contributions may according to *Miller; McFarlane* have this effect but only in exceptional cases. In *Charman v Charman*,[33] the Court of Appeal confirmed that such a contribution was not necessarily a financial one and declined to indicate a threshold which would separate the exceptional financial contribution from the unexceptional. It did, though, delimit the departure from equality in special contribution cases to awards of no lower than one third and no higher than 45 per cent of the relevant assets.

Although it was stated that short marriages will not per se post-*Miller; McFarlane* justify a departure from equality, it seems they may still have the same effect. There may be a narrower band of 'family assets' to divide (per Lord Nicholls); or given the duration of the marriage is factor to which the court must have regard, there may be cases where departure from equality is justified such as where the family assets are not jointly generated (per Baroness Hale).

[32] In *White v White*, the fact that the husband had inherited the farmland was a reason to depart from equality in what was otherwise an equal partnership marriage. In *P v P (Inherited Property)* [2005] 1 FLR 576, the fact that the major asset was the husband's inherited farmland from which he earned his living again justified departure from equality even where this limited the wife to an award which only met her reasonable requirements.

[33] [2007] EWCA Civ 503.

How is compensation to be calculated in appropriate cases and when will it justify departure from equality? Does it apply to the primary carer who has also worked and, if not, does this provide a perverse incentive to remain financially dependent?

Increased Disparity with Cohabitation

Legal clarity is less of an issue in the informal cohabitation context. Here the problem is the increased disparity between what courts can and do order on divorce or partnership dissolution as compared with very limited remedies available on cohabitation breakdown to functionally similar couples, especially given the fact that 59 per cent of cohabiting couples falsely believe they have the same legal rights as married couples.[34]

Whereas under divorce legislation and now the civil partnership legislation, the court has a wide range of orders at its disposal on relationship breakdown, including orders for periodic maintenance for a partner which adjusts income distribution and also lump-sum orders, property transfer orders, pension sharing orders and settlement of property orders which adjust capital assets as between the parties, this is not the case for cohabiting couples, whether or not there are children of the relationship. Whilst applications for similar orders where there are minor children of the relationship can be made for the benefit of the child,[35] these have been traditionally restrictively interpreted. Although there has been some recent softening of the court's willingness to take the needs of the primary carer into account where there is an embarrassment of assets, there is certainly no overriding aim to achieve 'fairness' as between the cohabitants and no family law-guided redistribution of assets recognising non-financial contributions to the welfare of the family or redressing relationship-generated disadvantage.[36]

What does this mean in practice? In ordinary cases, a divorcing home-maker/primary carer spouse where the major assets including the home are in the name of the other spouse will usually receive at least half of the assets, whereas an equivalent home-maker cohabitant in a similar position must prove an interest under a constructive trust to retain any share of the home. This, as Valerie Burns in *Burns v Burns*[37] found to her cost, is often a difficult and always an unpredictable prospect for the economically weaker cohabitant. Whilst the courts have been more receptive to arguments which

[34] A Barlow, S Duncan, G James and A Park, *Cohabitation, Marriage and the Law: Social Change and Legal Reform in the 21st Century* (Oxford, Hart Publishing, 2005).

[35] See Sched 1 Children Act 1989.

[36] *T v S (Financial Provision for Children)* [1994] 2 FLR 883, *J v C* [1999] 1 FLR 152, *Re P* [2003] EWCA Civ 837 and *H v M* [2006] Fam law 927.

[37] [1984] 1All ER 244.

enable the court to take the couple's whole course of dealing into account alongside direct contributions to the purchase,[38] where there has been no direct contribution such as some payment towards the mortgage or improvements or other evidence of implied common intention to share ownership of the home, there will be no constructive trust.[39] Whilst transfer of property orders can be made for the benefit of a child under 18,[40] unless the primary carer is a joint owner or can prove an interest under a resulting or constructive trust, the best outcome is likely to be the right to occupy the home until the children finish full-time education with no transfer of capital whatsoever. Orders from income for the benefit of the child may have an element built in for the primary carer[41] but no right to maintenance exists as between the adult parties, however disadvantaged the primary carer may have been in the labour market as a result of the relationship.

The Law Commission has, however, recently recommended legislation embodying a presumptive approach to regulating informal cohabitation outside marriage or civil partnership, but one which does not mirror the fairness-based approach available on divorce or civil partnership dissolution.[42] Rather, financial provision would be available only to redress any retained benefit or economic disadvantage suffered which arises directly from the relationship. As has been seen, the legal treatment of this group is far from cohesive and is often complex and confusing for the growing number of couples it affects, and it seems this is likely to continue. However, European community of property jurisdictions have not generally taken a functional approach to regulating cohabitation either.

LESSONS FROM EUROPE?

With the exception of Sweden, few presumptive rights are extended to informal cohabitants in Europe. However, in jurisdictions where there is a community of property regime this has generally been extended to registered partners.[43] Even leaving aside Britain and Ireland, the effects of marriage and registered partnerships on money and property still vary

38 See *Midland Bank v Cooke* [1995] 4 All ER 562, *Drake v Whip* [1996] 1 FLR 826, *Le Foe v Le Foe* [2001] 2 FLR 970 *Oxley v Hiscock* [2004] EWCA Civ 546, Fam Law 569, *Cox v Jones* [2004] EWHC 1486 (Ch) [2004] Fam Law 698, *Stack v Dowden* [2007] UKHL 17.

39 In *Stack v Dowden* [2007] UKHL 17, a case involving joint legal ownership, Lord Walker, at [26], did suggest *obiter* that a common intention constructive trust may not be restricted to cases where there is proof either of agreement or of direct contributions to the purchase of the home vested in a cohabitant partner's sole name.

40 Sched 1 Children Act 1989.

41 See *Re P* [2003] EWCA Civ 837 and *H v M* [2006] Fam law 927.

42 Law Commission, 2007, above n 9.

43 K Boele-Woelki and A Fuchs (eds), *Legal Recognition of Same-Sex Couples in Europe*, (Antwerp, Intersentia, 2003).

considerably from one European state to another. Given the interests of the European Commission in harmonising family property law across the European Union, an empirical study funded by the Nuffield Foundation was undertaken to find out more about how community of property regimes operate in practice in the married and registered partnership context, and to explore whether it would be appropriate for a community of property regime to be introduced in England and Wales either for married couples and, if so, in what form; and/or for unmarried cohabitants and, if so, in what form?[44]

The first stage of the research[45] involved a series of semi-structured interviews with 30 family law notaries and lawyers in France, the Netherlands and Sweden, with 10 from each jurisdiction selected for their specialisation either in matrimonial regime advice or divorce law.

The European Research

These three jurisdictions were chosen as they broadly represent the range of community systems in Europe and each has different approaches to cohabitants. The Netherlands operates a full immediate community system, embracing all assets whether acquired before or after the marriage or registered partnership (both of which are open to same- and different-sex couples), and thus subject to contracting out, all assets effectively become jointly owned. However, there is no legislation in place to offering presumptive financial protection during or after an informal cohabitation relationship. The overall impression gained from notaries and family lawyers in the Netherlands was one of broad satisfaction with the system, and of a feeling that its all-embracing nature has the tremendous advantage of simplicity. The sharing of post-marriage debt was viewed as an acceptable quid pro quo for the sharing of assets. The position of informal cohabitants was acknowledged to be unprotected but considered justifiable where both marriage and partnership registration was available to all.

France, on the other hand, operates a different form of immediate community on marriage, embracing only property acquired after marriage. In the registered partnership context, France has not extended a form of marriage to same-sex couples. Rather its Pacte Civile de Solidarité (PACS) allows same- and different-sex cohabitants to register an agreement in which they agree their own property division on breakdown, although in default of declaring anything different, a form of equal joint ownership

[44] The research proposal was formulated prior to the Civil Partnership Act 2004 and thus did not specifically consider civil partners in England and Wales.

[45] Cooke et al, above n 1.

(*indivision*) was (until recently) imposed.[46] The French PACS is interesting in that it is available to same- and different-sex cohabitants and is not a marriage-mirror model of partnership. In this regard, it stands unique.[47] Once again, what is available to unmarried couples is mainly achieved through registration. Although it is possible to make a declaration that a couple are cohabiting without registering a PACS, this has little legal effect as there is hardly any presumptive legislation. In France we gained a rather more negative view of the practicalities of community of property from the sample of notaries and lawyers. In particular, while post-marriage debt-sharing was a fully accepted part of the immediate community regime, people in general were reported to be unaware of the need to take advice about opting-out of the default regime in appropriate situations.

Sweden, however, in common with the other Scandinavian jurisdictions, offers deferred community. Only on divorce or death does the equal sharing of community assets take effect and there is provision in short marriages of less than five years to depart from equal division where it appears unjust to the owner of the majority of assets.[48] In the cohabitation context, Sweden alone operates a limited form of presumptive (as opposed to opt-in) deferred community, extending only to the family home, for unregistered cohabitants.[49] Here the highest level of perceived client satisfaction among lawyers was found, although the position of informal cohabitants was acknowledged to be no more than a safety-net, a fact not always appreciated by cohabitants.

In considering the suitability of an immediate community of property regime for England and Wales, it was concluded from this first phase of the study that the automatic sharing of debt under such a system was unlikely to be appropriate and there might well be an ideological problem with an immediate community system. Whilst its original rationale was to protect women, by giving them an automatic share in the family's wealth to compensate for their inability to feather the nest because they were sitting on it, this sits uneasily nowadays with the independence of women. This has led Scandinavian jurisdictions to move to deferred community systems.

Overall, the Swedish system of deferred community of property had more resonance with the English system, already described as a judicially created system of deferred community of property,[50] and perhaps even more apt after the recent suggested distinction in the House of Lords

[46] Since conclusion of the empirical project this default position has been revised to one of separate property by Loi no 2006-728, 23 June 2006, implemented in 1 January 2007. See now French Civil Code art 515-1–515-7.

[47] See A Barlow, 'Regulation of Cohabitation, Changing Family Policies and Social Attitudes: A Discussion of Britain within Europe' (2004) 26 *Law and Policy* 57.

[48] Swedish Marriage Code, ch 12 and guidance in the Code's *Travaux Préparatoires*, 1986/87: I, 184–90.

[49] Swedish Cohabitees Act 2003.

[50] Cretney, above n 4.

between 'matrimonial/family assets' automatically shared on divorce and 'non-matrimonial/family assets' which are less likely to be redistributed on divorce.[51] Sweden's presumptive approach to the protection of cohabitants was also thought to chime with our own presumptive approach in this field.

ENGLAND AND WALES STUDY

These issues were probed in the second phase of the study, involving 74 interviews with a sample of men and women drawn in equal measure from three study areas: Reading, Swansea and Liverpool. These represented high-cost, mid-range and low-cost housing markets in England and Wales as it was felt that the value of the family home and the ability to rehouse both partners following divorce may affect people's views. Whilst this was not a nationally representative sample, the sample was purposively selected to reflect a whole spectrum of respondents balanced between different socioeconomic groups, age, gender and relationship status/ experience in order to access a wide range of views. Using a 'grounded theory'[52] approach, we were interested in particular in how the respondents considered financial matters *ought* to be regulated on divorce.

Views relating to the desirability or otherwise of immediate and deferred community of property and of automatic joint ownership of the family home for married and cohabiting partners were tested mainly using vignettes focused on first a married couple and then a cohabiting couple with some direct attitudinal questions where this seemed appropriate. In order to find out what triggered the respondents' views, they were asked to consider the same vignettes first where the couples had no children and then where children were involved.

Immediate Community

We used vignettes in order to probe the idea of sharing liability and then of automatic joint ownership of the family home, looking at a married couple, Rosie and Jim, and a pair of cohabitants, Bob and Wendy. We set the scene as follows:

[51] See *Miller v Miller*; *McFarlane v McFarlane* [2006] UKHL 24 per Lord Nicholls. Baroness Hale refers confusingly to family assets and non-family assets.

[52] BG Glasyer and AL Strauss, *The Discovery of Grounded Theory* (Chicago, Aldine de Gruyter, 1967).

Rosie and Jim/ Wendy and Bob have been married/cohabiting for seven years. Jim and Rosie/Bob and Wendy both work full-time. They live in a house which Jim/Bob bought before they were married/lived together; he has paid all the mortgage instalments and pays some of the utility bills. Rosie/Wendy earns significantly less than Jim/Bob but pays for their joint holidays, her clothes and some of the utility bills. The house is an average three-bedroom semidetached house and the mortgage amounts to two-thirds of its value.

They each have a separate bank account for their earnings.

We asked respondents to consider different events which have different outcomes in community of property and separate property jurisdictions during the relationship. We first looked at identical situations in which Jim/Bob contracted a large debt for the purchase of a yacht. Interviewees were asked whether or not his creditors should be able to satisfy the debt using the whole of the equity of the shared family home and whether or not they should be able to access his partner's earnings. Only 13 of the 73 respondents who answered this question thought that Rosie's earnings should be available to Jim's creditors, as they would in an immediate community system. Just four of our respondents thought that Wendy, the cohabitant, should share Bob's debt; all those respondents were married or divorced. No cohabitant (or former cohabitant) respondents thought Wendy should share Bob's debt.

There was therefore a clear rejection of the liability consequences of an immediate community system. We then went on to consider views on automatic joint ownership of the home along the lines suggested by the Law Commission in 1978.[53]

Automatic Joint Ownership

We found support, in a small rather than an overwhelming majority, for the idea in the abstract that marriage should entail automatic joint ownership of property, with 50 agreeing but 21 of whom had conditions or reservations such as the non-owning spouse making a contribution, or relating to the length of the marriage. A very similar majority (49 to 22) was in favour of automatic joint ownership of earnings, and a smaller one (45 to 28 with some qualified agreement) in favour of automatic joint ownership of the family home. Views were evenly divided as to whether or not an inheritance should be automatically (ie by law rather than by choice) shared with one's spouse.

[53] Law Commission, 1978, above n 18.

Responses to the matching scenario for cohabitants revealed a different pattern. A smaller majority was in favour of the automatic sharing of earnings (36 to 34), and a majority (43 to 29) was against the automatic joint ownership of the shared home. Interestingly, there was some unprompted suggestion by a few respondents that, over time, cohabitants could 'earn' a share in each other's property, but this was not explored systematically.

Most of those who were initially against shared ownership changed their view when asked, in the abstract, whether or not their views would differ if the couple had children. Most said yes and of those who were opposed to automatic joint ownership in general terms, only eight did not change their view. In doing so, most seemed to refer to the family home rather than to earnings, and many gave one or both of two reasons for their change of view. One common reason was in order to safeguard a home for the children; and the other was to ensure that the children would eventually inherit some or all of the family home. However, neither of these is actually particularly relevant in assessing whether or not automatic joint ownership is an appropriate reform of English law. Added to this are the practical difficulties allied to the conveyancing and Land Registration system that make it very difficult to effectively introduce legal joint ownership at the point of marriage or civil partnership registration without significant technological advances permitting successful and automatic data-sharing between computerised public record systems. As for cohabitants, this would pose even greater problems as there is no point at which a cohabitation status becomes formally recognised and could thus trigger registration of joint legal ownership.

Automatic beneficial joint ownership is a possibility but would only protect an interest in the proceeds of sale of the home against third parties. It would not secure a roof over the family's head, giving the protection that people seemed to want. It would also shroud home ownership in uncertainty, a matter viewed negatively by mortgagees and other interested third parties if not by the parties themselves.

On balance, it was felt that whilst it would have been a very useful reform in the late 1960s, it is not one where the gains outweigh the drawbacks at this moment in time. Might deferred community of property be a more practical proposition?

Deferred Community

First, a general question was posed about a deferred redistribution of assets for cohabiting couples. Later vignettes were developed to involve divorce and cohabitation breakdown, asking respondents for views on whether or not family assets should at that point be divided equally between the parties as is the norm under a deferred community of property regime.

A general question was really aimed at testing views on the Swedish system which uniquely imposes deferred community of specified property on cohabitants. The Swedish law aims to protect unregistered cohabitants where no cohabitation contract has been made. It applies to the joint home and household goods acquired after the relationship for all cohabitants. We asked:

> In some countries, when couples have lived together for a number of years, for example three, and then split up, the law pools their property and shares it between them.
> (a) What do you think about this and why?
> (b) If you think this is a good idea, what sort of shares do you think would be appropriate and why?

Perhaps surprisingly, a majority of our respondents (38 of the 73 answering this question) thought this was a good idea; 19 of them suggested an automatic equal division of the pooled assets on relationship breakdown regardless of whether there were children. A theme which came through the answers was that this was appropriate if both partners were working and were contributing to the couple's shared life. As one respondent expressed it:

> 50/50, yes it's a partnership isn't it? It can't be attributed to simply judging what you're putting into it. It's a relationship that has many assets, not just financial. (Interview AR49, married male 31–40)

Seven respondents were sure that this system was appropriate where there were children but were more equivocal in other cases, and a further eight, whilst certain that assets should be shared, were unsure of the appropriateness of equal division which they felt would depend on the merits of each case. Of the remainder broadly in favour (four), some felt that only the home should be shared or that inherited assets or assets acquired before the relationship should be excluded.

However, a significant minority (32) rejected outright such a system on the basis that it was inappropriate, open to abuse by 'gold-diggers' and unfair in the short-term cohabitation context where there were no children. Here the overwhelming view was that financial contribution should directly govern the post-relationship outcome.

Thus there seems to be some support for community of property for informal cohabitants and this is strongest where the relationship is a joint enterprise, a matter that may not be easy to judge. However there was also a keen awareness of the possibility of abuse of such a system, which is perhaps an argument in favour of retaining court discretion but extending it to cohabitation breakdown.

Deferred community of property was further explored by developing the vignettes for the married and unmarried couples (Rosie and Jim and Wendy and Bob, respectively) who had each been together for seven years. We asked what the outcome should be with regard to the family home owned by Jim/Bob if the relationship broke down, first where the couple had no children, and second where they had two children, aged six and four. We specified four options reflecting possible legal outcomes.

In the married context where there were no children, just under half (34) thought that the house should be sold and the proceeds divided equally in line with the idea of deferred community of property. Interestingly, though, even though this was a marriage, 37 thought the home should be divided according to contribution. Not surprisingly, in the cohabitation context deferred community of the home or even a lesser share in it for Wendy was less popular. Although over half the sample were in favour of the same treatment of Rosie and Wendy, whatever their views were on that, over a quarter (20) of the respondents who felt that Rosie should get some sort of share of the home thought Wendy was not entitled to anything at all because she was not married:

> Because to my mind marriage is a partnership. When you're co-habiting, although it is a partnership, there is still something missing, a certificate to show that you are married. It's just the way I feel about it. (Interview 11PL, female, married, 51–60, retired, Liverpool, C2)

Thus whilst deferred community was thought more appropriate in the marriage context than the cohabitation context, views were divergent about the extent to which marriage itself should trigger an equal division.

However, in exploring views where our couples had children, a marked consensus in favour of deferred community with an equal sharing of assets was identified. There was also very strong support for equal treatment of couples with children, regardless of whether they were married or cohabiting. Only 10 of our 74 respondents gave different views relating to the outcomes for the married Rosie and Jim, compared with the cohabiting Bob and Wendy, and this was a striking finding, given the very different legal consequences that currently exist.

This typifies the responses:

> I think she should be allowed to stay in the house until the children are older and then the property sold.
> Q: And in what sort of shares?
> A: Again, I think it should be an equal split.
> Q: And why do you feel that?
> A: Because she's had the major responsibility of bringing up the children.
> Q: Now what if it was Wendy and Bob, the co-habiting couple whose relationship breaks down? Would you feel differently if it was Wendy and Bob who went through that?
> A: No, no.
> Q: Why not?
> A: Because they've both still got the same responsibilities to each other and to their children. (Interview L23, female married 51–60)

However, when we broke down the respondents into different categories, fewer of the divorced men and former cohabiting men were in favour of this as compared with other groups. Rather, a purely contribution-based approach was felt more appropriate whether married or not and despite the presence of children, with Jim/Bob supporting the family in other ways. This again raises the question of whether the law has currently drawn the lines in the right places, given public perceptions.

Overall, there seemed therefore to be some support for the principles of a deferred community of property regime in the married and unmarried contexts where there were children of the relationship. However, there was also a strong feeling that preservation of a home for the children should take priority, an outcome that would not always fit with the property entitlement concept of community of property at the lower end of the asset scale.

DOES A DEFERRED COMMUNITY OF PROPERTY REGIME HAVE ANYTHING TO OFFER ENGLAND AND WALES?

First, having studied the characteristics of three European community of property regimes, it is clear that we do not have such a regime in England and Wales. There is, though, a move towards a deferred community of property approach in cases where assets exceed needs due to the judicially created requirements of the yardstick of equality and the new distinction between matrimonial and non-matrimonial assets. However, this is not to be confused with a true community of property regime. The next question then is whether a formal community regime would be useful to this jurisdiction given the criticisms of the discretionary system we have.

On the positive side, such a regime would reflect the approach in *Miller* and *McFarlane* of identifying 'matrimonial assets', but would put it on a statutory footing. We would then know exactly which assets were 'his', or 'hers' or 'theirs'. This could achieve greater simplicity and certainty, and could promote agreement or mediation rather than litigation in financial disputes on relationship breakdown.

Equal division does have an instinctive appeal in the popular imagination as a 'fair' solution, particularly where there are children in both the married and unmarried contexts and any formal regime would permit people (both married and unmarried) to contract out of the regime and substitute another arrangement with far greater certainty in cohabitation or premarital contracts. Finally, certainty might be the new fairness, given that uncertainty is viewed as unjust.[54]

[54] This is argued by Buckley in the Irish context as offering a measure of 'security, certainty, and transparency . . . likely to increase both justice and well-being both during and after the

However, perhaps we risk losing more than we gain by adopting a 'European' approach. Deferred community is an entitlement-based rather than a needs-based redistribution of assets. We would lose all semblance of fairness if, as in the European regimes, needs could not justify departure from the rules of property division. Another possible problem is that a deferred community regime might not be viewed publicly acceptable for all couples, especially cohabitants without children. The hostile public reaction to the *Miller* decision where a two-year childless marriage resulted in the wife being awarded £5 million (roughly a quarter of the total assets) perhaps also echoes this negativity in the childless married context. Although permitting contracting out can be seen to preserve parties' autonomy in the face of a statutory regime, this also carries the danger that it may disadvantage weaker economic partners. A deferred community regime with a principled egalitarian approach or even a Swedish-style sliding-scale approach (such as Eekelaar's accrual over time[55]) might in the English housing context be at the expense of meeting children's housing needs, which the project findings showed respondents were clear should not be the case.

Where, then, does the right balance lie? As has been seen, the project data send conflicting messages. An attempt to build a model of deferred community of property which incorporated need was made.[56] The principle involved identifying the community and non-community assets for all the parties and applying the community assets to meet the parties' needs. Any excess would be divided equally. Where the community was insufficient to meet all the needs, then each party's non-community assets were applied proportionately to meet the outstanding needs.[57] However, whilst this worked well at the top end of the asset scale, it did not improve upon the current system at the lower end, and it was reluctantly concluded that it could not be pursued to any good effect.

Perhaps the principal reason for the difficulties of adapting to a community regime lies in the English housing market. The heavy emphasis on owner-occupation, with affordable rented accommodation hard to find or of poor quality, means that most people require capital in some form to meet their need for a home. This in turn militates towards a needs-based redistribution at least at the lower end of the asset scale.

Traditionally, the housing market in other parts of Europe has been rather different. Far more people rent, and therefore meet their housing

marriage'. See LA Buckley, 'Matrimonial Property and Irish Law: A Case for Community? (2002) 53(1) *Northern Ireland Legal Quarterly* 76.

55 J Eekelaar, 'Asset Distribution on Divorce—Time and Property' [2003] 33 *Family Law* 828.

56 See Cooke et al, above n 1.

57 For worked examples see Cooke et al, above n 1, and E Cooke and A Barlow, 'Community of Property: Some Final Reflections', paper presented to University Staffordshire conference, February 2007.

needs out of income. In that environment, a system which divides capital without reference to needs, while responding to needs through maintenance awards, makes far more sense.[58]

CONCLUSION

In the marriage and civil partnership context, given that deferred community of property is premised on equal sharing of assets specified as matrimonial and never permits the weaker economic spouse to be awarded more than one-half of the assets, it is clear that such a system cannot be adopted in England and Wales without abandoning the principal priority guiding financial provision on relationship breakdown in the married context of meeting both parties' housing needs and those of the children. The project findings confirm that such a priority developed through the judicial interpretation of section 25 of the Matrimonial Causes Act 1973 is very much in line with what people believe should happen on heterosexual relationship breakdown and, where there are children, regardless of whether the parties were married or cohabiting.

Whilst equal division of assets is an attractive principle which fits well with the construct of marriage (and civil partnership) as an equal partnership, it by no means guarantees meeting the needs of the weaker economic partner and the children other than in the context of the very rich. Furthermore, we have seen there is significant equivocation about the equal sharing of assets following short, childless marriages, and so some adjustment along the lines of the Swedish model might need to be introduced to gain public acceptance. It therefore seems that only if we are satisfied that needs can be adequately met from income or, more radically, if we are prepared to abandon meeting needs as the safeguard focus of financial provision on relationship breakdown, can we move fully towards an entitlement model. For deferred community of property incorporates completely different presumed notions of fairness centred on contractual

[58] Available figures from 1999 show that in the UK only 10 per cent of households rent compared to 36 per cent in Germany, 21 per cent in France, 17 per cent in the Netherlands and 16 per cent in Sweden – see further A Oswald, 'The Housing Market and Europe's Unemployment', Warwick University, 1999 available at http://www2.warwick.ac.uk/fac/soc/economics/staff/faculty/oswald/homesnt.pdf. Owner occupation rates in 2001 were 43 per cent Germany, 63 per cent France, 53 per cent the Netherlands, 60 per cent Sweden compared to 71 per cent in the UK (see further ESRC Society Today Fact Sheet on Housing in the UK, 2005 available at http://www.esrcsocietytoday.ac.uk/ESRCInfoCentre/facts/UK/index43.aspx?ComponentId=12642&SourcePageId=14975. This means that there is greater cultural acceptance of renting in other European jurisdictions which combines with lower average house prices. Thus at the lower end of the income and asset scale, more people accept the need to rent, whereas in the UK this is resisted due to the very high pressured and generally rising owner occupation housing market, where the family home is also perceived as a financial investment for the future. The UK therefore has proportionately more owner occupiers who become financially stretched on divorce.

entitlement and certainty. At the present time, therefore, unless we are prepared to sacrifice common law pragmatic and flexible notions of fairness to a civil law principled concept of contractual fairness, there are no obvious advantages to introducing a classical model deferred community regime. This is despite the attractions of the Swedish system which, it should be remembered, is underpinned by a welfare state which reduces 'needs' considerations on divorce.

Having said this, however, any further serious consideration of community of property as a regime for England and Wales would need to look carefully at the New Zealand model which was outside the scope of our Europe-focused empirical project. This is a jurisdiction which recently transferred from a purely discretionary system of ancillary relief to a deferred community of property system. What is more, it incorporates many features that the project findings identified as being desirable. It takes a functional approach in that it extends both to married couples and cohabitants of at least three years standing but is subject to contracting out. It therefore avoids the complexity of differently premised parallel schemes for married and cohabiting couples. Critically, it has also managed to combine an entitlement principle of equal sharing with elements of need or at least compensation-based discretion,[59] although it has been the subject to criticism.[60]

In the absence of a Scandinavian-style welfare state, this perhaps offers the best hope for balancing the certainty of entitlement with the flexibility of discretion but within bounds which will enable the outcome of most cases to be agreed or at least predicted with greater accuracy than is currently possible in England and Wales.

What is apparent from the England and Wales study is that the sharp regulatory divide between married and unmarried couples was not seen as appropriate, in particular where there were children of the relationship. Clearly this is an area where law has not, as Smart[61] proposes, kept up with rapid changes in contemporary practices of kinship.

[59] The Property (Relationships) Act 1996 as amended has equal sharing as a starting principle but subject to a large number of exceptions. These include separate rules for short marriages (ss 14 and 14A); a discretion where equal sharing of community assets would be repugnant to justice to share assets according to contributions to the relationship (s 13); and a claim for compensation paid from separate property over and above the equal share of community assets in order to alleviate economic disparity but only where one party's income and standard of living is likely to be significantly higher than the other's and this is attributable to the division of functions during the relationship (s 15). Note that again 'needs' other than compensation are met out of maintenance awards out of income alone (s 64 Family Proceedings Act 1980) but that it is possible to allow the parent with care to remain in the family home with the children (ss 26, 26A, 33(d) Property (Relationships Act) 1976).

[60] See J Miles, 'Principles or Pragmatism in Ancillary Relief; The Virtues of Flirting with Academic Theories and Other Jurisdictions.' (2005) 19 *International Journal of Law Policy and and the Family* 242.

[61] C Smart, 'Making Kin: Relationality and Law', ch 2 in this volume.

4

Caring and Sharing: Interdependency as a Basis for Property Redistribution?

SIMONE WONG

INTRODUCTION

IN RECENT YEARS, an increasing number of jurisdictions have introduced legal reform to regulate cohabitation, both opposite and same sex. In some cases, for example in Australia, reform has even been extended to other non-couple domestic relationships involving the provision of care and support. In England, the question of whether legal reform should be introduced to regulate cohabitation was recently reviewed by the Law Commission for England and Wales.[1] The debate has in part been fuelled by recent changes brought about by the passage of the Civil Partnership Act 2004, which served to highlight the gaps in the law in terms of treatment of various types of domestic relationships. For the time being in the UK, only opposite-sex couples are permitted to marry, while same-sex couples may acquire rights and responsibilities that are analogous to those of married couples by registering a civil partnership. Briefly, two arguments were put forward by the government to support the enactment of the Civil Partnership Act: the equality argument—to provide legal recognition to same-sex relationships which hitherto had been invisible to the law; and the economic vulnerability argument—to address the economic vulnerability of parties at the end of a relationship.

However, the use of the economic vulnerability argument made it easy for that argument to be hijacked by others, as can be seen from the events that took place in the House of Lords during the passage of the Civil Partnership Bill. If, as argued by the government, the key concern of the Act is to provide fairness and justice to those who are left economically

[1] Scotland has already introduced changes in the law which provides some rights, albeit less extensive than those given to married couples, in the Family Law (Scotland) Act 2006. See Family Law (Scotland) Act 2006, ss 25–29.

vulnerable at the end of a committed relationship, whether sexual or not, rather than same-sex marriage (albeit labelled as a 'civil partnership'), why should the Act stop at same-sex relationships? Moreover, the use of equality and/or economic vulnerability arguments may not necessarily serve the interests of parties to a domestic relationship. For many feminists, equality is a problematic concept. As Diduck and O'Donovan succinctly put it, one of the key criticisms of equality is that, while it resolves the problem of treating people or situations differently, it does not necessarily redress dominance within a close intimate relationship and/or recognise that differential treatment may sometimes be needed to counterbalance institutional or structural disadvantages.[2] Economic vulnerability, on the other hand, limits the focus to patterns of dependency when we should in fact look beyond this to patterns of shared commitment as a ground for legal intervention.[3]

In this chapter, I am concerned with the way in which legal discourse on justifying intervention in certain types of domestic relationships has increasingly shifted towards 'interdependency'. This trend raises the question of how we should think of 'interdependency' in this area of the law. Because of the complexities involved in understanding and evaluating close personal relationships, one reason why framing any reform of this area of the law is problematic (and challenging) is that a myriad of meanings can attach to the words used to describe such relationships. Nor is it being suggested that there can (or should) be only one legitimate way of understanding and/or using these terms. It is therefore important to grapple with how, for legal purposes, we understand and use terms such as 'interdependency' and the ways in which, if any, connections may or ought to be made between commitment, interdependency and economic vulnerability.

Given that the focus of law reform in England and Wales is currently confined to cohabitation, the chapter seeks to analyse firstly the way that interdependency is being constructed as a basis for justifying legal intervention in these relationships, and, secondly, how the law responds, or ought to respond, to such interdependency at the end of the relationship in terms of property redistribution. I intend to argue that, even where legal reform has shifted towards interdependency, most such reforms have not truly maximised the potential for providing greater scope for the notion of shared commitment to flourish. Instead, most measures to date have been conservative, limiting their scope to dyadic relationships that in many ways

[2] A Diduck and K O'Donovan, 'Feminism and Families: *Plus Ça Change?*', in A Diduck and K O'Donovan (eds), *Feminist Perspectives on Family Law* (Abingdon, Routledge-Cavendish, 2006) 11.

[3] A Bottomley and S Wong, 'Shared Households: A New Paradigm for Reform of Domestic Property Relations', in A Diduck and K O'Donovan (eds), *Feminist Perspectives on Family Law* (Abingdon, Routledge-Cavendish, 2006) 52.

mirror the heterosexual marriage model. The approaches taken in resolving property disputes have been equally conservative. This stems from the fact that most systems continue to focus on patterns of economic vulnerability as *the* reason for legal intervention and have not really been able to move beyond that to interdependency—to a more interactive pattern of shared commitment—as the baseline. By shifting the focus to interdependency, attention may still be given to economic vulnerability but that must be seen in combination with the parties' shared commitment.

EQUALITY VERSUS ECONOMIC VULNERABILITY

Moves towards extending protection beyond marriage to other domestic relationships, especially cohabitation, have mainly been driven by arguments of economic vulnerability and more recently, equality. The use of equality as a justification for legal intervention has been more successful for same-sex couples in that there is generally greater acceptance that discrimination on the basis of sexual orientation is no longer acceptable. In the UK, this view has been reinforced by the emerging human rights climate since the passage of the Human Rights Act 1998 which gave effect to the European Convention on Human Rights within national law.[4] The successful argumentation of equality led to the passage of the Civil Partnership Act 2004 whereby same-sex couples who enter into a civil partnership will thus acquire rights and responsibilities analogous to those of married couples, including access to financial relief and property redistribution when the relationship ends. On the other hand, the use of equality arguments by opposite-sex cohabitants and other parties, such as siblings who are parties to a domestic relationship, to seek legal protection in relation to financial and property matters has met with less success. I am not aware of any case that has been brought before the English courts by opposite-sex cohabitants to mount a challenge under the Human Rights Act for the lack of, or their exclusion from, a property adjustment regime similar to that afforded to married couples. Such attempts, however, have been made before the European Court of Human Rights.[5] In those cases, equality is closely aligned with non-discrimination on the basis of marital status. However, in the light of countervailing arguments such as freedom

[4] See, eg, *Ghaidan v Mendoza* [2002] 4 All ER 1162 (CA), [2004] 3 All ER 411 (HL); *Wandsworth London Borough Council v Michalak* [2002] 4 All ER 1136. Very weighty reasons will now be needed to justify differential treatment on the basis of sexual orientation in order for Arts 8 and 14 not to be engaged. For recent European Court cases, see also *Smith & Grady v UK* (Nos 33985/96 and 33986/96) (27 September 1999) (Ct J); *Lustig-Prean & Beckett v UK* (Nos 31417/96 and 32377/96) (27 September 1999) (Ct J); *Karner v Austria* (2004) 38 EHRR 24.

[5] See, eg, *Johnston v Ireland* (No 9697/82) (18 December 1986) (Ct J); *Saucedo Gómez v Spain* (No 37784/97) (26 January 1999) (Ct A D); *Quintana Zapata v Spain* (No 34615/97) (4 March 1998) (Com A D).

of choice and autonomy, the European Court case-law suggests that there is generally some reluctance to view differential treatment of married couples and opposite-sex cohabitants with regard to financial and property matters as unjustifiable discrimination.[6] I am also aware of only one UK case to date where a human rights challenge has been mounted by non-couple domestic partners.[7] This complaint to the European Court has been brought by two elderly sisters, Joyce and Sybil Burden, who have lived together all their lives and, for the past 30 years, have lived in the house they inherited from their parents. Each sister has made a will leaving all her property to the other. The survivor who inherits the other's half share would be subject to inheritance tax and might have to sell the shared home in order to pay the tax. The European Court, however, found by a close majority of four to three (and three strong dissenting judgments at that) that the two sisters have not been discriminated against as there is no violation of Article 1 of Protocol 1 (peaceful enjoyment of possessions) in conjunction with Article 14.

With equality arguments having limited mileage, opposite-sex cohabitants are more likely to invoke the economic vulnerability argument to appeal to the law's sense of justice and fairness. The economic vulnerability argument is often bolstered by other arguments such as the functional similarity of opposite-sex cohabitation and marriage, and the need for 'realism' in the law[8] as a justification for extending some legal protection to unmarried opposite-sex couples, especially those with children. The dependency of a cohabitant who undertakes homemaking and childcare responsibilities, and the ensuing economic vulnerability often suffered due to her lack of, or diminished participation in, wage labour, call for some redress of the (economic) imbalance suffered at the termination of the relationship. Moreover, Barlow et al found in their recent research on cohabitation that many couples are increasingly choosing not to marry and that many also do not make informed decisions about whether to marry or not.[9] Their survey further revealed that more than 40 per cent of respondents believed that some form of family law protection would be available

[6] For a fuller discussion, see S Wong, 'The Human Rights Act 1998 and the Shared Home: Issues for Cohabitants' (2005) 27 *Journal of Social Welfare and Family Law* 265.

[7] See *Burden and Burden v UK* (No 13378/05) (12 December 2006). The sisters have appealed to the Grand Chamber and the decision of the Grand Chamber is pending as at the time of writing this chapter.

[8] See A Barlow, S Duncan, G James and A Park, *Cohabitation, Marriage and the Law: Social Change and Legal Reform in the 21st Century* (Oxford, Hart Publishing, 2005). See also A Barlow, 'Cohabitation Law Reform—Messages from Research' (2006) 14 *Feminist Legal Studies* 167; cf A Bottomley, 'From Mrs Burns to Mrs Oxley: Do Co-habiting Women (Still) Need Marriage Law?' (2006) 14 *Feminist Legal Studies* 181, where she argues that the 'realism' argument needs to be looked at more closely, especially with its evocation of the figure of Mrs Burns as a key reason for reforming the law.

[9] Barlow et al, above n 8.

to them, despite their lack of marital status. When combined with the perceived view that neither the common law nor equitable principles currently provide sufficient protection to cohabitants,[10] it seems all too clear that changes in the law of cohabitation are needed to deal with the financial and property matters of cohabitants on the termination of their relationships.

In jurisdictions such as Australia these themes have been played out: legal reform initially took the shape of providing only opposite-sex cohabitants with access to the law where their relationship closely mirrors marriage. Earlier sub-national legislation, eg in New South Wales, was clearly more concerned with providing protection on the basis of status (based on the marriage model) rather than interdependency. Thus, a cohabiting relationship would qualify only if it were a 'relationship between [a man and a woman] . . . living or having lived together as husband and wife on a bona fide domestic basis although not married to each other'.[11]

In 1994, the Domestic Relationships Act 1994 of the Australian Capital Territory was passed which, as the first sub-national legislation to shift the focus of domestic relationships from status to interdependency, was a ground-breaking piece of legislation. Firstly, the statute not only extends protection to cohabiting couples, both opposite and same sex, but also to non-cohabiting couples and other domestic relationships involving the provision of care and support. Secondly, in emphasising interdependency as the basis of legal protection, the 1994 Act also abandons a marriage-like definition of a qualifying relationship, adopting instead a gender- and couple-neutral definition that is applicable both to couple and non-couple domestic relationships.[12]

New South Wales followed suit in 1999, amending and renaming the De Facto Relationships Act 1984 as the Property (Relationships) Act.[13] The impetus for change was in part due to the gay and lesbian lobby arguing for extension of legal protection to them on the grounds of equality and non-discrimination. However, the New South Wales amendments did not go as far the Domestic Relationships Act in that the 1984 Act is limited to opposite- and same-sex couples and those in non-couple caregiving relationships who live together. More recently, Tasmania also repealed its De Facto Relationships Act 1999 and introduced the Relationships Act

[10] See, eg, P Clarke, 'The Family Home: Intention and Agreement' (1992) 22 *Family Law* 22; S Gardner, 'Rethinking Family Property' (1993) 109 *Law Quarterly Review* 263; N Glover and P Todd, 'The Myth of Common Intention' (1996) 16 *Legal Studies* 325; S Wong, 'Constructive Trusts over the Family Home: Lessons to be Learned From Other Commonwealth Jurisdictions?' (1998) 18 *Legal Studies* 369.

[11] See s 3(1) of the earlier De Facto Relationships Act 1984.

[12] Domestic relationships are defined in s 3 of the Domestic Relationships Act 1994 as 'a personal relationship between two adults in which one provides personal or financial commitment and support of a domestic nature for the material benefit of the other'.

[13] The amendments were effected by the Property (Relationships) Legislation Amendment Act 1999.

2003. Like the Domestic Relationships Act and the Property (Relationships) Act, the new Tasmanian statute provides legal protection on an ascription basis to a wider class of domestic partners. These include couples as well as parties to a non-couple domestic relationship of caregiving, whether they are living together or not.[14] However, while economic vulnerability arising from the interdependent nature of these close personal relationships forms the underlying rationale for the statute's presumptive system, there is interestingly a retreat to status as an alternative route to legal protection. The Relationships Act is the first Australian sub-national legislation to provide a registration scheme where domestic partners may, through a deed of relationship, register their relationship.[15]

The developments that have taken place in the Australian context reveal the manner in which economic vulnerability-linked arguments of interdependency have overtaken equality arguments to bring about changes to the law. We see how the equality argument initially used by same-sex couples can equally piggyback on the economic vulnerability argument. Thus, same-sex couples argued for sameness in treatment because they, just like their opposite-sex counterparts, could be equally economically vulnerable in close intimate relationships. The deployment of economic vulnerability arguments, however, evinces a subtle shift as well in the legal discourse—that the nexus between equality and economic vulnerability need not necessarily be based on functional similarity of other domestic relationships and marriage but commitment and interdependency. That being the case, there is no logical reason to limit access to the law to only couple-based relationships. Once this leap is made in legal discourse, it opens up space for other interdependent relationships to use economic vulnerability as a justification for extending legal protection to their relationships.

INTERDEPENDENCY

The shift from equality/non-discrimination to commitment/interdependency as a justification for legal intervention in cohabiting relationships is unsurprising. A clear strength of the equality argument, argues Bamforth, lies in its clear emotive appeal to the law for same treatment.[16] Although not premised on any appeal for same treatment, reference to undue hardship or injustice that one may suffer as a consequence of being in a committed and interdependent relationship similarly gives rise to a very strong emotive appeal to the law for justice and fairness. What is more

[14] Relationships Act 2003, ss 4(1) and 5(1).

[15] Relationships Act 2003, s 11.

[16] N Bamforth, 'Same-sex Partnerships and Arguments of Justice' in R Wintemute and M Andenas (eds), *Legal Recognition of Same-sex Partnerships: A Study of National, European and International Law* (Oxford, Hart Publishing, 2001).

elusive, though, is the way in which interdependency and commitment are to be defined legally. Drawing on various models of legal reform, we find that in Australia, for example, sub-national statutes began by initially adopting a marriage-like definition, ie a dyadic relationship (between a man and a woman) which necessarily involves a sexual relationship. Legislation set boundaries on the meaning of 'intimacy' in couple relationships in order to contain the types of relationships covered. In doing so, the basis upon which these boundaries are set become crucial. In many models, conjugality formed the fulcrum for providing protection. Adopting an assimilative approach is problematic for several reasons[17] but, more crucially, it presupposes that cohabiting and marital relationships are similar and/or that all cohabitants, whether opposite or same sex, want their relationships to be treated as (functionally) similar to marriage.

To counter these concerns, some reforms have moved away from a marriage-like definition to a looser one of 'coupledom' in order to include same-sex couples. This makes conjugality apparently less essential since eligibility is instead focused on the presence of commitment and interdependency. A move towards more gender-neutral definitions has, like in Australia, opened the space for the inclusion of other 'committed and interdependent' non-couple domestic relationships of care and support. This shift in definitional terms has, however, raised one problem, namely the lack of guidance given by most of the statutes to help our understanding of what exactly it is about particular types of domestic relationships that actually gives rise to interdependency and any concomitant economic vulnerability. Here, we need to separate commitment from interdependency. The issue of commitment is often dealt with by most law reforms through the imposition of a minimum duration requirement in order to distinguish the more stable (and thus perceived as being more committed) relationships from those that are contingent, especially when the parties do not have children. In the Australian context, for instance, the sub-national legislation requires a minimum duration of two years for a particular relationship to be eligible, unless the partners have children.[18] In the UK, recent statistics such as the British Social Attitudes Survey 2000 reveal that the median duration of cohabitation is four years while the mean duration is 6.5 years. While the data is clearly incomplete since it is not known

[17] For the Australian perspective, see J Milllbank and K Sant, 'A Bride in Her Everyday Clothes: Same Sex Relationship Recognition in NSW' (2000) 22 *Sydney Law Review* 181; J Millbank and W Morgan, 'Let Them Eat Cake and Ice Cream: Wanting Something "More" from the Relationship Recognition Menu', in R Wintemute and M Andenas (eds), *Legal Recognition of Same-sex Partnerships: A Study of National, European and International Law* (Oxford, Hart Publishing, 2001); R Graycar and J Millbank, 'The Bride Wore Pink . . . to the Property (Relationships) Legislation Amendment Act 1999: Relationships Law Reform in New South Wales' (2000) 17 *Canadian Journal of Family Law* 227.

[18] See Property (Relationships) Act 1984, s 17; Domestic Relationships Act 1994, s 12; Relationships Act 2003, s 37.

whether ongoing cohabiting relationships at the time of the interviews are likely to continue and/or be converted into marriage, the General Household Survey 2002 nevertheless indicates that, between 1986 and 1998, the median duration of cohabitation for single (never married) men has risen to just over three years, while the median duration for single women is now over three years.[19] It may therefore be suggested that a minimum duration of two years is a sufficient indication of the partners' commitment to their relationship.

The issue of commitment also raises a further question of, aside from minimum duration, what other factors surrounding the parties' relationship may be equally relevant. The Australian sub-national legislation, for example, attempts to address this by providing a list of factors that the courts may take into account in determining the presence of a qualifying domestic relationship.[20] A closer look at the factors often provided in such lists suggests that the lists in fact perform a twofold evidentiary purpose: as further indication of the existence of a committed relationship as well as interdependency.[21] However, by picking factors that tend to be the same as those previously used alongside a marriage-like definition of cohabitation, there is a misguided emphasis on commitment and not enough on interdependency. There is even less guidance when it comes to caregiving domestic relationships. Most definitions relating to such relationships either are very open-ended or have some parameters set through the provision of a separate non-exhaustive list of factors. But that list, although not identical, tends to mirror in many ways the one used for couple-based relationships. Not only is the suitability of such a list highly questionable, but the problem faced by legislators in defining what commitment and interdependency mean in disparate domestic relationships is further reinforced. Because of the definitional issues that non-couple domestic relationships pose, it is not surprising that the Law Society, for example, rejected the extension of legal protection to such relationships.[22] Notwithstanding the use of more neutral terms such as 'coupledom', law reform may thus continue to resolve the issue of commitment between cohabitants by drawing on characteristics that mirror to some extent those of marriage, and by confining eligible relationships to those of sufficient longevity through a minimum-duration requirement.

Even if one were to accept that couple-based interdependent relationships should be given greater priority over other forms of domestic relationships

[19] J Haskey, 'Cohabitation in Great Britain: Past, Present and Future Trends—and Attitudes' (2002) 103 *Popular Trends* 4, 10. At 4.5 years, the median duration of cohabitation for divorced men and women tends to be slightly longer than for single men and women.

[20] See, eg, the lists found in s 4(2) of the Property (Relationships) Act 1984 and s 4(3) of the Relationships Act 2003.

[21] I am using 'interdependency' here in the manner discussed in more detail below, although not all of the factors, eg conjugality, that appear of such lists are necessary indicia of interdependency.

[22] Law Society, *Cohabitation: The Case for Clear Law* (2002).

in terms of legal protection, it still leaves unresolved the question of how concepts such as interdependency ought to be legally constructed. The use of a list of factors tends to obscure the second evidentiary function that such lists can perform and to subsume interdependency under commitment, rather than see them as separate but not necessarily mutually exclusive aspects of close personal relationships. Drawing on the theory of interdependency in the field of psychology, interdependency in a close relationship appears to describe:[23] 'the quantity and quality of that interdependence [between two persons] over time and in identifying the causal factor that both affect and are affected by interdependence'. This suggests that 'interdependency' is a relatively broad concept which relates to the interconnection of the activities of the parties to the relationship, and the way in which each partner's conduct has an impact on the other and affects their respective choices, outcomes, etc. A question that arises is the extent to which such an understanding of 'interdependency' may possibly be applied in legal discourse, especially when addressing the questions of whether a close relationship is interdependent and why it should be protected by the law. The theory of interdependency also requires us to look at the roles undertaken by the parties to the relationship. As Peplau explains, affect influences behavioural patterns in that the roles that people undertake within a relationship are influenced by one's emotional investment in a relationship.[24] Psychologists similarly observe that love and commitment often go together in opposite-sex relationships.[25] Kelley, for instance, suggests four components to love:[26] needing (a desire to be in the other's presence and to be cared for by the other); caring (anticipation of wanting to help the other); trusting (willingness to establish mutual trust through the exchange of confidence); and tolerance (willingness to tolerate the other's faults).[27] 'Love' must also be distinguished from 'commitment'—that 'love' does not necessarily involve a commitment to maintain a relationship. However, Kelley's research suggests that, for many couples, caring often came before need and trust, and was viewed by them as being

[23] E Berscheid and LA Peplau, 'The Emerging Science of Relationships', in HH Kelley et al (eds), *Close Relationships* (New York, WH Freeman and Co, 1983) 12.

[24] LA Peplau, 'Roles and Gender', in HH Kelley et al (eds), *Close Relationships* (New York, WH Freeman and Co, 1983) 228.

[25] It should be noted that these commentators make reference to opposite-sex cohabitation since their research focused only on this group. That is not to say that these notions of love and commitment fall within the exclusive purview of opposite-sex cohabitation, and cannot, and do not, apply to same-sex cohabitants.

[26] HH Kelley, 'Love and Commitment', in HH Kelley et al (eds), *Close Relationships* (New York, WH Freeman and Co, 1983) 273.

[27] Ibid, 285. Kelley also describes how these four components fit within three models of 'love': passionate love which emphasises needs; pragmatic love which emphasises trust and tolerance; and altruistic love which emphasises the caring features of love and views such behaviour as intrinsically motivated rather than performed with reciprocation in mind. In reality, many close personal relationships are capable of exhibiting more than one of these models of love at a time.

the most distinctive aspect of a committed and loving relationship. In the light of this, it may be suggested that, when attempting to define which types of close relationships ought to be protected through regulation, an important signifier of commitment should be the affective component of caring (as opposed to the physical act of caregiving which may or may not involve affective 'caring' for the recipient of the care given). Any list of factors to be included in a proposed legislation as guidance to the courts in determining whether a particular relationship is eligible should thus place greater emphasis on aspects of 'caring' rather than others such as conjugality.

Interdependency is also closely linked to the roles that the parties undertake within the relationship. Here, three specific features of role performance require consideration: diversity, specialisation and complementarity. Of these, 'complementarity' is of particular interest, not only for determining the extent of interdependency but also for assessing the range of contributions, financial and non-financial, made by the parties to the relationship for the purposes of making an award on separation. Peplau accepts that complementarity can occur through diversity as well as specialisation, and identifies two distinct types of complementarity: firstly, there is the interweaving of individual activities in face-to-face interaction; and secondly, where there is coordination of activities to accomplish shared goals or functions, or in 'managing' causal conditions influencing a relationship.[28] In other words, complementarity refers to the way in which the roles of the parties mesh; it concerns reciprocity of rights and obligations between the partners as a consequence of undertaking certain roles. Moreover, the theory of interdependency further observes that, within interdependent (couple) relationships, there is also a positive, linear relationship between commitment and willingness to sacrifice, and that the cost level of making sacrifices forms an important factor in moderating the relationship between commitment and willingness to sacrifice.[29] Where the cost level of the interdependence dilemma[30] is high, research reveals that couples in high-commitment relationships are more willing to make sacrifices because they are motivated by the dyad and less by the self than those in low-commitment relationships.[31] Thus, the willingness to make sacrifices (and take risks in making one more vulnerable) in a relationship is influ-

[28] Peplau, above n 24, 230.

[29] C Powell and M Van Vugt, 'Genuine Giving or selfish Sacrifice? The Role of Commitment and Cost Level upon Willingness to Sacrifice' (2003) 33 *European Journal of Social Psychology* 403.

[30] Ibid, 404. Powell and Van Vugt describe this as when the partners' preferences do not match and each partner is forced to choose between the option most beneficial to them and the one most beneficial to the dyad or the group (eg partner and children).

[31] Ibid. The research carried out by Powell and Van Vugt further reveals that, where the cost level of the interdependence dilemma is low, low-commitment couples may be equally willing to make sacrifices at levels comparable with, or even sometimes higher than, high-commitment couples since the dilemma involves a low cost and it may be beneficial to make the sacrifice.

enced by the couple's level of commitment as well as the cost (to the relationship) in making such sacrifices. The complex manner in which factors such as commitment, role performance and willingness to sacrifice interweave with interdependency influences the ways in, and the extent to, which partners 'care' for each other and adjust their conduct, both for the self and for the dyad (complementarity), in promoting the survival of the relationship.

It strikes me that 'complementarity' may thus be a useful notion upon which to base legal analysis of interdependency as it provides the scope for the consideration of role diversity as well as specialisation within a cohabiting relationship. It further enables us to consider role-coordination in a relationship and the way in which that can lead to one partner being directly or indirectly (inter)dependent on the other. In that way, interdependency for legal purposes may be couched in the following terms: firstly, whether, and the extent to which, the conduct and actions of the parties including the undertaking of roles (which remain gendered in many relationships) reflect a sufficient level of complementarity, ie working towards shared goals or functions in the relationship; and secondly, whether that complementarity has become skewed in favour of one partner so as to cause greater dependency, emotional and financial, on the part of the other partner which results in his or her economic vulnerability, should the relationship terminate. Adopting a notion of complementarity will better enable us to focus on patterns of shared commitment—something that has been argued elsewhere[32]—and how that shared commitment has caused one partner to become (or be more willing to become) economically vulnerable. The justificatory basis for legal intervention in such cases lies in the nexus between shared commitment and economic vulnerability, so that where there is limited evidence of caring and complementarity in the parties' relationship (interdependency), there is less reason for the courts to intervene.

PROPERTY REDISTRIBUTION ON THE BASIS OF INTERDEPENDENCY

Shifting to interdependency as the basis for legal intervention does not of itself tell us very much about the manner in which the financial and property matters of cohabitants ought to be resolved and the basis upon which property, for instance, should be redistributed. Relatedly, there may be several possible approaches to effecting property redistribution. Firstly, one could adopt a property law contributions-based approach where the question of redistribution is assessed wholly in the light of the contributions

32 Bottomley and Wong, above n 3.

made by the parties to the relationship. Legal reform can, for example, address the shortcomings of the common intention constructive trusts approach by providing statutory recognition to a wider range of contributions. Indirect financial and non-financial contributions may thus be taken into consideration by the courts in determining whether to make a property adjustment order.[33] However, a property law-based approach may be of limited effect since the focus remains on contributions. Aside from concerns about the potential for gender bias to remain and the problematic of placing value on non-financial contributions such as homemaking and childcare,[34] a contributions-based approach may, as the Law Commission has observed, be too inflexible to operate fairly and evenly across a diverse range of domestic relationships.[35]

A second possible approach is a rule-based one, eg a community of property regime which will allow for the division of specific assets that fall within the scope of the regime. Community of property, however, is not something that English family law is familiar with.[36] The existing system for married couples and civil partners remains based on statutory discretion.[37] The Law Commission further expresses doubts about the suitability of a rule-based approach for cohabitants.[38] One reason is the difficulty of providing a sufficiently comprehensive definition of assets that would fall within the category of 'relationship property', given the problem of pinpointing the start and end of cohabitation. Thus, a rule-based system may not be sufficiently flexible to respond to the diversity of cohabiting

33 This approach can be found, eg, in the Property (Relationships) Act 1984 of New South Wales.

34 See, eg, Bottomley and Wong, above n 3; A Diduck, 'Fairness and Justice for All? The House of Lords in *White* v *White* [2000] 2 FLR 981' (2001) 9 *Feminist Legal Studies* 173; S Wong, 'Property Regimes for Home-sharers: The Civil Partnership Bill and Some Antipodean Models' (2004) 26 *Journal of Social Welfare and Family Law* 362; S Wong, 'The Shared Home: A Rational Solution Through Statutory Reform?', in H Lim and A Bottomley (eds), *Feminist Perspectives on Land Law* (Abingdon, Routledge-Cavendish, 2007).

35 See Law Commission, *Sharing Homes: A Discussion Paper* (Law Com No 278, Cm 5666, 2002); and Law Commission, *Cohabitation: The Financial Consequences of Relationships Breakdown* (Law Com Consultation Paper No 179, 2006).

36 Cf the Family Law (Scotland) Act 1985, ss 9(1)(a) and 10, which provide for community of property in relation to 'matrimonial property', ie assets belonging to the spouses or either of them which were acquired by them or one of them before or during the marriage for use by them as a family home or as furniture or plenishings for such home. See also the Family Law (Scotland) Act 2006, ss 26 and 27, which provide cohabitants with the right of equal sharing but only in respect of a much narrower category of assets, eg household goods acquired during the period of cohabitation, money derived from any allowance made towards the parties' joint household expenses or any property acquired from such money, but excludes the shared family home.

37 Matrimonial Causes Act 1973, Part II; Civil Partnership Act 2004, schedule 5.

38 Law Commission, 2006, above n 35, paras 6.32–40; Law Commission, *Cohabitation: The Financial Consequences of Relationship Breakdown* (Law Com No 307, Cm 7182, 2007), paras 4.11–14. Cf E Cooke, E, A Barlow and T Callus, *Community of Property: A Regime for England and Wales?* (Bristol, Policy Press, 2006) where, based on their survey, the authors found that most cohabitants are not in favour of a community of property regime, and that there is greater support for such a system among couples with children. See also chapter by Barlow in this collection regarding the issues that arise with different models of community property.

relationships. Given this lukewarm reception, a third possibility is the discretion-based approach, with which English family law is more familiar.

A discretion-based approach allows for the exercise of judicial discretion in determining the appropriateness and the scale of making any property redistribution order. The approach is more flexible where the circumstances of individual relationships are taken into consideration. There is therefore greater scope for the consideration of a wider range of financial and non-financial contributions when determining whether a property redistribution order ought to be made. In some cases, legal reform may also provide scope for other matters beyond contributions to be taken into consideration. For example, the Domestic Relationships Act 1994 and the Relationships Act 2003 allow the relevant Australian sub-national courts to take into account other matters—a limited version of the 'needs and means' factors usually applied to marital proceedings[39]—such as the parties' financial resources, their earning capacities, their financial needs and obligations, and their responsibilities to support any other person.[40] Notwithstanding the possibility of legal reform extending the scope of factors which courts may take into account when exercising their discretion, one of the problems that remains is that the courts are often still required to perform the exceedingly difficult, and often impossible, task of placing value on contributions, especially non-financial contributions such as caregiving, in order to weigh these against other factors. To avoid this dilemma and in order to build on the discretion-based approach taken in family law, we may consider a fourth possibility—a broader relational approach where there is possibly greater scope for the complementarity of the parties' conduct in an interdependent relationship to play out.

An example of this approach may be seen in the principled discretion model recommended by the Law Commission which is based on the principles of economic advantage (retained benefit) and disadvantage.[41] The scheme proposes to recognise a wider range of contributions made to the relationship and, more importantly, the economic impact of those contributions. Thus the grant of relief seeks to address the positive value of contributions made by one partner during the relationship which leads to the retention of a benefit by the other partner on separation. Alternatively, relief may be granted where the applicant continues to suffer an economic disadvantage. That relates to the partner's impaired economic position stemming from the sacrifices made by him/her as a result of making contributions to the parties' shared lives, or the welfare of members of their family and may include continuing childcare responsibilities after separation. The Law Commission's model proposes the reversal of any retained

[39] See Family Law Act 1975 (Commonwealth), s 75. Similar provision is also found in the UK Matrimonial Causes Act 1973, s 25.

[40] Domestic Relationships Act 1994, ss 15 and 19; Relationships Act 2003, ss 40 and 47.

[41] Law Commission, 2007, above n 38.

benefit in so far as that is reasonable and practicable having regard to the Commission's suggested discretionary factors.[42] Relief for economic disadvantage, on the other hand, is subject to both the 'economic equality ceiling' and the discretionary factors, and any such disadvantage is to be shared equally by the partners.[43] However, unlike other schemes, the Law Commission's approach eschews a full retrospective inquiry[44] to identify and value each and every qualifying contribution[45] made by each party during the relationship for the purposes of determining the existence of any retained benefit and/or economic disadvantage at the time of separation. The assessment of contributions under this approach therefore excludes claims relating to matters such as housekeeping money provided and spent, rent-free accommodation provided during the relationship, or loss of earnings as a result of homemaking and/or childcare responsibilities—all matters that the Law Commission describes as 'water under the bridge'.[46]

Rather, the approach sets out to provide redress where an applicant shows that his or her contributions during the relationship have given rise to either a disadvantage in terms of a present or future diminution in savings, assets, income or earning capacity, or the respondent retaining an economic benefit in terms of assets, income or earning capacity. Instead of attempting to place economic value on individual contributions—a problem that exists in many of the models—the proposed retained benefit/economic disadvantage test goes further to look at the overall impact those contributions have had on each party's economic position at the time of separation. In doing so, the approach is more nuanced: it does enable the courts to take into consideration the ways in which the partners 'care' for each other and the family constituted by them, if any—'care' being used along the lines of the theory of interdependency discussed above—and how that 'caring' has affected each party's economic position on separation. The approach provides greater scope for looking at the complementarity of that 'caring' such as the way in which the couple's relationship is structured, the undertaking of roles, the possible career sacrifices made and the resulting loss of earnings, the financial and non-financial contributions they each make towards the relationship, etc. While the discretion-based family law approach arguably does allow many of these factors to be taken into consideration, what is significantly

[42] Ibid, paras 8.14 and 8.15. For a fuller discussion, see Part 4 of the Law Commission's 2007 Report.

[43] Ibid, para 4.65. The Law Commission had initially proposed in its 2006 Consultation Paper, above n 35, that the award of any relief would depend on weighing economic advantage and disadvantage, and providing redress for any (economic) imbalance that remains on separation.

[44] Some level of retrospection will nevertheless be necessary but the proposed scheme avoids the need for a protracted, and often hotly disputed, accounting of the value of individual contributions made, which is particularly problematic with non-financial contributions.

[45] See Law Commission, 2007, n 38, paras 4.43 and 4.44.

[46] Law Commission, 2006, n 35, para 6.131.

different with this more relational approach is that these various aspects of the relationship are now being viewed as complementing each other. What the courts are more concerned with under such an approach is not the intrinsic value of each of these matters—the Law Commission is particularly mindful of the problems courts face in trying to place value on various contributions which are often incommensurable. Instead, the focus is on the overall effect of the parties' interdependency and, more importantly, its effect on the position and ability of each partner to acquire assets, income and/or earning capacity. This forms a significant break from previous discretion-based models which, by attempting to continue to place value on matters such as the contributions themselves, remain stuck in an analytical loop that can never shift, or at least begin to challenge, issues such as sexual division of labour and gender bias.

A downside, though, of the Law Commission's relational model is the narrow view taken in relation to the parties' needs. This is not to say that the question of needs is wholly irrelevant; there is also some degree of acceptance of the Commission's reasons for not allowing needs alone to form a basis for the award of relief.[47] Rather, the question of needs is subsumed under the heading of retained benefit or economic disadvantage. For example, the applicant's needs due to continued childcare responsibilities after separation may be taken into account for the purposes of determining the extent of her economic disadvantage on separation. The scheme thus allows some scope for the consideration of her needs which are related to what Fineman describes as derivative dependency.[48] This type of dependency arises in situations where undertaking a caregiving role (eg looking after the children of the parties, or the other partner who suffers from a disability or illness, or an elderly relative) places a burden on the caregiver; there are material costs and consequences to the caregiver for undertaking that burden, both before and after separation. However, the Law Commission rejects a partner's needs which flow from inevitable dependency such as illness and disability, since this type of dependency, according to the Law Commission, is unrelated to the relationship.[49] The justificatory basis of needs must therefore be limited in order to avoid so-called concerns of encouraging dependency and to promote independence, the mantra of neoliberal policies, by seemingly providing partners with the means of becoming self-sufficient and autonomous individuals. However, Fineman explains:

[47] Law Commission, 2006, n 35, paras 6.62–77; Law Commission, 2007, n 38, paras 4.18–25.

[48] MA Fineman, *The Autonomy Myth: A Theory of Dependency* (New York, The New Press, 2004). Fineman describes two types of dependency: inevitable dependency where one is dependent on others due to some impediment, which includes physical, biological, economic, psychological and emotional dependency (examples of which are: being a child; illness; disability; and ageing); and derivative dependency where one undertakes the role of taking care of an inevitably dependent person.

[49] Law Commission, 2006, n 35, para 6.68.

> Autonomy is only possible when one is in a position to be able to share in society's benefits and burdens. And sharing in benefits and burdens can only occur when individuals have the basic resources that enable them to act in ways that are consistent with the tasks and expectations imposed upon them by the society in which they live.[50]

By upholding autonomy as *the* end in itself, dependency becomes a societal problem that must be avoided and those who are dependent are stigmatised and punished. The valorisation of independence, argues Fineman, serves to increase the pressure on the attainment of independence and the simultaneous resistance to responding to the dependency of others.[51]

While the relational approach proposed by the Law Commission does provide space for the consideration of derivative dependency-related needs, the lack of space for taking into account inevitable dependency-related needs requires closer scrutiny as insufficient weight is being given to the notion of 'needs', or its relationship with interdependency (as opposed to dependency) and any ensuing retained benefit or economic disadvantage of the parties. There is greater potential for polarisation of the issue as it may be easier to identify granting relief on the basis of either economic disadvantage or retained benefit to a cohabitant who provides care (derivatively dependent) rather than is inevitably dependent. In addition, one may argue that the needs of the inevitably dependent partner should more appropriately be met by public funds rather than privately through the grant of financial relief. However, given the 'caring' aspect of interdependent relationships, it may be extremely difficult in some cases to separate the needs generated by either of these two types of dependencies. Even though inevitable dependency such as disability or illness is not directly related to the parties' relationship, it necessarily becomes part of a relationship issue for the partners that, more often than not, can have an impact on their respective economic position (eg unemployment for the disabled partner and/or reduced employment for the caregiving partner). The decisions made by partners to deal with issues of dependency, whether inevitable or derivative, are thus closely intertwined with the level of commitment and the act of caring in a particular relationship. The extent to which both or either dependencies may affect the economic choices made by the parties to the relationship as a result of the interdependent nature of their relationship may not be so readily translated into 'retained benefit' and/or 'economic disadvantage'. The consequence is that the sacrifices made in relation to either dependency may thus be much more complex than a simple assessment of disadvantage or retained benefit, and should focus more broadly on the sharing of lives by the parties.

50 Fineman, above n 48, 29.
51 Ibid, 30.

This, however, does not mean that redress must be provided in all cases to inevitable dependency-related needs. Rather, coming back to the central notion of 'caring' argued above, what is being suggested is that the issue ought to be looked at more holistically. In order to do that, there should be more scope for the courts to consider the parties' needs, and not just derivative dependency-related needs, as a result of their sharing and caring for each other as well as other family members. The aim is to consider an appropriate award that addresses the consequences faced by each partner as a result of being part of a joint relationship of caring and the extent to which that creates mutuality of dependency. This therefore becomes a matter of weighing the extent of 'caring' and, relatedly, the level of complementarity in a given relationship and their causal links with the economic disadvantage or retained benefit of either party on separation. Moreover, the question of needs should also not be limited to the time of separation as it might be necessary in some cases to consider future needs as well. An approach that emphasises the former lacks flexibility to adapt to situations where the nature of the applicant's economic disadvantage may have a longer-term effect and extends beyond the point of separation. Thus, any remedy given will only be a short-term solution, with the applicant being eventually put back in a position of economic vulnerability post separation.

CONCLUSION

The experiences of other jurisdictions such as Australia in relation to reform of cohabitation law demonstrate a growing awareness of the unsuitability as well as resistance to defining eligibility in marriage-like terms. The changes in definitions—from marriage-like (opposite-sex) cohabitation to gender neutral notions of 'coupledom' and domestic relationships of 'care and support'—highlight more important shifts in legal discourse. Whereas the equality argument has been useful to, and more successfully deployed by, same-sex couples to argue for access to the law, the limited success offered to opposite-sex cohabitants means that alternative arguments, such as economic vulnerability, have to be constructed. However, to avoid concerns over (and resistance to) the assimilation of cohabitation with marriage, a growing trend in legal reform is to premise the justification for legal intervention on a desire to provide fairness to the parties in terms of redressing any economic vulnerability that might flow from their having been in a committed and interdependent relationship. A problem with this approach is that the reform models themselves often fail to provide or attempt to construct clear understandings of what 'interdependency' means. What often happens is a backdoor retreat to the marriage model through the use of a list of factors that seeks to look for characteristics of a cohabiting relationship that mirrors marriage.

The theory of interdependency in the field of psychology and its identification of 'caring' as being an important element of commitment in close personal relationships may provide the useful first step in rethinking both 'commitment' and 'interdependency' within law. It suggests that 'caring' may make a partner more willing to make 'sacrifices' for the relationship—sacrifices which, for example, involve the willingness to undertake particular roles within the relationship, to make certain financial and non-financial contributions for the benefit of parties to the relationship as well as any family constituted by them, etc, all of which can and may have an impact on his or her economic position on separation. By formulating a more coherent concept of interdependency, legal reform can begin to articulate a clearer definition of which types of relationships ought to be eligible without the problem of slippage into marriage-like definitions.

Developing the notion of 'caring' will further facilitate the formation of a more principled basis for addressing the parties' interdependency and any specific needs and/or economic vulnerability of cohabitants on separation which is not divorced from the reality of the parties' relationship. It paves the way for developing further a more relational approach to the resolution of financial and property matters of cohabitants that the Law Commission has begun in its project on cohabitation. Moreover, a relational approach should provide slightly more scope for consideration of the parties' needs. Needs should not be seen as either reinforcing dependency (of the economically vulnerable partner) or antithetical to interdependency. More importantly, there should be some scope as well to consider the extent to which both inevitable and derivative dependencies may, or may not, have any effect on the parties' economic positions and their respective needs on separation. A re-visioning of interdependency along the lines of caring therefore provides us with the space to develop a much more nuanced and flexible approach to addressing the financial and property matters of cohabitants on separation. In order for this legal project to go further, what is now needed is for more sociolegal research to be carried out to ascertain more precisely when and to what the extent couples are prepared to undertake 'caring' in a close personal relationship and, more significantly, what the moral hazards of 'caring' are and how far they do indeed expose one to economic vulnerability. Such research will help us form a better understanding of the complexities of sharing lives and how the law ought to respond when relationships end.

Part II

WHAT IS FAIR AND TO WHOM?

INTRODUCTION

THE PREVIOUS SECTION focused on potential starting points for the redistribution of property at the end of a relationship. This section shifts the focus to an examination of the impact of 'recognising' relationships through contextualisation within a broader frame of social policy issues.

Diduck's chapter explores the potential of utilising the concept of 'fairness'. She argues that the use of 'fairness' in recent English case-law, and also by the Law Commission in proposing reform for cohabitants, is too limited in that it only takes into account what is fair between the two individuals in the relationship, and fails to engage with evaluating broader interconnections between the parties and with other external (public) actors. Drawing on Fraser's work on the multidimensionality of fairness, she argues that extending the current, limited, notion of what is 'fair' would not only be more substantively 'just', but would also allow us to move beyond being confined to using a model based upon 'family', into a model more readily applicable to any relationship of interdependence.

Young's chapter extends this concern through an examination of the way in which Canadian tax provisions take into account marital or familial relationships. She acknowledges the significant struggle by lesbians and gay men to gain legal recognition of their relationships on the grounds of equality, but points out that the extension of the definition of 'spouses' to same-sex couples does not confer benefits to all. Tax provisions that make reference to 'spousal' and 'common law' status obscure the classed and gendered impact of the consequences of such provisions. More often than not the provisions tend to favour not only couples with high incomes, but reinforce the tendency of neoliberal governments to pass responsibility for the economic security of individuals to the private family. Extending the categories of recognised domestic relations based on a model of spousal status does not provide greater equity to the intended constituents, and, she argues, it is women who are generally discriminated against and encouraged to remain economically dependent. Her chapter provides a cogent example of the problems of extending recognition through a combination of 'equality' arguments and a marriage model.

5

Relationship Fairness

ALISON DIDUCK[1]

INTRODUCTION

> The [Matrimonial Causes Act 1973] does not state explicitly what is to be the aim of the courts when exercising these wide powers [of financial adjustment on divorce]. Implicitly, the objective must be to achieve a fair outcome. The purpose of these powers is to enable the court to make fair financial arrangements on or after divorce.[2]

THE HOUSE OF LORDS reminded us in the landmark case of *White v White*[3] that the court's discretion in untangling and distributing the financial consequences of marriage and divorce, and now also of forming and dissolving civil partnerships, is not unfettered. It is to be guided by fairness. But the Lords reminded us also that fairness is an elusive concept:

> [E]veryone's life is different. Features which are important when assessing fairness differ in each case. And, sometimes, different minds can reach different conclusions on what fairness requires. Then fairness, like beauty, lies in the eye of the beholder.[4]

Undeterred, however, the Lords continued to refine the means for its search. In *Miller v Miller; McFarlane v McFarlane*[5] it offered the following restatement from *White*:

[1] My sincere thanks go to Abbie Bright who provided research assistance, editorial assistance and, most importantly, insightful comments and suggestions. Thanks also to Susan Boyd, Robert Fine, Felicity Kaganas and David Seymour who read early drafts of this paper and offered detailed and thoughtful comments. Finally, I am indebted to the participants at the workshop in Onati who offered constructive criticism, engaging discussion and encouragement to pursue these ideas.

[2] *White v White* [2001] 1 AC 596, per Lord Nicholls, at [1].

[3] [2001] 1 AC 596.

[4] Ibid, per Lord Nicholls at 599.

[5] [2006] UKHL 24.

> [I]n seeking a fair outcome there is no place for discrimination between a husband and wife and their respective roles. Discrimination is the antithesis of fairness. In assessing the parties' contributions to the family there should be no bias in favour of the money-earner and against the home-maker and the child-carer.[6]

Beyond avoiding discrimination on the basis of familial/gender roles, Lord Nicholls identified several strands to finding fairness in a particular case.[7] The first strand is financial needs: 'This element of fairness reflects the fact that to greater or lesser extent every relationship of marriage gives rise to a relationship of interdependence'.[8] The second is compensation: 'This is aimed at redressing any significant prospective economic disparity between the parties arising from the way they conducted their marriage.' A third strand of fairness is sharing:

> This 'equal sharing' principle derives from the basic concept of equality permeating a marriage as understood today. Marriage, it is often said, is a partnership of equals. . . . The parties commit themselves to sharing their lives.[9]

We thus have some direction from the House of Lords as to the meaning of fairness on the breakdown of marital relationships. But 'most people would agree that the division of property between cohabitants when they separate should [also] be "fair"',[10] and so in 2006 the Law Commission was charged with the task of identifying a means of redressing unfairness on the breakdown of cohabiting relationships.[11] It acknowledged that 'reaching a consensus on what fairness comprises may be elusive',[12] yet it saw its challenge to be 'to find a satisfactory compromise between the goals of fairness, flexibility, certainty, clarity and practicality'.[13] In 2007 it met this challenge by proposing a scheme for adjustment of cohabitants' finances which is distinct from that which applies to divorcing couples, at least in part because cohabitants have not made the 'legal and public commitment that marriage entails'.[14] The scheme would, for eligible[15] couples only,

> seek to ensure that the pluses and minuses of the relationship were fairly shared between the couple. The applicant would have to show that the respondent retained a benefit or that the applicant had a continuing economic disadvantage,

[6] *Miller v Miller*, per Lord Nicholls at [1].
[7] Ibid, per Lord Nicholls at [10].
[8] Ibid, per Lord Nicholls at [11].
[9] Ibid, per Lord Nicholls at [16].
[10] Law Commission, *Cohabitation: The Financial Consequences of Relationship Breakdown* Law Com No 307 Executive Summary (London, Law Commission, 2007) para 6.25.
[11] Law Commission *Cohabitation: The Financial Consequences of Relationship Breakdown* (London, Law Commission, 2006) Consultation Paper No 179.
[12] Law Commission, above n 10, para 6.25.
[13] Ibid, para 6.31.
[14] Ibid, para 1.10.

> as a result of contributions made to the relationship. The value of any award would depend upon the extent of the retained benefit or continuing economic disadvantage.[16]

We see in these recent statements about financial fairness in personal relationships the House of Lords and the Law Commission each attempting to give meaning to an indefinite concept. Their attempts take account of social conditions and changing social and legal norms and therefore allow that the meaning of fairness is not fixed, yet they still represent a particular way of thinking about fairness that remains within a particular discourse. This chapter is an attempt to reflect upon that way of thinking about fairness in this area of family law. This means that I am less interested in the *meaning* of fairness from time to time in the family courts than I am in *ways of thinking* about it.[17] Different ways of thinking about a concept obviously have their own theoretical presuppositions and normative concerns and my aim in this chapter is to reflect upon both the current way of thinking about fairness in family law and alternatives to it.

I begin with the observation that the current way of thinking about fairness, as flexible as it is, remains within the discourse of the private: it accepts that the role of family law is to regulate relations between private individuals and is therefore concerned primarily if not exclusively to do fairness only between them. While assessments of fairness might, therefore, include 'public' norms such as equality or non-discrimination or might locate the parties' claims and circumstances in their social and economic context,[18] it is still thought about in the context of the traditional 'family law as private law' paradigm and therefore sustains particular familial and structural norms. I then speculate about other ways of thinking about fairness and illustrate one possible alternative which does not presuppose that this area of family law is 'private' and which reveals the underlying normative consequences of that presupposition. This way of thinking about fairness in determining the financial consequences of our partnering behaviour takes seriously family law's role in regulating our relationships with public institutions, the state and civil society as much as our relationships with each other. It impels family law to acknowledge its concurrent public nature and public consequences and therefore its role in achieving fairness in that realm as well.

To those who say that promoting this type of *social* fairness is not within

[15] Couples who had a child together would be eligible, as would couples who had cohabited for a minimum period of time. No recommendation was made as to the required duration of cohabitation. See Law Commission, above n 10, para 1.14.

[16] Law Commission, above n 10, para 1.19.

[17] R Fine, 'Europe and Antisemitism: Whither Postnationalism?' University of Warwick, paper on file with the author, 2008.

[18] A Diduck, 'Rights, Fairness and the Financial Consequences of Partnering and Separating' unpublished paper on file with the author, 2008.

(this part of) family law's remit, I would respond that family law has always been concerned about the social consequences of its rules. The government hoped, for example, that the Civil Partnership Act 2004 would help to combat homophobia and discrimination in society.[19] The Child Support Acts were intended to instil a sense of responsibility in non-resident parents and alleviate pressure on the public purse.[20] And the very fact that family law privileges certain relationships over others and thus determines the population entitled to make claims under it, the types of claims entitled individuals are permitted to make, and the factors that are relevant in deciding those claims, reveals the relative value it attaches first to that population vis-à-vis others, secondly to the claims it designates as permissible vis-à-vis those that fall outside it, and third to the consequences for those who are and are not captured within it. It seems to me that these relative values must have social as well as personal consequences.

I am interested in the potential link, for example, between this area of family law and social phenomena such as the decrease in wives' and children's income and the increase in husband's income on divorce,[21] the fact that older women receive disproportionate amounts of Pension Credit,[22] and that lone-parent families, 90 per cent of which are headed by mothers, are the second largest group (after disabled people) that claims income support.[23] I am interested, in other words, in exploring ways of thinking about fairness that implicate it in these social phenomena and are thus distinct from that adopted by the House of Lords and the Law Commission.

My examination proceeds from an overtly feminist orientation. This means that it is attentive to hierarchies of value and power within and between different forms of personal living arrangements. Without this lens we run the risk not only of overlooking the ways in which our personal living and public living are connected, as illustrated by the examples above of the increasing feminisation of poverty, but also of suppressing or ironing out the inconsistencies, contradictions and complexities in our personal living. A feminist orientation immediately challenges the cultural and legal idealisation of marriage that is accepted by both the Matrimonial Causes Act and the Law Commission. It begins from the joint assumptions that

[19] Department of Trade and Industry, *Final Regulatory Impact Assessment (RIA): Civil Partnership* (London, DTI, 2004), cited in C Stychin, 'Family Friendly? Rights, Responsibilities and Relationship Recognition', in A Diduck and K O'Donovan (eds), *Feminist Perspectives on Family Law* (London, Routledge-Cavendish, 2006).

[20] Department of Social Security, *Children Come First, The Government's Proposals on the Maintenance of Children* Cm 1264 (London, HMSO, 1990).

[21] G Douglas and A Perry, 'How Parents Cope Financially on Separation and Divorce—Implications for the Future of Ancillary Relief' (2001) 13 *Child and Family Law Quarterly* 67.

[22] A Diduck and F Kaganas, *Family Law, Gender and the State* (Oxford, Hart Publishing, 2nd ed, 2006) 194–97.

[23] ESRC, *ESRC Society Today—Welfare and Single Parenthood in the UK*, Fact Sheet, 2005.

there are many ways to arrange domestic or private lives, that these may change from time to time as individuals' lives and circumstances change, and that each may create or sustain relations of power, dependency and obligation.

A feminist starting point for thinking about fairness also frees us from problematic assumptions about marital and non-marital obligation, commitment and responsibility.[24] Much recent empirical research reveals that for many couples obligation and commitment to a shared life-project are fundamental to a good relationship, marital or non-marital.[25] In other words, cohabitants may be as committed to a relationship or to a partner as married people, even though their commitment may take a slightly different form or be perceived as coming from within rather than imposed normatively.[26] Duncan et al,[27] for example, found that most of their cohabiting respondents felt 'as good as married'; they had embarked upon and were committed to a shared life-plan or experience and had constructed what the authors call a 'DIY marriage'. Their choices about whether to marry or not had less to do with the level of commitment, love or obligation they felt to their partners, than with the personal and structural contexts in which they were able to express those values.[28]

Thirdly, a feminist orientation reveals that, for many, obligation felt or owed to another is not created only in conjugal or co-residential relationships. Researchers in Sweden and Korea, for example, have concluded that living apart together (LAT) is 'not so much a stage but a different kind of partnering',[29] and the Law Commission of Canada published a report in 2002[30] seeking ways in which rights and responsibilities might be allocated

[24] See Diduck, above n 18, and the comments of the House of Lords in *Stack v Dowden* [2007] UKHL 17 in which they reject fairness as the objective in determining the respective shares in the former family home of separating long-term cohabitants because those cohabitants had chosen not to marry.

[25] See, eg, J Eekelaar and M Maclean, 'Marriage and the Moral Bases of Personal Relationships' (2004) 31 *Journal of Law and Society* 510; S Duncan, A Barlow and G James, 'Why Don't They Marry? Cohabitation, Commitment and DIY Marriage' (2005) 17 *Child and Family Law Quarterly* 383; J Lewis, *The End of Marriage? Individualism and Intimate Relationships* (Cheltenham, Edward Elgar, 2001).

[26] Lewis, above n 25. See also J Pahl, 'Individualisation in Couple Finances: Who Pays for the Children?' (2005) 4(4) *Social Policy and Society* 381 and C Vogler, 'Cohabiting Couples: Rethinking Money in the Household at the Beginning of the Twenty First Century' (2005) 53 *Sociological Review* 1 on the way in which married and cohabiting heterosexual couples organise their intra-household economies.

[27] Duncan et al, above n 25. See also L Jamieson, M Anderson, D McCrone, F Bechhofer, R Stewart and Y Li, 'Cohabitation and Commitment: Partnership Plans of Young Men and Women' (2002) 50 *Sociological Review* 356.

[28] See also C Smart and P Steven, *Cohabitation Breakdown* (London, Family Policy Study Centre, 2000); J Lewis, 'Perceptions of Risk in Intimate Relationships: The Implications for Social Provision' (2005) 35 *Journal of Social Policy* 39.

[29] J Haskey and J Lewis, 'Living Apart-Together in Britain: Context and Meaning' (2006) 2(1) *International Journal of Law in Context* 37, 38. See also J Haskey, 'Living Arrangements in Contemporary Britain: Having a Partner Who Usually Lives Elsewhere and Living Apart Together (LAT)' (2005) 122 *Population Trends* 35.

independently of relational status, specifically excluding conjugality as a relevant factor in the allocation. Personal and financial interdependencies may be created between non-conjugal homesharers, friends and non-co-resident intimates, and thinking about fairness from this starting point thus permits us to take account of the social and personal economic effects of these interdependencies.

Finally, a feminist orientation values our social and individual needs for both connection and autonomy and our consequent need to protect and promote both. It dissolves the pernicious link between demand for respect for our private lives and the reification and isolation of a separate sphere in which they are said to be lived. It accords social and cultural respect and economic value to a variety of personal living choices, while at the same time demanding the public conditions that are necessary to sustain their value and to dismantle hierarchies of power that are attached to them. It acknowledges the intimate relationship between public and private responsibility for individual and social well-being. A feminist way of thinking about fairness in determining the economic consequences of forming and ending relationships implicates the social and the political; it reinforces the ideas, first, that the source of familial obligation is both social and personal,[31] and second, that obligation arises not only from private individual choices but also from the moral and social conditions in which those choices are expressed.[32] It supports the courts' concern to seek fairness between divorcing partners and the Law Commission's concern to seek fairness between separating cohabitants, but does not accept as self-evident that fairness's reach ends there.[33]

Thinking about fairness from a feminist ethos, in sum, exposes its different dimensions. Fairness has an economic dimension: it is about the fair allocation of the economic burdens and benefits and power that accrue from relationship choices. It also has a cultural dimension: it is about the inherent dignity of persons and the choices they make about their personal relations, and demands social and cultural respect for that dignity. And finally, it is about the ways in which dignity and economic power in personal relations are related to dignity and economic power in public relations and to the legitimacy of claims upon social, political and legal institutions for both.

[30] Law Commission of Canada, *Beyond Conjugality: Recognizing and Supporting Close Personal Adult Relationships* (Ottawa, Law Commission of Canada, 2002).

[31] L Ferguson, 'Family, Social Inequalities and the Persuasive Force of Interpersonal Obligation' (2008) 22(1) *International Journal of Law Policy and the Family* 61.

[32] D Cooper, *Challenging Diversity, Rethinking Equality and the Value of Difference* (Cambridge, Cambridge University Press, 2004).

[33] See also on this, J Herring, 'Why Financial Orders on Divorce Should be Unfair' (2005) 19 *International Journal of Law, Policy and the Family* 218.

NANCY FRASER: JUSTICE AND MULTIDIMENSIONALITY

It seems to me that the multidimensional approach to social justice offered by the political theorist Nancy Fraser might provide an interesting model from which to explore just one alternative way of thinking about fairness at the end of personal relationships. For Fraser, justice resides in the domains of the economic, the cultural/symbolic and the political.[34] Her analysis draws attention to the importance of each dimension as well as to their interconnection. It offers a way into another way of thinking about fairness in family law which is concerned with the private and public consequences of family living and their implication with economic and status hierarchies. I wish, therefore, to draw an analogy between Fraser's view of social justice and a new way of thinking about relationship fairness not necessarily to advocate that it is always a better view, but as an illustration that there *are* other ways of thinking about fairness.

Part of what is compelling about a multidimensional framework is that it makes visible the concern about the way in which feminist strategies in family law reform appear to be caught within a dilemma created by polarising two of the dimensions: the economic and the cultural. Although both are fundamental to the feminist project, too often they are cast as dichotomous. Susan Boyd, for example, highlighted this difficulty in 1999,[35] suggesting that feminist analysis of private 'family law' issues must ignore neither family law's heteronormativity (recognition) nor its instantiation of the gender division of labour in the family and the political economy more generally (redistribution). 'Reaffirming "the family", even by including same-sex spouses within it, will not necessarily stop the ways in which the "holy family" constrains the routes by which property interests are regulated and distributed',[36] and in which 'family work remains privatised and largely in women's hands'.[37] Any feminist view of fairness, in other words, must ignore neither its cultural element which would expose and dismantle family law's 'institutionalised patterns of status inequality' that 'constitute some actors as excluded, inferior, wholly other or simply invisible, hence as less than full partners in social interaction'[38] nor its economic element which would require family law to do its part to

[34] N Fraser, 'Reframing Justice in a Globalizing World' (2005) 36 *New Left Review* 69 (hereafter 'Reframing'); N Fraser, 'Mapping the Feminist Imagination: From Redistribution to Recognition to Representation' (2005) 12 *Constellations* 295 (hereafter 'Mapping').

[35] SB Boyd, 'Family, Law and Sexuality: Feminist Engagements' (1999) 8 *Social and Legal Studies* 369.

[36] Ibid, 376.

[37] Ibid, 377.

[38] N Fraser, 'Social Justice in the Age of Identity Politics: Redistribution, Recognition and Participation', in N Fraser and A Honeth (eds), *Redistribution or Recognition? A Political-Philosophical Exchange* (London, New York, Verso, 2003) 29.

reposition in relation to the political economy those who are denied the resources necessary to interact as peers in social life.

For Fraser, however, justice also requires a third element, which she calls representation. Representation resides in the realm of the political. 'The political in this sense furnishes the stage on which struggles over distribution and recognition are played out.'[39] Introducing the realm of the political means something similar to this 'Fraserian' way of thinking about family law's fairness. It means examining the 'family stage' and the ways in which it is constructed and delimited. Let me offer an example. Both the courts and the Law Commission operate upon a particular 'stage' when they think about fairness as reserved only for the individual separating parties. While redistribution between individuals also is important in my example of an alternative way of thinking about fairness, my enquiry does not end there. First, it requires that we scrutinise the limitations of the 'stage' which reserves claims to fairness for individuals within accepted/acceptable familial partnerships only. Second, it requires that we question the apparently self-evident fairness of shifting to those individual family members more and more responsibility for care and financial support of the weak and the dependent and for the costs of social reproduction generally. It recognises that the increasing privatisation of the costs of social reproduction disproportionately disadvantages women and children relative to men in the public sphere as much as in the familial sphere[40] and thus illuminates the interdependence and mutuality of public and private living. It implicates misrepresentation in the unfairness of maldistribution and misrecognition.

Third, the problem with the orthodox way of thinking about fairness is not that the public interest is not considered at all, but rather is the way in which the public and its interest are conceived. The public becomes conceived increasingly as merely a collection of other 'private' entities—families—rather than as a collectivity or number of collectivities based on other affinities or connections.[41] On this view, the public becomes nothing other than a collection of private families, each responsible only for its own,[42] and none responsible for another or for those who are left out entirely. The way in which family law becomes a tool for social ends[43]

[39] Fraser, 'Reframing', above n 34, 75.

[40] See on this Boyd, above n 35; B Cossman, 'Family Feuds: Neo-Liberal and Neo-Conservative Visions of the Reprivatization Project', in J Fudge and B Cossman (eds), *Privatization, Law and the Challenge to Feminism* (University of Toronto Press, 2002); MA Fineman, *The Autonomy Myth: A Theory of Dependency* New York and (London, The New Press, 2004); C Young and SB Boyd, 'Losing the Feminist Voice? Debates on the Legal Recognition of Same Sex Partnerships in Canada' (2006) 14 *Feminist Legal Studies* 213; A Diduck, 'Shifting Familiarity' (2005) 58 *Current Legal Problems* 235.

[41] See Diduck, above n 40; Cossman, above n 40; Young and Boyd, above n 40. This conception also means, increasingly, that the norms of 'the private' come to regulate 'the public'; see Cooper, above n 32; Diduck, above n 40.

[42] Diduck, above n 40.

[43] Ferguson, above n 31.

either deliberately, eg by encouraging marriage, or inadvertently, eg by contributing to the marginalisation of those not on the 'family stage', is obscured. Finally, and importantly, the interests of even this skewed vision of the public and the interests of the families that comprise it are deemed to be at odds. There is little recognition of the ways in which social well-being and private well-being are connected.

Viewed in this way, unfairness through misrecognition and maldistribution results from what Fraser identifies as the injustice of 'misframing' in the political:

> Establishing criteria of social belonging, and thus determining who counts as a member, the political dimension of justice specifies the reach of those other dimensions; it tells us who is included in, and who is excluded from, the circle of those entitled to a just distribution and reciprocal recognition. Establishing decision rules, the political dimension likewise sets the procedures for staging and resolving contests in both the economic and cultural dimensions: it tells us not only who can make claims for redistribution and recognition, but also how such claims are to be mooted and adjudicated.[44]

Misframing as a form of injustice is sometimes a problem of boundary setting: who counts as a member of the community of those entitled to make claims and who counts in the community to whom those claims can be made. Other times it is a problem of the mode in which the boundaries are constituted, as these may operate so as to define and delineate the substance and limits of what those claims may be. It is a 'gerrymandering of political space' at the expense of the disadvantaged.[45] When translating these ideas of political misframing into the family law context, unfairness in the allocation of the economic consequences of relationship breakdown is the result not only of misrecognition and/or maldistribution between parties but also of misrepresentation or misframing. This means it is a problem both of boundary setting, limiting the constituencies by and to whom claims can be made, and of the ways in which the boundaries are constituted, shifted and reconstituted. Before I go on to elaborate upon each of the three elements of this way of thinking about fairness, I wish to adopt and adapt one more part of Fraser's approach to social justice, ie her objective.

In the discussion above we saw that courts and the Law Commission have imported into the orthodox way of thinking about fairness the concepts of gender equality and non-discrimination, equal sharing of marital finances, compensation, and the meeting of individual needs. Fairness is individual and personal. Alternative objectives for fairness also might be to achieve a form of equality between the parties, to compensate them and/or meet their needs, but they might then go on to draw upon

[44] Fraser, 'Reframing', above n 34, 75.
[45] Ibid, 78.

ideas of social justice and include, for example, securing the parties' rights,[46] their autonomy or their capabilities.[47] For Fraser, social justice means participatory parity[48] and there is no reason why participatory parity could not be adopted as a reasonable objective for relationship fairness. Again, however, it requires thinking about fairness in an entirely different way. In aiming for participatory parity, courts would seek to address the ways in which the intimate relationships individuals forge or do not forge may, in both the public and the private, devalue them culturally and disadvantage them economically. A multidimensional way of thinking about fairness would attend to an individual's ability or inability to participate effectively in social and intimate life[49] and maintain respect for their intimate life choices. Clearly it is not the role of family law exclusively to do this, and equally clearly it could not do it in all cases. The point is that by exposing the partiality of the orthodox way of thinking about fairness, we may see the role it plays in promoting or inhibiting participatory parity. This way of thinking about fairness does not allow family law to abdicate responsibility for the part it plays in determining the social as well as the personal consequences of private living choices.

THE IMPORTANCE OF RECOGNITION

Here I wish to illustrate that there are alternative ways of thinking about fairness by drawing a detailed analogy with Fraser's social justice. It begins with the realm of the cultural. Fraser argues that misrecognition, status subordination or the hierarchical valuing of differences creates injustice when social 'interaction is regulated by an institutionalized pattern of cultural value that constitutes some categories of social actors as normative and others as deficient or inferior'.[50] She offers by way of example the way in which 'gender codes pervasive cultural patterns of interpretation and evaluation, which are central to the status order as a whole'[51] in which traits and work associated with masculinity are privileged and those associated with femininity are devalued. In the family law context, these gender meanings code nurture, care and homework as 'devoid of intelligence and skill' and as connected 'with dependency and powerlessness'.[52]

[46] For a discussion of rights-based approaches, see S Harris-Short, 'Family Law and the Human Rights Act 1998: Judicial Restraint or Revolution?' (2005) 17(3) *Child and Family Law Quarterly* 329.

[47] See, eg, M Nussbaum, 'Capabilities as Fundamental Entitlements: Sen and Social Justice', paper delivered at the London School of Economics, 13 March 2002.

[48] Fraser, above n 38; Fraser, 'Reframing', above n 34.

[49] M Minow and ML Shanley, 'Relational Rights and Responsibilities: Revisioning the Family in Liberal Political Theory and Law' (1996) 11 *Hypatia* 4.

[50] Fraser, above n 38, 30.

[51] Ibid, 20.

[52] Ibid, 66.

And indeed, in the divorce cases preceding *White v White*[53] we see courts relying precisely upon these gender-coded meanings. They accepted the hierarchical cultural value attributed to the work traditionally done by women in the home and by men outside it, and the way in which this value, indeed cultural values generally, shaped definitions and claims about 'proper' patterns of mutuality and interdependence between husband and wife.[54] Then came fairness in *White v White*:

> In seeking a fair outcome, there is no place for discrimination between husband and wife and their respective roles. . . . [W]hatever the division of labour chosen by the husband and wife, or forced upon them by circumstances, fairness requires that this should not prejudice or advantage either party when considering . . . the parties' contributions. . . . If, in their different spheres, each contributed equally to the family, then in principle it matters not which of them earned the money and built up the assets. There should be no bias in favour of the money-earner and against the homemaker and child carer.[55]

This is an important statement of gender status recognition in which the House of Lords appears deliberately to wish to enhance the status value of 'the feminine' vis-à-vis 'the masculine'.[56] It accepts that law has a role to play in doing this; that statements of law are important in reshaping gender relations in both 'traditional' and new patterns of work, care and well-being in intimate relations,[57] while also recognising the part played by cultural and social values in that reshaping process. Indeed Lord Nicholls in *Miller* later categorised 'fairness' as an 'instinctive response to a given set of facts'. Ultimately it is grounded in social and moral values, which 'change from one generation to the next'.[58]

Few would suggest, however, that gender status recognition in this way can, of itself, achieve the type of fairness that a feminist interrogation demands. Consider *White* itself, and indeed most of the cases following it. The fairness (as recognition) mantra was repeated by the courts in *Lambert*[59] and *Charman*[60] and before them in *H-J v H-J (Financial Provision: Equality)*;[61] *H v H (Financial Provision: Special Contribution)*[62]

[53] [2001] 1 AC 596.

[54] S Irwin, 'Interdependencies, Values and the Reshaping of Difference: Gender and Generation at the Birth of Twentieth Century Modernity' (2003) 54 *British Journal of Sociology* 565; see, eg, *Dart v Dart* [1996] 2 FLR 286.

[55] *White v White* [2001] 1 AC 596, per Lord Nicholls at 605.

[56] A Diduck and H Orton, 'Equality and Support for Spouses' (1994) 57 *Modern Law Review* 681.

[57] Irwin, above n 54, 581.

[58] The value of Lord Nicholls's 'prevailing social and moral values' approach had been acknowledged years earlier in *Porter v Porter* [1969] 1 WLR 1155 at 1159, where Sachs LJ observed that the discretionary powers available to it enabled the court to take into account 'the human outlook of the period in which they make their decisions'.

[59] *Lambert v Lambert* [2002] EWCA Civ 1685.

[60] [2006] EWHC 1879 (Fam), now see [2007] EWCA Civ 503.

[61] [2002] 1 FLR 415.

[62] [2002] 2 FLR 1021.

and *G v G (Financial Provision: Equal Division)*,[63] each of which extolled the cultural value of 'women's' care work but left wives with less than the 'equal' sharing, or redistribution fairness, that recognition of their equally valued roles would have required. We see in these cases the fundamental integration of recognition and redistribution fairness, yet even to concede this is a long way from saying recognition in this form should not have occurred, or indeed is not a part of fairness. It is important to this way of thinking about fairness that the moral, cultural and social statuses of caring and earning, of carer and earner, those (still) gendered differences, be recognised and reordered. These imperfect cases attribute value to 'traditionally private and therefore unvalued labour'[64] and may help to make visible the ways in which assisting and caring for others is a feature in all public and private living. As Nussbaum says,

> any real society is a care-giving and care-receiving society and must therefore discover ways of coping with these facts of human neediness and dependency that are compatible with the self-respect of the recipients and do not exploit the caregivers.[65]

Recognition fairness within relationships may also be promoted by the financial and property claims separating civil partners make when their registered civil partnerships end. The terms of the Matrimonial Causes Act 1973 (MCA), and the case-law interpreting them, including *White* and *Miller,* will be applicable to these cases. The roles undertaken in same-sex relationships sometimes fall into gendered patterns, and thereby will be familiar for an MCA analysis, and sometimes they do not, and will require a more reflective determination of MCA fairness. Same-sex partners, for example, more frequently than opposite-sex partners, share roles on a more diverse and equal basis.[66] Weeks and Dunne both describe 'doing' non-heterosexuality in intimate partnerships often as a rejection of gender roles in the domestic division of labour and finances. At the end of these relationships financial fairness may thus confound gender status and civil partnership cases generally may thereby offer an opportunity to challenge the cultural value ascribed to gendered definitions and patterns of work.[67]

It will be recalled that in this way of thinking about fairness one looks beyond the individual parties. Status fairness is important therefore, not

[63] [2002] EWHC 1339; [2002] 2 FLR 1143.

[64] Diduck and Orton, above n 56, 701.

[65] Nussbaum, above n 47, 22–23.

[66] J Weeks, 'Elective Families: Lesbian and Gay Life Experiments', in A Carling, S Duncan and R Edwards (eds), *Analysing Families, Morality and Rationality in Policy and Practice* (London and New York, Routledge, 2002); GA Dunne, 'A Passion for "Sameness"? Sexuality and Gender Accountability', in EB Silva, and C Smart (eds), *The New Family?* (London, Sage, 1999); L Jamieson, 'Intimacy Transformed? A Critical Look at the "Pure Relationship"' (1999) 33(3) *Sociology* 477.

[67] G Wilson, 'Financial Provision in Civil Partnerships' (2007) 37 *Family Law Journal* 31.

only within relationships, but also between them and so the very existence of the Civil Partnership Act 2004 might be said to advance fairness in the cultural realm. The Act challenges the way in which 'institutionalized patterns of cultural value construct heterosexuality as natural and normative, homosexuality as perverse and despised'.[68] As Young and Boyd observe, such a change in 'normative ideas of family would have been difficult to foresee even a decade ago'.[69] Further, the fact that the Law Commission of England and Wales was charged with the task of determining the extent to which economic consequences may attach to a potentially new range of relationships is also important for advancing recognition fairness socially. Together, these initiatives achieve some form of status recognition for non-marital and non-heterosexual relationships. Indeed the Civil Partnership Act 2004 may go further and revalue monogamy and conjugality as well as heterosexuality.[70]

Despite their expansive potential, however, both the Civil Partnership Act 2004 and the Law Commission's proposals were designed to accommodate those who fit within the marriage model. The Civil Partnership Act 2004 was intended to provide (a spurious form of) equality for stable, monogamous same-sex couples and the Law Commission is concerned to assist long-term cohabitants who arrange their domestic lives as though they were married or civilly partnered. And so, rather than challenge the marriage/not marriage dichotomy, they may strengthen it: 'by naturalizing and universalizing marriage rather than heterosexuality, I fear we are simply in danger of replacing compulsory heterosexuality with a regime of compulsory matrimony'.[71]

The orthodox way of thinking about fairness, then, applicable only to those who choose that regime, has significant consequences for those who do not. Those who refuse monogamy, conjugality, co-residence or partnership entirely continue to suffer from misrecognition unfairness. Their personal and intimate living arrangements are still seen as abnormal or deficient and remain outside the culturally privileged 'family'.

So, while cultural recognition must reflect the importance to individuals and to society of the opportunity for intimacy with another or others, for sharing the burdens and joys of one's life, it must also respect the different ways those opportunities may be taken. We might see this respect reflected in public law rights discourse, but it has yet to become a part of fairness. Alternative ways of thinking about fairness, however, might incorporate them so that recognition extends beyond law simply creating a new

[68] Fraser, above n 38, 18.

[69] Young and Boyd, above n 40, 214; See also Diduck, above n 40.

[70] N Barker, 'Sex and the Civil Partnership Act: The Future of (Non)Conjugality?' (2006) 14 *Feminist Legal Studies* 241.

[71] R Robson, 'Assimilation, Marriage and Lesbian Liberation' (2002) 75 *Temple Law Review* 709, 819. See also Young and Boyd, above n 40 and Boyd, above n 35.

plurality of 'authorised' relationships,[72] which, among other things, give rise to entitlement to claim on the resources of another. Further, that recognition, in fairness, might vary in different circumstances which have less to do with the official category into which a relationship falls than with the way in which it is lived. We may, for example, have a claim against our employer for recognition of one person for family leave applications, against the state for recognition of another as a spouse, and against a different person, for example a home-sharer, for recognition of ways in which we lived interdependently with them. Recognition claims in this sense eliminate hierarchies of 'the proper' relationship[73] by recognising that we may sometimes forge different connections with different people, each of which may serve a different yet valuable function for us and for society. Wong's response to the Law Commission captures this claim for recognition: 'the question of legal reform should not be looked at in isolation as being relevant only to cohabitants but also to other forms of intimate interdependent relationships, whether couple or non-couple based'.[74]

It is also possible that we may, from time to time, refuse intimate partnerships entirely. This way of thinking about fairness would reinforce the legitimacy and cultural value of living outside of a relationship. Living singly currently falls out of the realm of the 'proper' for adults. Seen to be, among other things, a sign of emotional immaturity, selfishness or pathology, independence from relationship is demonised for some, such as autonomous mothers, and pitied for others. Social and cultural value attaches to establishing a 'stable' intimacy with another, in short, to 'family' and the orthodox way of thinking about fairness only reinforces that value. Individual economic independence, which in effect means interdependence with one's employer or with the state or with different friends or extended family members for different purposes from time to time, is devalued. Connection/dependency is only recognised as occurring in families and the important connections between non-familial individuals and between the individual and the state and civil society are disregarded. In thinking about fairness as only important for couples or spouses, we not only demarcate couples from friends, we *demote* friends and other intimacies[75] and connections.

A new way of thinking about fairness would also work to dethrone marriage culturally by breaking down the marriage/not marriage divide. It allows that the culturally privileged obligations, commitments and responsi-

[72] Cooper, above n 32.

[73] Ibid.

[74] S Wong, 'Response to the Law Commission Consultation Paper No 179 "Cohabitation: The Financial Consequences of Relationship Breakdown"' (2006), unpublished paper on file with the author.

[75] Cooper, above n 32, 111.

bilities that are assumed to inhere in marriage and in marriage only, first of all may not exist in all or even the majority of contemporary marriages. Secondly, they may exist or not exist equally in non-marriages.[76] Recognition fairness, therefore, includes a revaluation of the status of gender, sexual and personal relations. Recognition as revaluation is not enough, however; attributing cultural or status value to differences and respect for dignity of choices made about relationships does little to concretise, in economic terms, the 'equal' value symbolically attributed to them.

THE IMPORTANCE OF REDISTRIBUTION

Let me now examine redistribution as a part of a reimagined relationship fairness. Again, my starting point is the *White* case. This decision acknowledges a form of redistribution first in its categorical renunciation of the reasonable requirements test, and secondly in its creation of the 'yardstick of equality' by which financial arrangements on divorce ought to be measured. First:

> If a husband and wife by their joint efforts over many years, his directly in his business and hers indirectly at home, have built up a valuable business from scratch, why should the claimant wife be confined to the court's assessment of her reasonable requirements, and the husband left with a much larger share? Or, to put the question differently, in such a case, where the assets exceed the financial needs of both parties, why should the surplus belong solely to the husband . . . [t]he mere absence of financial need cannot by itself, be sufficient reason. If it were, discrimination would be creeping in by the back door.[77]

And next:

> [A] judge would always be well advised to check his tentative views against the yardstick of equality of division. As a general guide, equality should be departed from only if, and to the extent that, there is good reason for doing so.[78]

The court finds a need here, in fairness, to redistribute the economic advantages and disadvantages of their marital living between husband and wife and further that fairness requires that that redistribution be measured against a gender-recognition-based yardstick of equality. The *Lambert* decision which followed in the Court of Appeal demonstrates also the link between redistribution and recognition fairness. Here the court strictly limited claims in which unequal division could be justified by one party (the breadwinner) demonstrating a special skill or exceptional contribution in the acquisition of the family wealth:

[76] See Diduck, above n 18.
[77] *White v White*, per Lord Nicholls at 992.
[78] Ibid, per Lord Nicholls at 989.

> The danger of gender discrimination resulting from a finding of special contribution is plain. If all that is regarded is the scale of the breadwinner's success then discrimination is almost bound to follow since there is no equal opportunity for the homemaker to demonstrate the scale of her comparable success.[79]

Most dramatically, however, consider *Miller; McFarlane*'s creation specifically of a place for compensation in the financial reordering of the post-marital relationship. While two of the 'strands' of fairness, need and sharing, were said to exist by virtue of the marriage, or, in reality, by virtue of the expectations, norms and assumptions about marriage, compensation (into which some need can be subsumed[80]) is not dependent upon the *fact* of the marriage. According to Baroness Hale, compensation was for 'relationship generated disadvantage'.[81] For Lord Hope, it was to compensate 'a women who has chosen motherhood over her career in the interests of her family'.[82] Lord Nicholls thought compensation must redress 'any significant prospective economic disparity between the parties arising from the way they conducted their marriage'.[83] Compensation is thus not about meeting all of a former spouse's needs, nor is it related to the form or definition of the relationship; it arises from the way the parties lived and arranged their relationship. Moreover, it ought to address 'real-world' disadvantage, because, 'although less marked than in the past, women may still suffer a disproportionate financial loss on the breakdown of a marriage because of their traditional role as home-maker and child-carer'.[84]

We see in the cases from *White* to *Miller* fair financial redistribution between husband and wife grounded at least partly in the principle of compensation for relationship-generated disadvantage. Compensation integrates the economic with gender status value and makes recognition meaningful economically rather than simply symbolically. It is a way of redressing economic disadvantage resulting from misrecognition and maldistribution arising from the way personal living was organised. There is no obvious reason why it, in fairness, could not extend beyond the marital relationship. The Law Commission appears to agree, even though the House of Lords in *Stack* did not.

The Law Commission's remedy for financial hardship suffered by qualifying separating cohabitants is based upon this compensation principle. It looks to the way the relationship was lived, including to the way in which gendered family norms and structural conditions might differentially affect the parties' opportunities and finds that fairness requires compensation for

[79] *Lambert v Lambert* [2002] EWCA (Civ), [45].

[80] J Eekelaar, 'Property and Financial Sharing on Divorce—Sharing and Compensating' (2006) 36 *Family Law Journal* 753.

[81] [2006] UKHL 24, [140].

[82] Ibid, [20].

[83] Ibid, [13].

[84] Ibid, per Lord Nicholls at [13].

ongoing advantage or disadvantage resulting from the roles undertaken in the partnership. The Law Commission does not ascribe all or even some of the obligations assumed to inhere in marriage to a particular form of cohabiting relationship; it looks only to the economic consequences of individual personal relationships. In this way, rather than importing assumptions about marital obligation into those consequences, it sees compensation, in fairness, as the limits of a claim against a former partner. There is no place in fairness in these relationships for other strands such as need or equality/sharing that would arise simply because someone once lived with someone else.

In the light of changing expectations and experiences of marriage and other forms of intimacy, this approach makes sense for the Law Commission. In the light, however, of those same changes *and* of the claims to recognition discussed above, it also makes sense for the divorce courts: a basis of entitlement dependent upon relationship status commits misrecognition unfairness. Once this is acknowledged, fairness between any formerly interdependent individuals and between different relationship arrangements may be promoted by seeking to compensate a party for disadvantage/advantage generated by status misrecognition and economic maldistribution. Meeting a former partner's needs might be fair compensation for the way in which the relationship was organised, and a yardstick of equality might then be useful to measure the value of the compensation, but both would be considered because they promote recognition fairness, rather than because of assumptions about their inherent place in marriage/civil partnership. This form of compensation redistributes between individual (former) partners some of the social costs and social benefits of the gender division of labour and gender-based dependency. And so, rather than the Law Commission's question about whether or not remedies for cohabitants ought, in fairness, to look like those available for the married and civilly partnered, this alternative offers the potentially more interesting question of whether remedies for the married and civilly partnered ought, in fairness, to look more like those proposed for cohabitants.

But just as recognition and redistribution are intertwined between parties, so are the personal and the social and the political intertwined. Our three-dimensional way of thinking about fairness demands that the costs of social reproduction be redistributed beyond merely between those who were once in acceptable intimacies.[85] It highlights the way in which heteronormativity and the gender order in the form of *the private family* are linked directly with the maintenance of a particular structure of production and reproduction in which maldistribution and misrecognition continue. So, while the status recognition of non-normative families and of gender roles within families are necessarily related to the redistribution of the

[85] Boyd, above n 35, 377.

economic benefits and burdens within and between them, on their own they will not disrupt the material role of the family itself in the maldistribution socially of those benefits and burdens. It is here that the third dimension of fairness becomes important.

THE IMPORTANCE OF REPRESENTATION

Fraser's idea of representation as the third element of justice involves rediscovering the importance of the realm of the political in addition to that of the economic and the cultural. In the same way, reinstating the importance of the political—the public—in claims to fairness in family law may help to highlight the role of family law in allocating the costs of social reproduction. Fraser examines what she calls the 'politics of framing' in a globalising world. She hypothesises misrepresentation injustice in Westphalian boundary setting and she looks to the global post-Westphalian 'community' to answer the claims of justice. Some claims, she says, simply cannot be addressed in the domestic political sphere. And so, frame setting, the creation of that sphere, is among the most consequential of political decisions.[86] Here, she is referring to the frame of the modern territorial state:

> Constituting both members and non-members in a single stroke, this decision effectively excludes the latter from the universe of those entitled to consideration within the community in matters of distribution, recognition and ordinary-political representation. . . . The injustice remains, moreover, even when those excluded from one political community are included as subjects in another—as long as the effect of the political division is to put some relevant aspect of justice beyond their reach. Still more serious, of course, is the case in which one is excluded from membership in any political community. . . . those who suffer it may become objects of charity or benevolence. But deprived of the possibility of authoring first-order claims, they become non-persons with respect to justice.[87]

Let us think of 'the family' as the equivalent for analytical purposes of Fraser's modern territorial state and of her post-Westphalian community as the sphere of the 'public' in relation to that family or couple. Fraser's territorial boundaries become family law's family/not family boundaries. Families (and non-families) or 'authorised' relationships (and non-authorised ones) are constituted by law in the public/political realm, immediately and simultaneously constituting the communities against whom one is or is not entitled to make claims for recognition or redistribution. On this view, it is misframing that confines issues of recognition and redistribution within the 'family' by rendering only certain claims and certain respondents legit-

[86] Fraser, 'Reframing', above n 34, 77.
[87] Ibid, 77.

imate. Misframing further creates subcategories of families, such as civil partners and cohabitants, who are able to claim only some aspects of fairness. Most seriously, misframing creates the 'stateless', those who live outside the authorised 'family'. The single mother or those in non-qualifying cohabiting relationships find a place in no political community and are therefore unable to voice redistribution and recognition claims at all. The fairness or otherwise of the consequences of their, indeed all of our, actual dependencies on a non-'family' member or on the state thus cannot be assessed by recognition or redistribution claims. The unfairness of misframing for the purposes of redistributing the economic consequences of relationship breakdown thus is a problem of boundary setting: the variable boundaries determining who counts as 'family' against whom we can claim recognition and redistribution affects the economic consequences of all forms of personal living.[88]

According to Fraser, misframing as representation unfairness is also a problem of the *mode* in which the boundary is constituted. Susan Boyd[89] reminds us that the *process of constituting* 'family' is fundamental to relations of production and reproduction: normative gender and normative sexuality serve the reproduction of the normative family which is 'systematically tied to the mode of production proper to the functioning of political economy'.[90] The normative family or relationship is increasingly important to neoliberalism, Labour's 'third way',[91] in which the costs of social reproduction are increasingly privatised.[92] In family law's selective boundary-setting exercise, creating more and more 'families', such as qualifying cohabitants and civil partners, we really do see a 'gerrymandering' of the political space into which responsibility for those costs can be loaded, and the increasing marginalisation of all those who remain outside.

And now, consider these words:

> Increasingly subject to contestation, the Keynesian-westphalian frame [or 'the family' frame] is now considered by many to be a major vehicle of injustice, as it partitions political space in ways that block many who are poor and despised from challenging the forces that oppress them. . . . [t]his frame insulates offshore powers [or 'the state'] from critique and control. . . . Also protected are the governance structures of the global [or state] economy.[93]

The constitution of more and more authorised relationships or families—this remaking of more and more public, political space as 'private'—also

[88] See Young, 'Taking Spousal Status into Account for Tax Purposes: The Pitfalls and Penalties, ch 6 in this book and Diduck, above n 40.

[89] Boyd, above n 35.

[90] Ibid, 375, 376, quoting J Butler, 'Merely Cultural' (1997/1998) 227 *New Left Review* 33.

[91] C Stychin, 'Couplings: Civil Partnership in the United Kingdom' (2005) 8 *NY City Law Review* 543.

[92] Boyd, above n 35; Diduck, above n 40; Cossman, above n 40.

[93] Fraser, 'Reframing', above n 34, 78.

has an effect on our vision of and understanding of the public or the social. Westphalian-type misframing means that the public becomes perceived as nothing other than private 'families' and 'stateless' individuals who are not 'citizens' of private families. Except in the most egregious circumstances, each family bears responsibility only for its own. And the interest of this 'public' is perceived only as the interest of the individual, insulated families who comprise it. The familial frame therefore ensures not only that the social costs of reproduction remain absorbed within the individual family components of the public, but that the social benefits are perceived to remain there as well. By thinking about fairness only in terms of its application to certain, albeit increasing forms of relationships, family law reinforces the insulation of the state and the political economy that sustains it from being held to account for the benefit they receive from the functioning normative family *and* from the unpaid reproductive labour of non-familial non-citizens.

If, however, we think about family law's fairness as a concept in which all three of Fraser's elements are linked, we make visible the links between social and personal living, between social and personal interests, and social and personal well-being to decentre the idea that little is owed to the 'stranger'[94] and we reveal the way in which the orthodox way of thinking about fairness in family law may contribute to broader social unfairness. Thinking about recognition and redistribution would also include thinking about inclusion/exclusion from the community of those entitled to make claims for them, about the substance of those claims, and about to whom they can be addressed. Fraser advocates a transformative approach to this task:

> [For proponents of a transformative approach to justice] the state-territorial principle no longer affords an adequate basis for determining the 'who' of justice in every case. They concede of course, that that principle remains relevant for many purposes: thus supporters of transformation do not propose to eliminate state-territoriality entirely. But they contend that its grammar is out of synch with the structural causes of many injustices in a globalizing world.[95]

And so, an alternative way of thinking about fairness in this area of family law might reflect that the conjugal couple family no longer can delimit the 'who' of fairness in every case while conceding that intimacy, care and sharing remain important to personal and social living. But while it may not want to eliminate family entirely, it would contend that its 'grammar', the rules that give it sense and coherence, eg about exclusivity, gender responsibility, heteronormativity and privacy, are out of synch with personal experience and the structural causes of injustice—unfairness—in civil society and the political economy.

[94] Cooper, above n 32, 111; see also Diduck, above n 40.
[95] Fraser, 'Reframing', above n 34, 81.

Fraser's pursuit of social justice includes seeking ways to democratise the process of frame setting—to challenge its 'deep grammar'.[96] Again, thinking about relationship fairness in this way, we might see the beginning of such a democratisation process in the incipient social, political and legal acknowledgement of the messy and diverse ways we practise family, friendship or caring, and concurrent acknowledgement of the ways in which these are a part of public living, including employment, tax paying and civic engagement.[97]

In sum, there are alternative ways of thinking about fairness that demand some accountability on the part of the law and the state for the mode in which the family frame is set *and* the form and extent of regulation that results. Reflecting upon those different ways of thinking, we see that personal living is also social and political living, and that it is possible to think about fairness in family law in a way which reveals its responsbility for fairness or lack of fairness in all three realms.

[96] Ibid, 81.

[97] A Diduck, *Law's Families* (London, Butterworths; Cambridge, Cambridge University Press, 2003). See also Young, above n 88.

6

Taking Spousal Status into Account for Tax Purposes: The Pitfalls and Penalties

CLAIRE FL YOUNG

INTRODUCTION

THE LAST 30 years in Canada have seen dramatic changes in the legal definition of 'family' and 'spouse' as well as our social understanding of these relationships. Today in Canada common law relationships[1] through ascription are recognised for many legal purposes. Based on a period of cohabitation many, but not all, of the rights and duties of marriage have been extended to common law cohabitants. Furthermore common law relationships include both heterosexual and same-sex relationships. Most recently in July 2005 the federal government legalised civil same-sex marriage across Canada. Both opposite-sex and same-sex partners can now choose whether to marry or not; even if they do not, they may still be ascribed spousal status for various purposes, based on a period of cohabitation. In other countries such as the US and the UK we are seeing a move towards taking the rules that apply to married couples and extending them to common law cohabitants or allowing couples to register their partnerships so that they can avail themselves of the rights and responsibilities accorded to that status.

These changes, and in particular, the recognition of same-sex relationships for tax purposes, have led me to re-examine how Canada treats spousal and common law relationships in tax law and policy.[2] It is

[1] 'Common law' is the term used in Canada to describe two people living in a conjugal relationship that is recognised in law for some purposes.

[2] Throughout this chapter I refer to 'spousal and common law relationships'. S 248 of the Canadian Income Tax Act, SC 1985, c 1 (5th Supp) defines 'spouse' as a married person and 'common law partner' as an individual living in a conjugal relationship with the taxpayer for at least one year.

important, however, to emphasise that I am not critiquing the inclusion of lesbians and gay men as common law partners. That change was an important part of the struggle for equality and indeed was a milestone in that quest. But, as I have discussed in other work, I argue that we need to rethink the broader issue of why we take marital or familial relationships into account at all for tax purposes.[3] There are two points that should be made at this juncture. First, neoconservative governments are increasingly using tax policies as they apply to married persons and common law spouses to reinforce the traditional family with the stay-at-home mother and the father as the breadwinner. We are seeing this trend in Australia, the US and Canada, all of which have either implemented or are discussing tax measures that effectively treat spouses or common law couples as one tax unit. Secondly governments are increasingly using tax measures that take spousal status into account to shift economic responsibility for the welfare of citizens from the state to the private family.

My analysis is in three parts. First I trace some of the recent developments that led to the inclusion of same-sex couples as common law partners for tax purposes in Canada. Then I turn to the political picture and consider the Canadian government's keen interest in taking familial or spousal relationships into account for tax purposes. Finally I turn to some of the particular tax rules that take spousal status into account. In a nutshell my question is: can these rules continue to be justified or should we be looking to eliminate all reference to spousal and common law relationships from our tax legislation? My conclusion is that many of these provisions should be removed from the Income Tax Act (ITA). The reason that they are no longer valid varies from rule to rule. For example, some rules are inequitable and discriminate without good reason against those couples with low incomes and in favour of those with high incomes. Others, including those that focus on dependency, are inherently flawed and poorly targeted so that they do not achieve their policy goals. Some rules can be critiqued on the basis that they are simply part of a neoliberal privatisation agenda that encourages individuals to rely on the private family for their economic security. These rules exclude those not in spousal or common law relationships from a variety of very important benefits delivered by the tax system.

CHANGING DEFINITIONS OF SPOUSE IN CANADA

In order to place Canadian tax rules in the broader social context of changing definitions of family and spouse, it is important to trace some of

[3] CFL Young, 'Taxing Times for Lesbians and Gay Men: Equality at What Cost?' (1994) 17 *Dalhousie Law Journal* 534–59.

these recent changes. Since the 1970s Canada has increasingly recognised common law heterosexual relationships through ascription. As mentioned, the result is that many of the rights and responsibilities accorded to married couples are now accorded to common law couples. During the mid-1990s the Charter of Rights and Freedoms,[4] and, in particular the equality provision, section 15(1), was used with great success to challenge heterosexist definitions of spouse. The result is that, since the mid-1990s, same-sex couples have increasingly, though unevenly across the provinces, been treated as common law couples. In 1999, the Supreme Court of Canada rendered the most important judicial decision to date on same-sex spousal recognition in *M v H*,[5] striking down as unconstitutional a definition of 'spouse' in a family law statute that had been limited to opposite-sex cohabitants. The result was that lesbians and gay men could now sue each other for spousal support on the breakdown of their relationships. This case generated many legislative changes at both federal and provincial levels to extend spousal or equivalent status to same-sex cohabitants.[6]

Meanwhile on the tax front, the Ontario Court of Appeal had held in 1998 in *Rosenberg v Canada (Attorney General)*[7] that the words 'or same-sex' should be read into the definition of 'spouse' in the ITA, for the purposes of registration of pension plans. The case was brought by two women who worked for one of Canada's large unions, the Canadian Union of Public Employees (CUPE). CUPE had a standard employment pension plan which included a provision for survivor benefits. Pension plans in Canada are heavily subsidised by the tax system, with deductions for contributions by employers and employees, and sheltering from tax of all income earned by the plan until the pension is received. In order to qualify for these subsidies the plan must accord with the requirements of the ITA and that included a definition at that time of spouse that was restricted to heterosexual couples. CUPE decided to extend its plan to its lesbian and gay employees on the same terms as it applied to its heterosexual employees, but the government refused to accept this amendment. By reading the words 'or same-sex' into the definition of spouse in the ITA for the purpose of pension plans the court effectively extended entitlement to survivor benefits under occupational pension plans to the partners of lesbians and gay men who die while covered by the plan.[8] Interestingly, unlike other cases involving successful Charter

[4] Charter of Rights and Freedoms, Part 1 of the Constitution Act, being Sched B to the Canada Act 1982 (UK) 1982, c 11 (hereinafter 'the Charter').

[5] *M v H* (1999) 171 DLR (4th) 577 (SCC), [1999] 2 SCR 3.

[6] Eg, the Definition of Spouse Amendment Act, SBC 1999, c 29 and the Definition of Spouse Amendment Act, SBC 2000, c 24; An Act to Amend Certain Statutes because of the Supreme Court of Canada's Decision in *M v H*, SO 1999, c 6.

[7] *Rosenberg v Canada (Attorney General)*, (1998), 38 OR (3d) 577.

[8] For an in-depth analysis of this case, see CFL Young, 'Spousal Status, Pension Benefits and Tax: *Rosenberg v Canada (Attorney-General)*' (1998) 6 *Canadian Labour and Employment Law Journal* 435–53.

challenges on the basis of sexual orientation, the federal government did not appeal this decision.

Both the *M v H* and *Rosenberg* decisions had other far-reaching consequences. In 2000 the federal government enacted the Modernization of Benefits and Obligations Act[9] which amended 68 pieces of legislation to include same-sex couples in an array of laws that assign rights and responsibilities based on spousal status. Sections 130–46 of the Modernization of Benefits and Obligations Act amended the ITA to redefine spouse to include married persons and to add a new definition of common law partner which includes a person cohabiting in a conjugal relationship with the taxpayer for a period of at least one year.[10] Meanwhile the Law Commission of Canada (LCC) launched a major research project titled 'Beyond Conjugality: Recognizing and Supporting Close Personal Adult Relationships' which entailed a 'fundamental rethinking of the way in which governments regulate relationships'.[11] In brief the LCC concluded that governments rely too heavily on marital and common law relationships in accomplishing state objectives. The LCC suggested that the government re-evaluate the way in which it regulates relationships and it devised a four-part methodology to facilitate this re-evaluation. One question posed by this new methodology was, 'Are the objectives of the legislation legitimate and, if so, are relationships relevant to achieving them?'[12] Included in the legislation reviewed in this research paper was the ITA.

In the early 21st century, a renewed struggle for same-sex marriage emerged. Several successful Charter challenges were raised to the common law rule that defined marriage as between one man and one woman.[13] As a result, same-sex couples acquired the right to marry in several provinces and one territory. In October 2004, the federal government sought the opinion of the Supreme Court of Canada on the question of whether same-sex marriage for civil purposes was consistent with the Charter; the Supreme Court of Canada held that it was. On 20 July 2005, Bill C-38, the

[9] Modernization of Benefits and Obligations Act, SC 2000, C-23, ch 12.

[10] S 248 provides that a 'common law partner' with respect to a taxpayer at any time, means a person who cohabits at that time in a conjugal relationship with the taxpayer and:

> (a) has so cohabited with the taxpayer for a continuous period of at least one year, or
> (b) would be the parent of a child of whom the taxpayer is a parent, if this Act were read without reference to paragraphs 252(1)(c) and (e) and subparagraph 252(2)(a)(iii),
> and for the purposes of this definition, where at any time the taxpayer and the person cohabit in a conjugal relationship, they are, at any particular time after that time, deemed to be cohabiting in a conjugal relationship unless they were not cohabiting at the particular time for a period of at least 90 days that includes the particular time because of a breakdown of their conjugal relationship.

[11] Law Commission of Canada, *Beyond Conjugality: Recognizing and Supporting Close Personal and Adult Relationships* (Ottawa, 2001), ix.

[12] Ibid, xix.

[13] Eg in *Ontario, Halpern v Canada (Attorney General)* (2003), 169 OAC 172 (CA); in *British Columbia, EGALE Canada Inc v Canada (Attorney General)* (2003), 228 BCCA 406.

Civil Marriage Act, received Royal Assent and was proclaimed into law, legalising civil same-sex marriage across Canada. Civil marriage in Canada is now defined as 'the lawful union of two persons to the exclusion of all others'.

PROGRESS AT WHAT COST?

Without diminishing the struggle that lesbians and gay men have endured to secure legal recognition of their relationships, or its potential to challenge heterosexual norms and definitions of family, I argue that the recent tax changes in Canada to include same-sex couples as common law partners have done nothing to challenge the socioeconomic inequalities embedded in the tax rules that apply to spouses and common law partners. Indeed expanding the definition of those who are treated as spouses for tax purposes has simply reinforced those inequalities. It is time to revisit and rethink why we take spousal and common law relationships into account for tax purposes. Other than the recent work of the LCC,[14] which was part of a larger project examining the numerous laws that take spousal status into account, no attention has been paid by legislators over the last four decades to the fundamental tax policy question of why we take spousal and common law relationships into account for certain tax purposes and whether such a policy can be justified.

While many see the federal government's decision to enact the Modernization of Benefits and Obligations Act and thus expand the group accorded common law status for tax purposes as progressive, some caution is necessary. Certainly there is an assumption by many that it is to their advantage to be treated as spouses and common law partners for tax purposes.[15] There is a sense that there are more tax breaks for couples and that the tax bill of a couple will be lower than it would be if they were taxed as individuals. As I have demonstrated in previous work, this is not necessarily true.[16] In fact the impact of being treated as spouses or common law partners varies depending on three factors: the amount of income of each of the partners; the nature of that income; and the relative distribution of that income as between the partners. As I shall discuss in more detail later, generally speaking, in Canada a couple comprised of two low-rate taxpayers pays more tax when they are treated as a couple rather than as individuals. A couple in which there are two high-rate taxpayers

[14] Law Commission of Canada, above n 11.

[15] The author spoke with several groups of lesbian and gay individuals about the impact on them of the changes to the definition of spouse, and generally speaking most of those individuals believed they would benefit from the change even though in fact many of them would pay more tax as a result of the change.

[16] Young, above n 3.

and a couple in which one person is a high-rate taxpayer and the other has little or no income both tend to benefit in terms of taxes saved when treated as a couple. It is also important to note that one cannot choose to be or not be a common law partner. If you meet the statutory test of common law partner, that status is ascribed to you and all the rules that apply to common law relationships apply to you. Thus it is vital that the rules that take spousal status into account operate in a fair and efficient manner.

In this chapter I focus on two distinct aspects of these recent developments. First, I contend that the Canadian government's decision not to appeal *Rosenberg*, and its willingness to include same-sex couples as common law partners for tax purposes, was a pragmatic political decision, a decision that was not based on any analysis of the change from a tax policy perspective. As I shall discuss in more detail, such a change resulted in a tax windfall for the federal government. Much of this windfall was due to a reduction in the amount of tax credits available to common law partners, a reduction that resulted from the aggregation of income when determining entitlement to those credits. At the same time including same-sex couples as common law partners accords perfectly with the neoliberal agenda of privatisation of the economic security of citizens. That is, the tax system is increasingly being used to encourage individual family members to care for each other, thereby relieving the state of its responsibility.

THE POLITICS OF IT ALL

A Tax Windfall

Income tax law is one of the most important political tools that a government has as its disposal. Tax laws are used to direct economic and social behaviour in a myriad of different ways. Many of the most important measures used to achieve social policy goals are tax expenditures. Tax expenditures are defined as any deviation from the benchmark personal income tax structure. They include measures such as deductions in the computation of income, tax credits, exemptions from tax and deferral of tax payable. Tax expenditures are the functional equivalent of direct government expenditures, with one main difference: instead of being delivered as a direct grant to an individual, tax expenditures are delivered by the tax system. The distinction is significant. While we tend to analyse the impact of a technical tax provision by reference to criteria such as horizontal and vertical equity, neutrality and simplicity, we apply different criteria to a tax expenditure. As the LCC has said: 'Could the objective be better served through the use of some other government policy instrument?'[17] To this question I would add, is the measure fair or does it discriminate in an inappropriate manner against some taxpayers and in favour of others?

As mentioned above, inclusion of same-sex couples as common law partners for tax purposes resulted in a tax windfall for the government because some individuals were required to pay more taxes when treated as part of a couple than they previously paid as individuals. While the federal government has not published the amount of this windfall, history tells us that it can be considerable. In 1993 when the federal government amended the definition of spouse to include 'common law' heterosexual spouses, the Department of Finance estimated that the change would result in increased tax revenues over a five-year period of $9.85 billion (all amounts in this chapter are in Canadian dollars).[18] The primary reason for the increased tax revenues is attributable to the rules that require the combining of spouses and common law partners' incomes for the purpose of computing entitlement to the refundable Goods and Services Tax (GST) credit and the Canada Child Tax Benefit. Entitlement to both these tax credits depends on one's level of income and, as income increases, the amount of the credit is reduced and eventually phased out completely. Therefore, for example, two individuals with incomes of $20,000 who are now included as common law partners will lose entitlement to either all or part of these refundable tax credits. The impact of this change is especially harsh on those with low incomes, the very group the tax credits are intended to benefit. There is also a gendered impact. Given that women tend to earn less than men and have lower incomes, it is likely that more women than men will lose these credits.[19]

The Privatisation Agenda

One of the cornerstones of neoliberalism and, more recently, neoconservatism is an increased reliance on the private sector, including the private family and the private market, rather than the state, to provide for the welfare of citizens. As Lisa Philipps has said, 'the drive towards privatization in Canada has at its heart one central claim: that private choice is better than public regulation as a mechanism for allocating resources and

[17] Law Commission of Canada, above n 11, 65.

[18] Canada, Department of Finance, Budget Papers, Supplementary Information, 25 February 1992, 138–39.

[19] In Canada, women who work full year, full time earn 73 cents for every dollar earned by men (latest figures available), see, C Wiggins,'Women's Work: Challenging and Changing the World', research paper prepared for the 2003 Canadian Labour Congress Women's Conference, May 2003, http://canadianlabour.ca/index.php/Women/548, accessed 26 May 2008.

ordering social affairs'.[20] Increasingly in Canada, law and in this context, tax law, is being used as a tool of privatisation.[21] Tax expenditures in particular are often used as a private mechanism to achieve social or economic goals. That is, while we see the state as 'public' in contrast to the private market or family, by using tax expenditures delivered to the private sector to reinforce private responsibilities, the state is to a certain extent abdicating its public responsibility for that social or economic goal.

In this chapter, I focus on just one aspect of that privatisation, namely the trend to place responsibility on individual family members to care for each other, thereby relieving the state of its responsibility in that regard. That 'caregiving' can take many forms, including the actual caregiving of the elderly and disabled and the economic support of family members. My contention is that by taking spousal and common law partner status into account with respect to entitlement to and allocation of a variety of tax expenditures, the tax system is one important tool in this privatisation. For example, the Canadian government has made it clear that the future for Canadians in terms of their economic security in retirement is to contribute to private pension plans such as occupational pension plans (Registered Pensions Plans, RPPs) and personal plans (Registered Retirement Pension Plans, RRSPs), and not to rely on the more universal Old Age Security or the Canada Pension Plan.[22] As a result these private plans are heavily subsidised by tax expenditures, including tax deductions for contributions to the plans, and a sheltering of all income earned by the plan from tax until either the contributions are withdrawn or the plan matures. The value of these tax expenditures is a staggering $31 billion for 2005, making tax expenditures for retirement savings the single largest tax expenditure in Canada.[23]

At a general level, the major problem for many is a lack of access to these plans. This is especially true for women whose lack of participation in the paid labour force in comparison to that of men means that many women are excluded from these plans.[24] In addition, the kind of work that women

[20] L Philipps, 'Tax Law and Social Reproduction: The Gender of Fiscal Policy in an Age of Privatization', in B Cossman and J Fudge (eds), *Privatization, Law and the Challenge to Feminism* (University of Toronto Press, 2002) 41.

[21] For a detailed discussion of the role of law in the drive towards privatisation, see Philipps, ibid, 30–36.

[22] The Old Age Security is a non-contributory plan consisting of a flat-rate monthly sum paid to those over 65, although as income increases there is a clawback through the income tax system of part of the pension. Nevertheless it is the most 'universal' pension plan in Canada. The Canada Pension Plan is a contributory income replacement plan and benefits are based on labour force participation. Both these plans are described as 'public' pensions in contrast to the private RPPs and RRSPs.

[23] Canada, Department of Finance, *Tax Expenditures and Evaluations, 2005* (Ottawa, 2005) Table 1.

[24] Only 57 per cent of women over 15 are employed in Canada, compared to 68 per cent of men (latest figures available), see Housing, Family and Social Statistics Division, 'Women in Canada: Work Chapter Updates' (Ottawa: Statistics Canada, 2004); available online at http://www.statcan.ca /english/free pub/89F0133 XIE/89F01 33XIE2003000.pdf.

do is a major factor. Only those who work for relatively large employers, economically able to provide a pension plan, will benefit. Those who work part-time, in non-unionised jobs or for small employers unable to finance these plans do not benefit. In Canada women have consistently formed 70 per cent of the part-time labour force since the mid-1970s.[25] Similarly, in order to access RRSPs, one must have the discretionary income to make the contribution. Given that women earn less than men,[26] it is not surprising that more men than women make these contributions and thereby benefit from the tax expenditure.

To a certain extent the government has recognised and attempted to remedy women's unequal access to private pension plans and the accompanying tax subsidies. Consequently, the ITA permits contributions to a 'spousal' RRSP. A taxpayer may contribute to a plan in their spouse or common law partner's name and receive the same tax benefits that they would have received had they made the contribution to their own plan. Thus there is the opportunity to establish a pension plan for one's spouse or common law partner, and the ability to income split with that person by diverting future income to them. The advantages can be significant where the spouse or common law partner has little or no other income when they retire.

While the Canadian 'spousal' RRSP is a well-intentioned measure, it remains a highly private and limited response to a public issue: women's lack of access to pension and superannuation plans. This lack of access in turn contributes to the fact that so many elderly women live in poverty.[27] Essentially the private family is encouraged to provide for its own economic security in retirement, albeit with a tax break to encourage it to do so. But many cannot take advantage of this opportunity. Low-income taxpayers may not have the discretionary funds to contribute on their spouse's behalf. Additionally, single women have no access to this expenditure. Given that 43 per cent of single women over 65 live below the poverty line compared to 5 per cent of women over 65 who have a spouse, it appears that the subsidy in being misdirected.[28] By linking this tax expenditure to spousal status, the government is directing the benefit to a very limited group of people, a group that may not be the neediest. Furthermore, in Canada at least, statistics show that fewer people than ever are living in a married or common law relationship.[29] As the Women and Taxation Working Group of the Ontario Fair Tax Commission stated: 'the

[25] Ibid.

[26] See n 19 above.

[27] In Canada in 2000, 71 per cent of those over 65 living below the poverty line were women; see See Statistics Canada, 'Analysing Family Income'; available on-line at http://www12.statcan.ca/english/census01/products/analytic/companion/inc/canada.cfm#4.

[28] Ibid.

[29] Statistics Canada, '2001 Marital Status, Common-Law Status, Families, Dwellings and Households', *The Daily* (Ottawa: 22 October 2002).

concept of a couple as a life-long economic unit with joint income, wealth, and expenses may no longer be appropriate given changing family structures, increasing divorce rates, and falling marriage rates'.[30] As I have demonstrated, reliance on the private sector for the economic security of individuals is problematic for a variety of reasons. At a general level such privatisation policies tend to diminish the role that the state plays in ensuring a fair level of income for all its citizens. The state is delegating its responsibility to the private sector with virtually no strings attached. Encouraging the private family to fill the role previously taken by the state leaves gaps in the social security network, gaps that those without spouses or common law partners often fall through. As discussed in the pension context, the result is often a retirement lived in poverty. The current privileging of private pension plans also reduces the resources available for the more universal state pensions, pensions on which women in particular depend for their economic security in retirement.[31] Applying tax expenditure analysis to these provisions, one can conclude that they are not the best way to achieve the policy goal of ensuring that Canadians, and women in particular, are economically secure in their retirement. As I have discussed, they are too limited in scope and benefit some at the expense of others with no rational justification for that discrimination.

OTHER TAX EXPENDITURES

In this part of the chapter I take a variety of tax expenditures and analyse their impact by reference to the policy underlying them. They include measures that take dependency into account and provide a subsidy to the person who supports a dependent person; measures that assume an economic mutuality in relationships; and measures that reduce entitlement to certain tax expenditures because they take the perceived economies of scale that arise in relationships into account.

The Dependent Spouse and Common Law Partner Credit

The spousal and common law partner tax credit is available to a taxpayer who supports their spouse. Put simply, the taxpayer is entitled to a tax

[30] Ontario Fair Tax Commission, Women and Tax Working Group, *Women and Taxation* (Toronto, Ontario Fair Tax Commission, 1992) 22.

[31] During the past 20 years, 99 per cent of the income gain of the 10 per cent of elderly women living alone with the lowest incomes was from higher direct government payments. For the 20 per cent of women in the middle of the income distribution, direct government transfers accounted for more than 80 per cent of their gain, see Statistics Canada, 'Analysing Family Income', last modified 3 March 2004; available on-line at http://www.12.statcan.ca/english/census01/products/analytic/companion/inc/canada.cfm#14.

credit of just over $1,000 which is reduced in amount if the spouse or common law partner's income exceeds approximately $680, with the credit being eliminated once the spouse or common law partner's income exceeds approximately $7,000. As the LCC has said, 'the credit appears to be designed to promote economic dependency in conjugal relationships'.[32]

There have been many critiques of the spousal and common law partner tax credit.[33] First, because more women than men work in the home and not in the paid labour force, it is men who predominantly claim the spousal and common law partner tax credit. Several issues arise when one considers the impact on women of provisions such as the spouse and common law partner tax credit. Provisions based on dependency are a disincentive to women's participation in the paid labour force. When the tax costs, such as the loss of the credit, are taken into account, there is a real disincentive to women in spousal or common law relationships to enter the paid labour force. This disincentive is exacerbated by other costs incurred by women who choose to work outside the home, such as childcare, travel, clothing and the monetary and non-monetary costs (such as performing the labour oneself) associated with replacing the household labour. Furthermore, when one considers that many women are the secondary earners in their relationships, and that they work for relatively low wages, the combination of these factors and the loss of the tax credit have a particularly detrimental effect on women's choice to work outside the home.

Another important critique of dependency provisions is that rules such as the spousal and common law partner tax credit affirm that a woman's dependency on man deserves tax relief. Again, this undermines the autonomy of women and results in a certain privatisation of economic responsibility for dependent persons. Tax policy has responded to women's lack of economic power by leaving it to the family (the private sector) to assume responsibility for women's lack of resources. Furthermore the tax subsidy is delivered to the economically dominant person in the relationship and not the 'dependent' person who needs it. This manner of delivery assumes that income is pooled and wealth distributed equally within the relationship. However, research has shown that such pooling is not the norm in relationships, with one study demonstrating that it only occurs in one-fifth of households surveyed.[34] Many women do not have access to or control over income earned by their spouse and predicating tax policies on the assumption that they do is unfair.

The spousal and common law partner tax credit is a measure that can be

[32] Law Commission of Canada, above n 11, 74.

[33] See, eg, Law Commission of Canada which recommended that the spousal tax credit be repealed and replaced with 'enhanced or new programs that more carefully target caregivers and children', ibid, 77.

[34] C Vogler and J Pahl, 'Money, Power and Inequality within Marriage' (1994) *Sociological Review* 263, 285.

viewed as one that gives public recognition to the work done by women in the home. Indeed it is the only measure (tax or otherwise) that places a 'value' on household labour. But if it is intended to recognise the contribution made by those who work in the home, then, as mentioned above, the tax credit should go to the person who performs that labour and not the person who benefits from it. Further, viewing the tax credit as a measure that values household labour is problematic. Because the 'value' placed on the labour is so low, the measure can only be considered to reinforce the perception that household labour, including childcare, has little value. That in turn contributes to the undervaluation of work such as childcare, even when it is performed in the open market, as evidenced by the low salaries paid to childcare workers.

Another justification for the spousal or common law partner tax credit is that it recognises the reduced ability to pay tax of an individual who supports a person who is economically dependent on them. But this argument is not persuasive. It ignores the benefit that accrues to the individual from work performed in the home, such as housework and childcare, by the person whom they support. Indeed this home labour may well increase the individual's ability to pay because there is no need to have recourse to the private market in order to obtain the services provided in the home by the spouse he/she supports. This point was not lost on the Royal Commission on the Status of Women in 1970 when it rejected the Carter Commission recommendation that the family be the unit of taxation. At that time the Royal Commission on the Status of Women noted that

> in most cases the wife who works at home as a housekeeper, far from being a dependent, performs essential services worth at least as much to her as to her husband as the cost of food, shelter and clothing that he provides for her.[35]

Given all these problems it is not surprising that various individuals and organisations have called for the repeal of the spousal or common law tax credit.[36]

As mentioned earlier in this chapter, the impact of the rules that take spousal or common law status into account vary depending on the level of income of the spouses or common law partners and the distribution of income within the relationship. There is no question that those couples with high incomes and significant wealth can benefit tremendously from some of the tax rules. One example is the ability to transfer capital property to your spouse or common law partner on a tax-free basis, either

[35] Royal Commission on the Status of Women in Canada, Report (Ottawa, Information Canada, 1970) 293–94.

[36] See, eg, the Law Commission of Canada, above n 11, 77; M Maloney, 'What Is the Appropriate Tax Unit for the 1990s and Beyond?', in A Maslove (ed), *Issues in the Taxation of Individuals* (Toronto, University of Toronto Press and the Ontario Fair Tax Commission, 1994) 146; C Young, *What's Sex Got To Do With It? Tax and the Family* (Ottawa, Law Commission of Canada, 2000) 113.

inter vivos or on death. Canada's tax treatment of capital differs from that of most other jurisdictions. There are no estate taxes, succession duties or gift taxes in Canada. Rather when capital property is transferred from one person to another, either by way of a gift or bequest, the general rule is that the transferor is deemed to have disposed of the property at fair market value.[37] The result is that if the fair market value of the property at the time of transfer is more than the cost of the property to the transferor, a capital gain arises and one-half of the gain is included in the transferor's income. A significant exception to this rule is that if the transfer is to a spouse or common law partner a rollover of the property occurs with the taxpayer deemed to dispose of the property for proceeds of disposition equal to their cost for the property; the spouse or common law partner then effectively acquires the property at an amount equal to those proceeds of disposition. The result is a significant deferral of tax until the spouse or common law partner ultimately disposes of the property. The rollover is available both on an *inter vivos* basis and on death and is also available with respect to a transfer to a former spouse or former common law partner in settlement of rights arising from the marriage or common law partnership.[38]

These rules serve a variety of purposes. From a practical perspective, if transfers between spouses were taxable events, the Canada Revenue Agency (CRA) would have to trace all such transactions in order to ensure that any tax owing was paid. Given the informal context in which these transactions occur, such a task would be difficult. Another problem is that because these transactions do not take place in the open market, there may be a liquidity problem with no cash available to pay the tax. The rollover rules are also intended to encourage the redistribution of property within the relationship, especially from men, who tend to own more capital property than women, to their spouse or common law partner. It is questionable, however, how effective the rules are in this regard. There are many reasons why an individual may choose not to transfer property to their spouse on an *inter vivos* basis, including concern about transferring control of that property to the spouse or common law partner. These rules are also affected by the operation of the attribution rules. If capital property that is transferred to a spouse or common law partner at less than fair market value generates income, that income is attributed to the transferor and not taxed to the spouse or common law partner, thereby preventing income splitting with respect to income from property.[39] Given that most of these transfers are presumably gifts, the attribution of income may well operate

[37] S 69 of the ITA.

[38] S 70(6) of the ITA provides the rollover for transfers as a consequence of death to a spouse or common law partner or to a spouse trust and ss 73(1) and (1.01) of the ITA provides the rollover for *inter vivos* transfers to a spouse or common law partner.

[39] S 74.1 of the ITA.

to deter taxpayers from entering these transactions.[40] It is impossible to determine whether the rollover rules do encourage the redistribution of wealth on an *inter vivos* basis in spousal and common law relationships. While CRA classify these provisions as tax expenditures, they do not put a value on the expenditures because 'the data is not available to support a meaningful estimate/projection'.[41]

These rules can be critiqued on a variety of grounds. First, they only benefit those couples with considerable wealth who own capital property. In the absence of gift taxes or estate taxes, these rules provide a huge benefit to those couples because there is no taxation of any appreciation in the value of the capital property owned by the couple so long as it is owned by either of the spouses or common law partners. Second, while it may be difficult to trace intra-spousal *inter vivos* transfers, the same cannot be said of transfers on death where the will or other documents relating to probate or intestacy will provide information about the transfer.

The rollover rules are predicated on an assumption of economic interdependence[42] and economic mutuality, ie what is mine is yours and what is yours is mine. Yet not all spousal and common law relationships are founded on economic interdependence, nor is there an economic mutuality within the relationship with respect to property. Thus the rollover rules can be said to be overinclusive. They are rules that apply in situations which do not reflect their underlying policy. This problem led the LCC to recommend the extension of the rules to all persons living in economically interdependent relationships.[43] I disagree with their recommendation and believe that the *inter vivos* rules at least should be repealed outright. First, as mentioned above, the application of the attribution rules may deter taxpayers from entering into these transactions, thereby obviating the need for the rollover rules. Secondly, tracing problems are not unique to intra-spousal or common law partner transfers. Transfers to adult children or close friends can be equally difficult to trace. Furthermore, the ITA provides for a self-assessing system in which taxpayers are required to declare a variety of transactions that cannot always be traced, including gifts to third parties. Finally, there is, of course, always the problem of defining 'interdependence' if one goes down that road.

[40] S 74.2 of the ITA also provides that a transfer of capital property to a spouse or common law partner must be at fair market value in order to avoid the attribution of any capital gain arising from that transfer to the transferor when the spouse or common law partner disposes of the property.

[41] Canada, Department of Finance, *Tax Expenditures: Notes to the Estimates/Projections, 2004* (Ottawa, 2004) 15.

[42] The Law Commission of Canada described economic interdependence as the 'raisin d'etre' of the rollover rules, above n 11, 89.

[43] Ibid, Recommendation 25.

Provisions that Are Based on an Assumption of Economies of Scale in Relationships

Some of the provisions that apply to spousal and common law relationships take into account the economies of scale in terms of consumption and household production that are assumed to arise from spouses and common law partners living together. These economies of scale arise from sharing the cost of certain items, such as rent, household expenses, including durable consumer assets such as furniture and kitchen appliances as well as the benefits from shared household work. The theory is that the savings from these shared expenses and labour increase a taxpayer's ability to pay tax. In some instances the assumption of an enhanced ability to pay means that entitlement to certain tax credits and deductions is reduced for a couple. For example, the childcare expense deduction provides a deduction in the computation of income of a limited amount of child care expenses.[44] In spousal or common law relationships, however, the deduction must be taken by the taxpayer with the lower income. This rule effectively reduces the value of the deduction because that value is tied to the rate at which tax is paid: high-rate taxpayers save more in terms of taxes payable than low-rate taxpayers.

Other provisions take into account the assumed increased ability to pay that flows from economies of scale by aggregating the incomes of spouses and common law partners for the purposes of determining entitlement to tax credits. For example, the GST credit is intended to compensate low-income individuals for the regressive impact of the GST, a flat-rate sales tax. Because it is targeted at low-income individuals, the tax credit is reduced by 5 per cent of the amount by which the individual's income exceeds approximately $30,000. However, the income of spouses and common law partners is aggregated to compute the entitlement to the GST credit with the result that the amount they receive as a couple will be less than they received as two individuals.[45] As mentioned earlier, this reduction in the amount of the GST credit is one of the reasons why the inclusion of lesbians and gay men as spouses resulted in a tax windfall for the government.

The issue of aggregating the income of families or spouses when determining entitlement to tax credits is complex. But to the extent that is based on an assumption of economies of scale, it is highly problematic. First, economies of scale arise in a variety of situations other than spousal or common law relationships. As the LCC noted,

[44] S 63 of the ITA.

[45] The Law Commission of Canada noted that the 'GST credit received by each member of a cohabiting couple is reduced to about 65 percent of the amount that would be received by them as individuals', above n 11, 79–80.

> even if consumption economies exist when individuals live together and share resources, and even if one takes the view that they should be taken into account in government transfers, conjugal cohabitation has become an increasingly poor proxy for the identification of such economies.[46]

Many others, such as students or good friends, share accommodation and the associated expenses. The tax system takes no account of their economies of scale when determining entitlement to tax credits. In addition, individuals enter into all kinds of arrangements that produce economies of scale, such as car pooling, sharing a babysitter and recycling consumer durables by passing them on to a friend when new purchases are made. Again the tax system takes no account of these transactions. Given that it is virtually impossible to identify when household economies arise or to define the nature of the relationships in which they do arise, tax provisions should not be based on an assumption that such economies exist and enhance the ability to pay of spouses and common law partners.[47] I agree with the LCC which concluded that 'income security programs should not assume that the benefits of individual income are always shared with others in conjugal relationships and that sharing never occurs in other relationships', and share its view that entitlement to tax credits such as the GST credit be determined by reference to individual income and not spousal or family income.

It is interesting to note how arguments based on economies of scale are used (or not used). The example of the GST credit indicates that those with relatively low and equal incomes lose a tax benefit because of assumed economies of scale. One does not, however, hear much talk of the advantages of economies of scale when looking at the tax treatment of the couple with one high-income earner and a spouse or common law partner with little or no income. Two recent developments in Canada demonstrate this inconsistency in policy.

In 2007 the federal government introduced rules that permit the splitting of pension income between spouses or common law partners,[48] and also hinted that it was contemplating introducing rules that would allow spouses and common law partners to split all their income 50/50. Income splitting benefits the couple in which one partner has a high income and the other no income. The reason is that income that would be taxed at a high marginal rate of tax is taxed at a much lower rate because it is effectively taxed in the hands of the partner who had no income. Income splitting can generate a huge tax saving for such couples: a saving of approximately $8,000 for the couple in which one partner has an income

[46] Law Commission of Canada, above n 11, 80.

[47] Ibid, 82.

[48] See Canada, Department of Finance, 'Legislative Proposals and Explanatory Notes Concerning Specified Investment Flow-Through Trusts and Partnerships', http://www.fin.gc.ca/drleg/ITA-l_ftt1206e.html, accessed 26 May 2008.

of over $120,000 and the other partner has no income. But of course the couple with relatively equal incomes (regardless of how high or low they are) will save nothing. It is also important to note that there is no requirement that the income that is split between the partners actually be transferred to the low-income spouse or common law partner: the income split is purely fictional.

The possibility that the Canadian government might permit the splitting of all income between spouses or common law partners is especially troubling. Such a measure would accord perfectly with a policy that encourages women to remain in the home to perform household and childcare labour rather than working outside the home in the paid labour force. The reason is that loss of that tax benefit would be a considerable deterrent to women's participation in the paid labour force. For the couple with relatively equal incomes there is, of course, no tax saving, meaning that this measure is very specific in its target. It is designed to encourage a return to the 'traditional' family where the mother stays at home. Finally as with the pension income splitting, the income splitting is simply a fictional event for tax purposes, there is no requirement that the income be transferred to the spouse with the low income.

CONCLUSION

In this chapter I have used the recent developments in Canada to extend the definition of spouse in the ITA to include lesbians and gay men as a catalyst to rethink why we take spousal relationships into account at all for tax purposes. In no way do I intend to diminish the remarkable struggle of lesbians and gay men for equality, but I would argue that the consequences of attaining spousal status for tax purposes are both classed and gendered in their impact. The result is a reinforcement of some of the existing inequities which privilege those with high incomes at the expense of those with low incomes. As I have demonstrated, the incentive for the Canadian government to make this change was strong. Not only did tax revenues for the government increase in amount, but the change also bolstered the ongoing policy of placing the responsibility for the economic security of citizens on the private family rather than the state. It is time that we reconsidered all the tax rules that take spousal status into account and ensure that they are in fact operating in an equitable manner and are based on sound tax policy principles.

Part III

HETERONORMATIVITY AND MARRIAGE FUNDAMENTALISM

INTRODUCTION

THIS SECTION CONTAINS two chapters that examine the ways in which neoliberal politics of governance engender the heteronormalisation of intimate couple relationships, both opposite and same sex. The authors of each of these chapters demonstrate the ways in which the extension of legal rights and obligations to unmarried couple relationships are often premised on an assimilative approach whereby such relationships are aligned with heterosexual marriage. In the first of the two chapters, Boyd and Baldassi consider the important question of the extent to which the extension of legal recognition to unmarried couples, opposite and same sex, reaffirms the privileged position of marriage in law—which they describe as 'marriage fundamentalism'. Drawing on the developments that have taken place in Canada, Boyd and Baldassi show how equality arguments have been more successfully deployed to enable opposite- and same-sex cohabitants to access the law for spousal support than property division.

In the latter situation, the fundamental essence of marriage is reaffirmed by denying access to cohabitants on formal equality grounds, ie there is the choice of entering marriage; access to rights such as property division therefore remain specifically contingent on marital status. Boyd and Baldassi then turn their attention to examining cases brought in 2002 and 2006 to investigate the extent to which marriage fundamentalism informs spousal support claims, and whether there are any significant differences in the judicial treatment of claims made by married and unmarried couples. The authors discern a tendency to place greater emphasis on the 'marriage-like' quality of cohabitation, where cohabitants are less likely to succeed in making a claim for spousal support unless they are able to prove that their relationship closely mirrored marriage. In addition, Boyd and Baldassi allude to how these claims are highly gendered in that most of the claims were brought by women. Their chapter provides a cautious reminder that the extension of legal recognition to other forms of familial relationships such as opposite- and same-sex cohabitation may, on the one hand, seem 'progressive' but, on the other hand, serve to reaffirm marriage fundamentalism by assisting only those who can fit themselves within the marriage model.

Nan Seuffert continues this theme of heteronormativity in her chapter which draws on the immigration laws of New Zealand. Seuffert demonstrates how, notwithstanding the extension of legal recognition to same-sex couples for the purposes of immigration, the law in New Zealand adopts an assimilative approach in relation to the recognition and inclusion of new identities within national norms. She describes how the process of assimilation homonormatises same-sex relationships which in turn serves to perpetuate differential treatment of same-sex couples who do not, or cannot, fit within such homonormativity. The chapter analyses the implications of reinscribing and reprivileging marriage and long-term stable relationships as the cornerstone of society. By adopting an assimilative approach that involves recognition of, and inclusion of the 'sameness' in, same-sex relationships that look most marriage-like, any residue, or mark of difference, will remain unrecognised and excluded. Thus only same-sex couples who demonstrate the domestication of their relationship by being homonormatised are most likely to benefit and gain immigration into New Zealand.

Both chapters illustrate the limiting effect of legal intervention in intimate domestic relationships as a consequence of the reinforcement of the marriage model as a starting point for recognition. They resonate with concerns raised by other feminist scholars about the way in which the marriage model is consistently being stretched to accommodate as well as extend legal privileges to unmarried couples, both opposite and same sex, on the basis of a 'logic of semblance'.[1] This fails to acknowledge the diversity of intimate relationships, recognising only those that can be mainstreamed with marriage.

[1] See A Bottomley and S Wong, 'Shared Households: A New Paradigm for Reform of Domestic Property Relations', in A Diduck and K O'Donovan (eds), *Feminist Perspective on Family Law* (Abingdon, Routledge-Cavendish, 2006).

7

Marriage or Naught? Marriage and Unmarried Cohabitation in Canada[1]

SUSAN B BOYD AND CINDY L BALDASSI

INTRODUCTION

BEFORE CANADA ATTRACTED attention in 2005 as one of the first countries in the world to legalise same-sex marriage, it was better known for its legal recognition of unmarried relationships. This recognition began in the late 1970s when the social fact of unmarried relationships became more obvious and it became less tenable to define children born outside marriage as 'illegitimate'. Recognition proceeded incrementally by drawing unmarried opposite-sex cohabitants into family law regulation for certain purposes. Some statutory definitions of 'spouse' were expanded to include partners who had cohabited for a certain period—usually between one and three years, and sometimes a shorter period if the couple had children. In the late 20th and early 21st centuries, many Canadian jurisdictions extended similar recognition to same-sex cohabitants, especially after a Supreme Court of Canada decision declared unconstitutional the exclusion of same-sex cohabitants from a spousal support regime.[2] To the surprise of many, the Supreme Court of Canada stemmed the evolutionary tide in its 2002 decision in *Nova Scotia v Walsh*,[3] by declaring that distinctions drawn between married and unmarried couples in relation to property division did not offend the equality rights guarantees of the Canadian Charter of Rights and Freedoms.[4] Unmarried partners can therefore be excluded from matrimonial property statutes without contravening the Constitution.

[1] We are grateful for funding from a UBC Hampton Research Grant and to Jessica Metters for final editing work.

[2] *M v H* [1999] 2 SCR 3.

[3] *Nova Scotia (Attorney General) v Walsh* [2002] 4 SCR 325.

[4] Canadian Charter of Rights and Freedoms, Part I of the Constitution Act, 1982, being Sched B to the Canada Act 1982 (UK), 1982, c 11.

This chapter was inspired by questions arising from these contradictory trends. Has the power of marriage been reasserted in Canadian law? Now that gay men and lesbians have gained access to legal marriage, is unmarried cohabitation constructed as a lesser status? Has traditional familial ideology been reinforced as a result of the legalisation of same-sex marriage and the reinscribing of a constitutionally valid legal distinction between married and unmarried partners? Does case-law reveal a distinction between these types of partnership? Or is the story one of formal equality, which includes those who fit a marriage model, whether they are married or not, and leaves others out in the cold?

We address these questions by bringing feminist critiques of familial ideology in a neoliberal state to bear on the legal treatment of married and unmarried cohabitants. We first outline to what extent marriage remains a relevant distinction in relation to statutory family law remedies in Canada. We then suggest that the legalisation of same-sex marriage is a triumph of formal equality that may not eradicate the ideological premises of patriarchal relations or marriage fundamentalism. As a case study, we examine judicial decisions in 2002 and 2006 regarding claims for spousal support brought by married and unmarried partners in one Canadian province in order to assess whether marriage fundamentalism can be detected in that context. Very few claims for support were in fact made by unmarried partners and no meaningful differences were found between judicial treatment of unmarried versus married claims. The cases did, however, reveal some troubling themes in relation to women's inequality and the use of spousal support in an era of eroded state support for those in economic need. We conclude that the ways in which both married and unmarried cohabitants are discursively constructed in spousal support claims suggest reaffirmation of a marriage model that plays a particular role in a neoliberal system of governance.

STATE REGULATION OF MARRIED AND UNMARRIED INTIMATE RELATIONSHIPS

Canada remains an uneven patchwork quilt in terms of the access that unmarried cohabitants have to family law remedies, although the pattern of this quilt has changed considerably in recent years.[5] Many Canadian jurisdictions still distinguish between married and unmarried cohabitants, with

[5] Canada's federal system literally renders family law jurisdiction a patchwork. The federal government has jurisdiction over the definition of marriage, divorce and matters corollary to divorce. Federal statutes may also govern certain benefits (eg federal pensions) that couples receive. Provincial governments are, however, accorded jurisdiction over most family law matters, including property and questions to do with child custody, child support and spousal support outside of divorce. Treatment of married versus unmarried partners varies considerably from province to province.

the highest degree of 'inclusivity' of unmarried cohabitants being seen in relation to spousal support. Even here, marriage is significant because only partners with a marriage licence gain automatic entry (without proving a period of cohabitation) into statutory regimes. Moreover, in relation to property claims, unmarried partners encounter extra hurdles in several jurisdictions. Persuading one's partner to make the *choice* of formalising a relationship or opting into a property regime through a contractual measure (marriage, registration or domestic contract) is often a condition precedent to taking advantage of legislated norms of fairness regarding property. Some jurisdictions, such as British Columbia and Ontario, still allow only married partners to benefit from statutory property provisions.[6] As a result, unmarried partners who have not contracted into the statutory regime, but feel they have a claim to a share in their partner's property, must resort to the more cumbersome mechanisms of constructive trust doctrine.[7]

Despite the Supreme Court of Canada decision in *Walsh*, not all property regimes exclude unmarried cohabitants. Some jurisdictions had already changed their statutes before the Supreme Court decision to include unmarried cohabitants.[8] At the time of writing, Saskatchewan, Manitoba, the Northwest Territories and Nunavut include unmarried cohabitants in their matrimonial property statutes once a period of cohabitation ascribes them spousal status.[9] A few other jurisdictions, Nova Scotia and Newfoundland & Labrador, for example, allow unmarried cohabitants to register as partners and thereby opt into statutory property regimes.[10]

Since 2005, same-sex partners can choose to legally marry,[11] in which case they are included in all laws applicable to married partners, including property regimes. Those same-sex partners who do not choose to marry will be treated the same as unmarried opposite-sex partners in most, but not all, jurisdictions, with Nunavut and the Yukon Territories being the exceptions at the time of writing.

Marriage as an important contractual marker and social institution thus appears to have retained some special status in Canada as the 'gold standard' of intimate partnerships, despite the country's considerable recognition of unmarried cohabitants. Indeed, the struggles of same-sex partners for the right to legally marry have succeeded based partly on the argument that marriage *is* the gold standard and that nothing short of marriage (eg civil union or registered partnership) will adequately provide

[6] Family Relations Act, RSBC 1996, c 128; Family Law Act, RSO 1990, c F3.

[7] For a critical analysis of this remedy, see the dissent in *Walsh*, above n 3.

[8] Eg Manitoba's Family Property Act, RSM 1987, c M45, s 2.1; Saskatchewan's Family Property Act, 1997, SS 1997, c F-6.3, s 2.

[9] Of these four, only Nunavut excludes same-sex cohabitants from ascribed status.

[10] Vital Statistics Act, RS, c 494, s 1; Family Law Act, RSNL 1990, c F-2, s 63.

[11] Civil Marriage Act, SC 2005, c 33.

the equality rights guaranteed in the Charter of Rights and Freedoms.[12] As a result, marriage has been expanded and offered to a population living outside the heterosexual norm. As Katherine Silbaugh suggests in her discussion of the Massachusetts same-sex marriage case, *Goodridge v Department of Public Health*,[13] marriage has retained its symbolic resonance as a unique marker of intimate relationships. Moreover, she suggests, a state monopoly has been asserted over marriage by incorporating into it relationships that formerly constituted a threat to that monopoly.[14]

MARRIAGE FUNDAMENTALISM, FORMAL EQUALITY, AND CHOICE

Several Canadian authors have also suggested that even in the face of increased social and legal acceptance of non-marital and same-sex relationships, legal marriage is still held out—problematically—as a unique sociolegal institution.[15] Bringing such relationships within legal parameters does unsettle the special status of legal marriage,[16] but overall, a traditional approach to marriage may nevertheless be reinforced. Writing from a feminist perspective on what she calls 'marriage fundamentalism', Hester Lessard notes that 'the same socially conservative discourse that a short time ago was marshalled to justify denial of same sex claims'[17] was used to justify the liberalisation of marriage to include same-sex partners. For instance, the Ontario Court of Appeal decision on same-sex marriage constructed marriage as 'a basic element of social organization in societies around the world' and 'a fundamental societal institution'.[18]

Similarly, Shelley Gavigan writes about the 'enduring appeal of familial ideology even in relation to "non-traditional" families and the novel context of "equal marriage for same sex couples".'[19] Like other Canadian feminist authors, Gavigan is troubled by the ways in which the same-sex marriage campaign in Canada has proceeded without a critique of gender inequality within the family and with a seemingly shared understanding among litigants, supporters and judges that marriage is a fundamental social

[12] C Young and SB Boyd, 'Losing the Feminist Voice? Debates on the Legal Recognition of Same Sex Partnerships in Canada' (2006) 14 *Feminist Legal Studies* 213, 224–25.

[13] 798 NE2d 941, 948 (Mass 2003).

[14] KB Silbaugh, 'The Practice of Marriage' (2005) 20 *Wisconsin Women's Law Journal* 189, 210.

[15] Eg Young and Boyd, above n 12.

[16] Silbaugh, above n 14, 198.

[17] H Lessard, 'Charter Gridlock: Equality Formalism and Marriage Fundamentalism' (2006) 33 *Supreme Court Law Review* (2d) 291, 296.

[18] *Halpern v Canada (Attorney General),* [2003] OJ No 2268 (QL) paras 5–6.

[19] S Gavigan, 'Equal Families, Equal Parents, Equal Spouses, Equal Marriage: The Case of the Missing Patriarch' (2006) 33 *Supreme Court Law Review* (2d) 317, 319.

institution.[20] Indeed, Gavigan asks whether 'equal marriage' should perhaps be understood as a classic oxymoron.[21] Among other things, many of the arguments in favour of same-sex marriage were premised on a notion that marriage would give the children of lesbian couples 'legitimacy'. This formal equality argument for giving same-sex couples the same rights as opposite-sex couples reinvoked a now-obsolete notion of marriage and legitimacy as important signifiers for the status of children.[22]

Formal equality has, of course, played an important role in relation to some progressive struggles, not only for equal marriage, but also for women's family law remedies. As Gavigan says, formal equality for women has historically represented a formal (albeit uneven) inhibition of patriarchal relations. For instance, legal recognition of unmarried partners has provided remedies to women who emerge from these relationships financially disadvantaged, just as legal recognition of same-sex partners has provided economic remedies to those who were formerly excluded on the basis of their sexual orientation. Formal equality is, however, far from sufficient. What is now required is to think about the pursuit of systemic or substantive equality *after* equal marriage, which in turn raises questions of public versus private remedies for economic inequality.[23]

Moreover, different *forms* of formal equality are at play in family law, some more troubling than others. The more progressive 'public' form of making spouses formally equal under the law (eg wives equal to husbands; same-sex spouses equal to opposite-sex) can be contrasted with the less progressive formal equality of 'private' contract law. Under the latter, for instance, parties to domestic contracts that limit a spouse's access to property division or spousal support are often deemed to be on a formally equal footing with each other. This formal equality in turn makes it more difficult for less powerful parties to challenge contractual arrangements that might otherwise be found to be unfair. As Gavigan writes: 'the purpose of formal equality in this context is to pretend that the spouses are free and equal parties, which allows the Court to permit them (actually him) to leave—*ie*, contract out of—the terrain of family law'.[24] This contractual language of 'choice', so prevalent within neoliberalism, also influenced recent decisions of the Supreme Court of Canada, and, ironically (given its liberal roots), may also entrench a socially conservative conception of family.[25] For instance, that same-sex partners should be able to *choose* the institution of marriage was an important argument, rooted in liberalism

20 Young and Boyd, above n 12.
21 Gavigan, above n 19, 320.
22 Ibid, 336.
23 Ibid, 320. See A Diduck, 'Relationship Fairness', ch 5 of this book.
24 Gavigan, above n 19, 330.
25 Lessard, above n 17.

and formal equality, in the same-sex marriage debates.[26] Lessard takes up the question of contract and 'choice', looking specifically at the line drawn between married and unmarried partners in the *Walsh* and *Hodge* decisions.[27] The Supreme Court first reaffirmed the fundamental essence of marriage in the same-sex marriage litigation, even as its heterosexual exclusivity was undone. The Court then redeployed marriage's essence in *Walsh* and *Hodge* to constitute marriage as a fundamentally different institution and reject claims by unmarried cohabitants to legislative remedies that remain contingent on marital status—namely property division and pensions. Gender inequality can result from this renewed constitutional respectability accorded to marriage.

The Supreme Court's increasing use of the discourse of 'choice' plays out discursively in ways that may obscure constraints on choice. First, in the Supreme Court's rationale for excluding unmarried cohabitants from property regimes in *Walsh*, marriage represents: 'a conscious choice of self-actualizing, formally equal actors who deliberately enter the relationship with full knowledge and acceptance of the entire range of their present and future responsibilities and obligations'.[28] Yet in reality these actors may not be fully aware of the legal implications of either choosing or rejecting marriage. Moreover, one partner can insist on a marriage contract that diminishes the rights and responsibilities that supposedly flow from marriage, as in another recent Supreme Court decision that precluded a wife from challenging a prenuptial agreement severely limiting her economic remedies.[29] Second, a decision *not* to marry is respected in the name of both partners' freedom of choice, even if this decision represents the will of only one of them, often the propertied one. Consequently, a property regime requiring a fair division of assets will not be available to the economically disadvantaged partner. This reasoning represents the essence of the majority decision of the Supreme Court of Canada in *Walsh* that limited property remedies to married spouses. As one family law scholar put it: 'Liberty trumps equality in Charter values.'[30]

In addition to valuing choice and liberty, reaffirmation of marriage reflects another type of neoliberal influence—the realignment of the public/private divide. Neoliberal policies of familialisation and privatisation in Canada include putting increased reliance on families to perform the work of social reproduction and to care for those in need, in the face of a

[26] Young and Boyd, above n 12, 228.

[27] Lessard, above n 17. The Supreme Court decided marriage makes a difference for pension rights based on spousal status in *Hodge v Canada (Minister of Human Resources Development)* [2004] 3 SCR 357.

[28] Gavigan, above n 19, 330.

[29] See *Hartshorne v Hartshorne* (2004) 236 DLR (4th) 193 (SCC). See SB Boyd and C Young, 'Feminism, Law, and Public Policy: Family Feuds and Taxing Times' (2004) 42 *Osgoode Hall Law Journal* 545, 565–67.

[30] DAR Thompson, 'Annotation *Walsh v Nova Scotia*' (2002) 32 RFL (5th) 81.

reduction in public social programmes.[31] But some non-normative family forms that do not fit the socially conservative vision of family still remain excluded under many aspects of the newly realigned public and private ordering:

> The newly located line between public and private, which now positions some gay and lesbian families as insiders, implicitly authorizes the exclusion of a reconfigured group of outsiders: those who are single, lone parents; in multi-person intimate relationships; in non-conjugal but intensely interdependent familial relationships, which may or may not be kin-based; and in common-law relationships with their same- or opposite-sex partners.[32]

Neoliberal governance and neoconservative images of the family are, thus, interrelated, as a traditional definition of family still prevails for some purposes even in the face of neoliberal neutrality. Members of non-normative families tend to be cast on the mercy of a now-shrunken social safety net.

Moreover, under the new governance schemes related to neoliberalism, individuals have been constituted as autonomous, responsible citizens, in a subtly different manner than under classical liberal theory. The self-actualising responsible citizen is now a vehicle for pursuing various policy practices and agendas, rather than being the object of these agendas.[33] In the context of family law, the responsible citizen makes good choices and stands by them. Notably: 'The responsibilized citizen of neo-liberalism fits quite comfortably into the shoes of the self-interested citizen of classical liberalism who is typically evoked by constitutional rights discourse. Both are *choosing* subjects.'[34]

The majority decision in *Walsh* discounts the historical disadvantage and stereotyping that cohabiting partners (especially women) have suffered in favour of the principle that 'choice must be paramount'.[35] Despite the functional similarities between unmarried and married conjugal relationships, the failure of unmarried partners to *choose* marriage prevents them from being considered as similarly situated. Marriage, in this view, has become one among many lifestyles the market citizen can choose.[36] Nonetheless it remains a favoured choice, at least in relation to claims for a share of property.[37] If one chooses poorly (against marriage) one may be

[31] Ibid, 298. See also B Cossman and J Fudge (eds), *Privatization, Law, and the Challenge to Feminism* (University of Toronto Press, 2002).

[32] Lessard, above n 17, 296.

[33] Ibid, 301. Lessard draws on N Rose, *Inventing Our Selves: Psychology, Power, and Personhood* (Cambridge, Cambridge University Press, 1996), 155; see also H Reece *Divorcing Responsibly* (Oxford, Hart Publishing, 2003).

[34] Lessard, above n 17, 301. Emphasis added.

[35] *Walsh*, above n 3, para 43.

[36] Lessard, above n 17, 306–07.

[37] H Conway and P Girard, '"No Place like Home": The Search for a Legal Framework for Cohabitants and the Family Home in Canada and Britain' (2004–05) 30 *Queen's Law Journal* 715, 719.

excluded from economic remedies. The socially conservative privileging of marriage appears in *Walsh* to have trumped the neoliberal impulse to expand that allocation of financial responsibilities to the private sphere of the family. In his concurring reasons in *Walsh*, Gonthier J suggests that these private financial responsibilities should, in the case of unmarried cohabitants, be enforced through spousal support law, rather than matrimonial property regimes. Accordingly, we now turn to our case study of spousal support claims. We found little concrete evidence that Gonthier J's approach has been adopted by lower courts and less difference between married and unmarried cases than anticipated. We did, however, find evidence of the gendered impact of the discourses of neoliberalism and marriage fundamentalism that we have just reviewed.

CASE STUDY: SPOUSAL SUPPORT CLAIMS IN BRITISH COLUMBIA

As mentioned above, most Canadian jurisdictions define unmarried partners as 'spouses' in spousal support statutes provided they have cohabited in a conjugal relationship for a certain length of time. In theory, then, married and unmarried spouses *should* be treated the same in relation to spousal support claims. Still, given the re-emergence of marriage fundamentalism, it seemed plausible that judges might take a different approach to claims brought by unmarried as opposed to married cohabitants, and give negative weight to the fact that a claimant never married the person from whom she or he is claiming support. Would judges assess those who chose to marry as being more committed to their relationship, and therefore grant spousal support claims more often, or make larger awards? Or, to the contrary, might the fact that unmarried cohabitants are often excluded from matrimonial property regimes because they have not 'chosen' to opt into those regimes mean that judges might feel it even more important to treat their claims the same as those emanating from married spouses? We also wondered to what extent same-sex cohabitants were bringing claims for spousal support and how their claims were treated.

We explored these questions by studying all spousal support cases decided in British Columbia in 2002 (just before the Supreme Court decision in *Walsh*) and in 2006 (after *Walsh*). We chose British Columbia because this province excludes unmarried cohabitants from the matrimonial property regime unless they have opted in by signing a property agreement.[38] Using the electronic database Quicklaw, we searched for all interim or final spousal support awards, including variations and appeals made under either the Divorce Act[39] or provincial legislation. The

[38] Family Relations Act, above n 6, s 120.1.
[39] RSC 1985, c 3 (2nd Supp), D-3.4.

provincial Family Relations Act permits claims by either married spouses or unmarried cohabitants who have lived with another person in a marriage-like relationship for a period of at least two years, provided the application is made within one year after they ceased to cohabit. Since 1998, these cohabitants can be either same sex or opposite sex; to quote the statute, 'the marriage-like relationship may be between persons of the same gender'.[40]

The vast majority of claims for spousal support were brought by a married spouse and far more were brought under the Divorce Act. Only nine of the 99 cases (9.1 per cent) we found for 2002 involved cohabitants (although five cases were unclear as to marital status). Only 10 of 144 cases (6.9 per cent) in 2006 involved cohabitants, with one case being unclear as to marital status. Moreover, only one same-sex case was found for 2002 and none for 2006. Although our numbers are too small to offer any statistical significance, the snapshot that these cases provide suggest some troubling trends in relation to marriage fundamentalism and neoliberalism.

Why Don't Unmarried Cohabitants Bring More Claims?

We can only speculate about the small number of claims by unmarried cohabitants. In common law Canada (excluding Québec), only 13.4 per cent of Canadian couples cohabit without marrying[41] but unmarried cohabitations are generally less stable than marriages.[42]

Unmarried cohabitants who wish to claim spousal support do suffer from two special evidentiary burdens related to having to prove their spousal status before they can even present a claim. Whereas married spouses can simply file their marriage licence as proof of spousal status, unmarried partners must prove two elements under the British Columbia statute. First, they must provide evidence that they lived in a 'marriage-like relationship' for at least two years. Second, they must show that they have brought their claim within one year after they ceased to live together. Two of the 2002 cases illustrate that this latter hurdle can defeat a claim.[43] The party with the greater income or assets will often dispute the spousal nature of the relationship (eg the length of cohabitation) or, if it is proven, the point at which the spouses began to live separate and apart. As a result, cohabi-

[40] Family Relations Act, above n 6, s 1(1).

[41] Statistics Canada, *Family Portrait: Continuity and Change in Canadian Families and Households in 2006: Findings* (Ottawa, Statistics Canada, 2007) 35. The figures are much higher at 34.6 per cent for Québec, where spousal support remedies are not available to unmarried partners.

[42] Statistics Canada, *Changing Conjugal Life in Canada* (Ottawa, Statistics Canada, Housing, Family and Social Statistics Division, 2002, Catalogue No 89-576-XIE) 6.

[43] *James v Burns*, 2002 BCSC 1750; *Sese v Ledesma*, 2002 BCSC 544 (this is the case involving a same-sex relationship).

tation is a far less secure form of relationship than marriage when it comes to making support claims.

Married spouses in our cases cohabit for periods of greater than 15 years more often than unmarried spouses.[44] Nevertheless, a short period of cohabitation did not necessarily preclude a spousal support award for an unmarried partner, so long as the minimum two-year period of cohabitation was proven. For instance, in *KCS v RWQ*,[45] a female cohabitant received an award of $2,000 a month after a 3.5-year period of cohabitation (all monetary values in this chapter refer to Canadian dollars). The considerable disparity of income and the male cohabitant's failure to file documents or appear at the hearing likely dictated against him.

Unmarried spouses may be less likely than their married counterparts to bring legal action when their relationships break down. Expectations of such relationships may be lower. It appears that education and income levels are lower than those of married partners.[46] It is also possible that some cohabitants may not be aware of their legal rights to claim spousal support. Around the time of the *Walsh* decision in 2002, there was discussion about a false assumption on the part of the lay public that unmarried cohabitants *did* have rights to claim both property division and spousal support under statutory regimes.[47] In terms of our 2006 cases, one can speculate but never know for sure—that some cohabitants thought that if they were precluded from making matrimonial property claims after *Walsh* (there was a great deal of media coverage of that decision[48]), then they were also precluded from making a spousal support claim. Alternatively, unmarried cohabitants may simply pursue out-of-court settlements rather than risk their claim being denied in litigation—which is a possibility given the extra evidentiary burdens they face. Since the vast majority of family law claims are settled out of court, a study such as this one cannot tell us much about how most people actually settle their disputes.

[44] For couples divorcing in 2002, the average duration of marriage was 14.2 years. Statistics Canada, *The Daily* (4 May 2004), http://www.statcan.ca/Daily/English/040504/d040504a.htm, accessed 28 May 2008.

[45] *KCS v RWQ*, 2006 BCPC 301.

[46] AM Ambert, *Cohabitation and Marriage: How are They Related?* (Ottawa, Vanier Institute of the Family, 2005) 8.

[47] Eg K Busby, 'Common Law Partnerships and Marital Property: Time for a Change?' (2004) 23 *Jurisfemme: News from the National Association of Women and the Law* 2; M Orton, 'Common Law? Learn the Rules' [2003] *Ottawa Citizen* 6 April, D1. A UK study suggests that cohabitants generally believe that some entitlement to property will accrue at relationship breakdown: G Douglas, J Pearce and H Woodward, *A Failure of Trust: Resolving Property Disputes on Cohabitation Breakdown* (Cardiff, Wales, Cardiff Law School, 2007).

[48] See, eg, J Tibbetts, 'Common Law not Equal to Marriage: Unmarried Couples Denied Right to 50/50 Asset Split' [2002] *National Post* 20 Dec, A1; T MacCharles, 'It's Not the Same as Being Married' [2002] *Toronto Star* 20 Dec, A1; K Makin, 'Common-law Property Rights Denied' [2002] *Globe and Mail* 20 Dec, A1.

Judicial Treatment of Unmarried Cohabitants

Due to the small number of cases involving cohabitants, it is difficult to draw meaningful comparisons between the relative success of claims made by married and unmarried partners. We cannot draw any serious inferences from the one or two cases where a cohabiting spouse claiming support appeared to receive less than the usual award.[49] Overall, we did not find obvious differences in judicial treatment of unmarried versus married relationships in either year, other than the ones dictated by statute. The diversity of fact scenarios in the cases combined with the multiple factors judges must consider in these cases also make it difficult to compare. Furthermore, it is impossible to draw any comparisons between opposite- and same-sex partner claims, given that only one case involved a same-sex (lesbian) couple, and this case failed at the outset due to failure to bring the claim within a year of the end of cohabitation.[50]

The distinction between marriage and cohabitation was actually blurred rather than highlighted in a number of respects in the cases we studied. In several cases, couples had cohabited prior to marrying, reflecting a trend that has been remarked upon by sociologists, especially in relation to recent generations.[51] When marriage followed cohabitation, judges tended to treat cohabitation time the same as time spent married, thus defeating arguments by defendants that the amount of support should be reduced based on a short marriage. For example, in *O'Keeffe v O'Keeffe*, the couple had cohabited for three years prior to the five-year marriage. The judge stated: 'It is not, of course, the length of the marriage that governs, it is the period of cohabitation. That was eight years and not particularly short.'[52] In some cases, judges combined the periods of cohabitation and marriage and referred to the total as the 'marriage'.[53]

Moreover, the British Columbia statute itself mandates that support can only be claimed by or from cohabitants who have lived in a 'marriage-like' relationship. As a result, far from cohabitation being contrasted to marriage, the focus is on the similarities between cohabiting and married couples. One judge even referred to unmarried cohabitation as 'marriage'.[54] Quite possibly, due to the bias built into this statutory definition of 'spouse', those cohabiting partners whose relationship appears less than 'marriage-like' will be discouraged in any attempt to pursue a claim for spousal support. Again, this study can tell us nothing about out-of-court settlements.

49 Eg *Cross v Larsen*, 2006 BCSC 420.

50 *Sese*, above n 43.

51 Statistics Canada, *Changing Conjugal Life*, above n 42, 3.

52 *O'Keeffe v O'Keeffe*, 2002 BCSC 337, para 63, per Clancy J. See also *Beese v Beese*, 2006 BCSC 1662.

53 *Smith v Smith*, 2006 BCSC 1655, para 26; *Wise v Wise*, 2006 BCSC 945, para 1.

54 *EKGD v LWP*, 2006 BCSC 1721, para 51.

We did not find much difference between judicial approaches to the small number of cohabitation cases as between 2002 and 2006, although there was some increased attention to the 'marriage-like' quality of the cohabitation in 2006. It is difficult to know whether the attention to the special nature of marriage in *Walsh* contributed to this increased attention. Even in cases where the point was not in dispute, judges sometimes stressed the fact that the parties used the terms 'husband' and 'wife', or that they became engaged, but never got around to marrying.[55] In *EKGD*, the couple had lived together for 21 years, and did on occasion use the terms 'husband' and 'wife'.[56] He had proposed and bought her an engagement ring, and the judge felt it was clear that they had intended to be married. A similar 18-year relationship also saw the judge stressing the use of terms such as 'common-law wife' by the man in his will, and the fact that he had 'proposed marriage and she accepted that proposal', even though the nature of the 'marriage-like' relationship was not in dispute.[57] In *Whale v Gregoire*, the cohabitation only lasted three and a half years and the partners were 'careful to maintain their economic independence in many ways'.[58] The fact that the man had bought a $7,500 engagement ring for the woman, and that they were formally engaged, served to prove the existence of a spousal relationship.

A discourse that reinforces marriage fundamentalism thus arguably features in spousal support cases, including those few involving unmarried cohabitation. Unmarried cohabitants whose relationships do not appear 'marriage-like' are likely to encounter barriers to spousal support claims. There has been debate about the amorphous yet assimilative 'marriage-like' or conjugality requirement that unmarried cohabitants must meet in order to be deemed 'spouses' in Canadian law.[59] Although it has been judicially altered over the years, the governing case in British Columbia still has influence. In his discussion of subjective and objective tests in *Gostlin v Kergin*, Lambert J referenced some traditional markers of marriage:

> In deciding whether a couple lived together as husband and wife . . . I would ask whether the unmarried couple's relationship was like the relationship of the married couple in that the unmarried couple have shown they have voluntarily embraced the permanent support obligations. . . . If each partner had been asked, at any time during the relevant period of more than two years, whether, if their partner were to be suddenly disabled for life, would they consider themselves committed to life-long financial and moral support of that partner, and the answer of both of them would have been 'Yes', then they are living together as

[55] *Wilson v McDougald*, 2006 BCSC 1155, para 1.
[56] *EKGD v LWP*, above n 54, para 34.
[57] *Mead v Wilson-Haffenden*, 2006 BCSC 851, paras 6 and 23.
[58] *Whale v Gregoire*, 2006 BCSC 735, para 161.
[59] B Cossman, and B Ryder, 'What Is Marriage Like? The Irrelevance of Conjugality' (2001) 18 *Canadian Journal of Family Law* 269.

> husband and wife. If the answer would have been 'No', then they may be living together, but not as husband and wife.
>
> Of course, in the particular circumstances of any case, the answer to that question may prove elusive. If that is so, then other, more objective indicators may show the way. Did the couple refer to themselves, when talking to their friends, as husband and wife, or as spouses, or in some equivalent way that recognized a long-term commitment? Did they share the legal rights to their living accommodation? Did they share their property? Did they share their finances and their bank accounts? Did they share their vacations? In short, did they share their lives? And, perhaps *most important of all*, did one of them surrender financial independence and become economically dependant on the other, in accordance with a mutual arrangement.[60]

This latter emphasis on economic dependence has since been diluted in favour of interdependence, but in this test marriage as a normative framework clearly influences legal determinations about whether unmarried cohabitants can make successful spousal support claims. As the following chapter by Nan Seuffert shows, heteronormative models of relationships tend to be reinforced even as formerly non-normative intimate relationships are assimilated into the legal system.

A Gendered Subtext

As our above discussion of marriage fundamentalism revealed, not far beneath the formal equality discourse characterising recent Supreme Court of Canada decisions on married and unmarried relationships lies a deeply gendered subtext. The spousal support cases we reviewed also reveal a highly gendered dynamic, but notably this arises in *both* the married and the unmarried cases. Despite the gender neutrality of modern spousal support law, and despite the fact that a few men feature as claimants and some had been primary caregivers of children, most claims were brought by women in both the unmarried and married categories. In the married category in 2002, 81 women claimed support in comparison to four men. Eight female cohabitants made a claim, whereas one male cohabitant did so. Overall, 94.9 per cent of the claimants were women. In 2006, 93.8 per cent of all claimants were women. In the cohabitant category, all 10 claimants were women. In relation to all claimants in both years, only 5.3 per cent were men; 94.2 per cent were women; and in 0.4 per cent of cases, both made a claim.

When evaluating whether a spouse should receive a spousal support award, judges must consider numerous variables, which are phrased in gender-neutral terms. For instance, under the Divorce Act, judges must take

[60] (1986) 3 BCLR (2d) 264 at 267–68 (CA). Emphasis added.

into consideration the condition, means, needs and other circumstances of each spouse, including (a) the length of cohabitation; (b) the functions performed by each spouse; and (c) any order, agreement or arrangement relating to support of either spouse. Under the Family Relations Act, judges are directed to take into account the needs, means, capacities and economic circumstances of each spouse, including factors such as the effect on the earning capacity of each spouse arising from responsibilities assumed by each spouse during cohabitation. Our cases indicate that judges will also consider factors such as whether a property division will occur, the age of each party, the age and number of children, and custody arrangements. Domestic contracts can be influential, but we found only two cases in 2002 and four in 2006 that involved contracts.

In addition, since 2005, judges may refer to the *Spousal Support Advisory Guidelines*, which give direction as to the amount and duration of spousal support once entitlement is established.[61] An income-sharing method is used to produce a range of amounts and durations for support, which leaves room for judicial discretion in assessing each particular case. The majority of our 2006 cases did not, however, invoke the *Guidelines*, perhaps in part due to their recent introduction and uncertainty as to their status. Even when they were invoked (in a total of 39, or 27.1 per cent, of cases), awards might be outside the recommended range. In 12 cases, awards were below the lower end of the *Guideline* amounts; in only four were they above the range. In just over half of the 39 cases, the support amount was within the range, but awards were more likely to be below than above the mid-range.

One factor that was dealt with inconsistently—and sometimes problematically—in both our marriage and cohabitation cases was the extent to which a female claimant is capable of earning a living, and the impact of responsibility for children on that capacity. Somewhere between 74 and 79 per cent of the cases mentioned that there had been children during the relationship. School-age children were mainly at issue. In one line of cases, judges and masters took into account the fact that a woman's ability to take paid work is significantly reduced if she has dependent children living with her. Even then, her spousal support award might be reduced or up for review once one or more of her children graduate from high school.[62] In another line of cases, judges appeared to take the view that a woman can work full time even when she has children at home.

[61] C Rogerson and R Thompson, 'Spousal Support Advisory Guidelines: A Draft Proposal' (Toronto, University of Toronto, 2005), http://canada.justice.gc.ca/eng/dept-min/pub/ss-pae/proj/ssag-idpa.pdf, accessed 28 May 2008. In *Redpath v Redpath*, 2006 BCCA 338, para 42, the British Columbia Court of Appeal indicated that if a particular award deviated substantially from the Guidelines range, with no exceptional circumstances to explain the anomaly, the standard of review should be reformulated to permit appellate intervention.

[62] Eg *AT v CT*, 2006 BCSC 240. This case involved a 23-year marriage. Her support was reduced by more than a third once the youngest child graduated.

These cases may reveal the influence of neoliberal expectations that everyone must be a responsible worker citizen, regardless of 'private' responsibilities, eg for children.[63] Financial dependency—especially of single mothers on the state—is now viewed as a pathological dependency, and measures must be taken to avoid this by encouraging women to make the correct choices. Income was sometimes imputed to women who were deemed not to be working to their full capacity. For instance, in *Cross v Larsen*,[64] the mother was expected to find full-time work despite the fact that she never worked full time during the 15–18-year cohabitation. The children were still only aged 10 and 13. She received an interim award of $600 a month, but the computation included an imputed income of full-time minimum wage work for her, despite the fact that she was currently on social assistance and her spouse made $87,000 a year (approximately double the average full-time wage in Canada, which in 2001 was $43,231[65]).

Furthermore, a 'market model' is evident in some spousal support cases. Although Canadian law is now clear that support can be awarded on both a needs basis and a compensatory basis (for advantages and disadvantages accrued as a result of division of labour during cohabitation), some judges have denied substantial or continuing support to women who were perceived not to have lost any economic opportunity as a result of the marriage. That is, if a woman was employed throughout the relationship, the fact that she shouldered the main responsibility for the children and/or that he had a much higher income might be deemed largely irrelevant to her claim, especially if she 'chose' her career path. For example, in *Jefferson*,[66] a 12.5-year relationship ended with the mother as sole custodian of two pre-teen boys and a restraining order against the father. Despite his income of nearly $58,000 a year and the fact that he was probably hiding assets, the mother was awarded only $500 a month for one year because 'there is no evidence before the court of career aspirations not pursued as a result of the marriage to the defendant'.[67] The mother had worked part time throughout the marriage and now ran a daycare business, but her annual income including the child-support payments was $23,000. The judge said:

> The fact is that at the time these parties began living together and eventually married the pattern of Ms Jefferson's life had been set, not by this marriage but

[63] B Cossman, 'Family Feuds: Neo-Liberal and Neo-Conservative Visions of the Reprivatization Project' in Cossman and Fudge, above n 31.

[64] Above n 49.

[65] *Earnings of Canadians: Making a Living in the New Economy* (Ottawa, Statistics Canada, 2003), 8, 24.

[66] *Jefferson v Jefferson*, 2002 BCSC 151.

[67] Ibid, para 81.

> by her previous decisions and her previous marriage. It is true that this marriage resulted in two children for whom she has shouldered the main responsibility. Despite that she has pursued employment of her *choice* while maintaining her family responsibilities.[68]

The husband's much higher income and the wife's childcare responsibilities were accorded no weight, despite his obvious ability to pay. Because she did not give up a high-paying career to be with him and always managed to work during the relationship, she was not entitled to an equalisation of incomes, even in a short-term transitional phase. The advantages that her household labour may have given him were not, apparently, taken into account.

In *SM*,[69] the mother was a dentist but had severe tendonitis and could not work full time for the time being. The judge acknowledged that she had done most if not all of the childcare during the 14-year marriage, and she still had custody of the children. Despite the fact that the husband's income was $135,000, whereas the wife's *imputed* income was $76,800 a year (from part-time work and disability payments), she was awarded no spousal support:

> I can make no finding that the Plaintiff has lost economic opportunity as a result of the joint decision to move from Edmonton or to raise the two children of the marriage. I am not satisfied that there has been any significant or any impact on the future earning capacity of the Plaintiff as a result of decisions mutually taken. Given the division of assets and the present ability of the Plaintiff to earn income, I am satisfied that no award of support is necessary.[70]

In both *Jefferson* and *SM*, asset division was equal. However, spousal support is an independent remedy intended to address both need and compensation, and not necessarily to be precluded by equal division of property. That the women in these cases had been 'responsible worker citizens' seemed to count against their claims, despite their clear economic inequality and disproportionate responsibility for children.

In a surprising number of cases—a full third in 2002 and 28.5 per cent in 2006—spousal support claimants argued that they suffered from a health problem, a disability or depression—all factors that impeded their ability to support themselves. Some such claims were made against partners who could hardly be regarded as wealthy. In *Rayvals v Rayvals*,[71] the woman had a disability that was deemed almost certain to be permanent and had arisen during a marriage in which she had been financially dependent. The marriage was for three years, preceded by four years of cohabitation. Her husband made $45,000 per year and was required to pay her $500 per

[68] Ibid (emphasis added).
[69] *SM v HA*, 2002 BCSC 1677.
[70] Ibid, para 85.
[71] 2002 BCSC 128.

month, indefinitely. In other cases, claimants were not so lucky. Their evidence might be lacking, or, even if evidence supported their claim about disability, their ex-spouse might not have the means to pay. In still other cases (about 4 per cent of all 2002 cases and 4.9 per cent in 2006), the defendant claimed a health or disability issue. In two cases in each of 2002 and 2006, both parties did so.

These disability cases raise the question whether individuals experiencing financial difficulties due to health problems that restrict their ability to work may resort to the spousal support system as a way to survive financially. Particularly where income levels of defendants were low, it may be that the spousal support system is being asked to do too much work in a climate in which public support networks are being eroded. Some judges acted as gatekeepers, taking very seriously their assessment of whether the health or disability was as serious as claimed, and whether the claimant could actually work or not.[72]

Lessard's analysis of the *Hodge* case may offer some insight into these claims. She suggests that *Hodge* can be read as an example of a woman attempting to challenge the fact that her access to a public pension (a regime of material support aimed at addressing age-related poverty) was premised on her conjugal relationship with a wage earner, rather than on her status as a citizen. Betty Hodge had lived with a violent, alcoholic man for 22 years. She finally left him and he died four months later. Her claim for a survivor pension failed because of a statutory requirement that unmarried cohabitants must reside with the contributor for 12 months *immediately* preceding death—a requirement not made of married spouses. Like many of the claimants in our case sample, it appears, Betty Hodge was arguing for recognition as a spouse in order to find a material basis on which to survive. These cases remind us that we must acknowledge the ways in which people act as agents within historically specific circumstances of social and economic hardship.[73] Women must be resourceful in a neoliberal context where it is increasingly difficult to rely on social assistance. Perhaps some make claims of former spouses in circumstances when they prefer to be autonomous. But in a neoliberal climate in which marriage and (sometimes) marriage-like relationships are privileged, they may increasingly fall between the gaps of remedies provided by family law and social welfare law.[74] And our case study suggests that family law remedies themselves increasingly incorporate neoliberal expectations—eg that even

[72] Eg *MacKenzie v MacKenzie*, 2006 BCSC 367.

[73] C Smart, 'Stories of Family Life: Cohabitation, Marriage and Social Change' (2000) 17 *Canadian Journal of Family Law* 20, 50.

[74] MJ Mossman and M MacLean, 'Family Law and Social Assistance Programs: Rethinking Equality', in P Evans and G Wekerle (eds), *Women and the Canadian Welfare State* (University of Toronto Press, 1997), 117.

married women be responsible worker citizens—that may well penalise claimants.

CONCLUSION

Few distinctions were drawn between married spouses and the few unmarried cohabitants in our spousal support case study. When high-profile constitutional rights claims under the Charter of Rights and Freedoms are not at issue, as they were in the Supreme Court decisions in *Walsh* and *Hodge*, judges may be less vigilant about marking marriage off as a special legal category. In adjudicating run-of-the-mill family law claims, they may simply try to balance the various factors involved in determining spousal support claims.

However, the points that Lessard and Gavigan have made about familial ideology and marriage fundamentalism are not irrelevant in these spousal support cases, which tell a story of reaffirmation of marriage—and marriage-like relationships—and of insiders and outsiders. The newly drawn line between public and private positions as insiders married same-sex partners and, for some purposes, unmarried cohabitants who are 'marriage-like'. But various others, such as single mothers and some unmarried cohabitants such as Betty Hodge, are cast as outsiders.[75] As we acknowledge the important victories that lesbian and gay couples have made in relation to marriage, we must also consider the defeats suffered by poor women, single mothers and some separating mothers (such as Susan Walsh) who do not fit within the relevant definition of 'spouse'.[76]

The questions raised by the shifting lines between married and unmarried persons, same sex and opposite sex, are complicated by broadening the analysis to consider the role that marriage (and relationships that are sufficiently marriage-like) are playing in law and society, and within a neoliberal state that places primary responsibility not with governments, nor even ultimately with families, but with individuals.[77] Individuals who have once been in a marriage, or marriage-like relationship, may be able to persuade a family law judge to grant their spousal support claim, at least for a while and so long as they can show that the relationship generated some loss of their 'market value'. Those who have not, or whose relationship did not fit within the relevant definition of 'spouse', will be left out in the cold. Unmarried cohabitants certainly have a higher burden of proof to satisfy before they can reach the threshold of an economic remedy. In some cases, individuals who are in economic need, eg those with mental or physical disabilities, or language difficulties, which impede their ability to

[75] Lessard, above n 17, 296.
[76] Gavigan, above n 19, 341.
[77] Lessard, above n 17, 316.

earn income, may be able to use the spousal support system as a social safety net of sorts, at least for a time. But others will have to rely—if they can—on the diminishing social safety net that characterises the neoliberal state. The different lines that are drawn in different statutory regimes between those who fall inside or outside of relevant definitions of spouse also place a heavy onus on individuals to garner knowledge about these definitions and make smart choices about the legal form of their intimate relationships.

When read in this manner, this story is not one of 'progressive' inclusion in the family system. Nor is it simply a story of exclusion of unmarried partners. Placed in its broader social context, it is a complex story of people (more often women) who face financial hardship at the end of a marriage or marriage-like relationship, and find that in the harsh climate of neoliberalism, their best bet is to turn to those who may be legally defined as their spouses. It is also a story that raises serious questions about those who cannot fit themselves within the paradigmatic marriage model, or did not make the 'correct' choice. In this economic climate, one is inclined to argue for inclusion of a broader range of relationships within the family law rubric. However, this reinforcement of private remedies takes the pressure off the state—the public—to provide for those citizens who are in economic straits. Moreover, it overlooks the extent to which family law remedies themselves are now limited by a neoliberal market mentality that emphasises choice and individual responsibility. Under such a mentality, the ongoing significance of inequalities based on gender or disability is too often obscured. Those who are engaged in policy-making in the family law realm must keep this complex story of economic remedies on relationship breakdown in mind as they struggle to formulate legal norms that generate fairness in a still unequal world.

8

Same-Sex Immigration: Domestication and Homonormativity

NAN SEUFFERT

INTRODUCTION

LAW- AND POLICY-MAKERS in New Zealand have taken what might be seen, from a conservative/liberal divide, as two contradictory stances on aspects of border control over the past decade. In one move, they have progressively tightened and whitened immigration policy generally, making the criteria and process for gaining residency more restrictive. At the same time, they have progressively opened the borders in relation to the immigration of same-sex couples, aligning immigration requirements for these couples with those of heterosexual couples. I argue that New Zealand's recent liberalisation of immigration law and policy for gays and lesbians aligns with, rather than contradicts, notions of neoliberal politics, progressive modernity and the current tightening and whitening of immigration. Same-sex couples who most easily fit the immigration criteria will be those from developed 'Western' democracies that also tolerate and recognise same-sex relationships according to an assimilative model, and who live together in long-term stable, monogamous, property-owning relationships, sharing domestic chores. The criteria require the production of subjects who fit highly prescriptive, heteronormative models of caring and sharing in domestic relationships. These criteria mean that immigration of same-sex couples is likely to favour properly homonormatised[1] lesbians and gay men, who are white, middle class and part of the 'new neo-liberal sexual politics' of a domesticated, depoliticised, privatised gay constituency.[2]

[1] L Duggan, 'The New Homonormativity: The Sexual Politics of Neo-liberalism', in R Castronovo and DD Nelson (eds), *Materializing Democracy: Toward a Revitalized Cultural Politics* (Durham, Duke University Press, 2002) 175–94.

[2] Ibid, 179.

HOMONORMATIVITY, NATION AND DOMESTICATION

In recent decades 'queer theory' has arisen from critiques of 'heteronormativity',[3] or the assumption that humans are divided into the categories of 'man' and 'woman', that these two categories represent opposite sexes that are natural and biological, that certain masculine and feminine traits, characteristics and actions flow from the fact of each biological sex, and that it is normal for the two sexes to enter into heterosexual intimate relationships. Disrupting and displacing heteronormativity has required recognising the biological diversity of human bodies and the existence of culturally marginal sexual identifications, including lesbian, gay, transgender, transsexual, bisexual, intersex, cross-dresser and others. In part in resistance to the historically fixed and entrenched categories of sex and sexuality, these identifications tend to be more fluid; some people identify only as 'queer', while others refuse any specific identification. Queer theory, which itself resists categorisation, might be seen as 'resistance to regimes of the normal'.[4] It radically challenges the use of fixed, reified categories, assumptions about what is natural and normal, and hierarchies of sexual identification. Indeed, it has been said that to categorise it as a school of thought 'is to risk domesticating it, and to fixing it in ways that queer theory resists fixing itself'.[5] I will return to the idea of domestication.

The term 'homonormativity' has been coined by Lisa Duggan to represent the normalisation of particular types of intimate homosexual relationships that reflect social hierarchies, including race, gender, class and other configurations of privilege.[6] Duggan argues that a gay politics has emerged in the United States that positions itself as mainstream, between the 'extremists' on the far left and the far right.[7] This gay politics seeks only formal equality rights.[8] It focuses on gay marriage and access to the military, adopting the idea that sexuality beyond formal marriage is a private matter. Duggan argues that the focus on the privatisation of lesbian and gay relationships of this politics embraces neoliberal economic policy, with its pro-business calls for downsizing government and the privatisation of many goods and services, in favour of the self-regulation of 'free markets'.[9] It is a 'politics that does not contest dominant heteronormative assumptions and institutions but upholds and sustains them while promising the possibility of a demobilized gay constituency and a privatized, depoliticized gay culture anchored in domesticity and consumption'.[10]

[3] M Warner, 'Introduction: Fear of a Queer Planet' (1991) 29 *Social Text* 3.
[4] Ibid, 16.
[5] A Jagose, *Queer Theory* (Dunedin, University of Otago Press, 1996) 2.
[6] Duggan, above n 1, 175–76.
[7] Ibid.
[8] M Davies, *Asking the Law Question* (Sydney, Law Book Co, 1994) 179–82.
[9] Duggan, n 1, 177–79.
[10] Ibid, 179.

Duggan is careful to acknowledge that her identification of homonormativity does not create a category that parallels and reflects heteronormativity, as there are no gay structures parallel to those supporting and sustaining heterosexuality; her project is the identification and naming of an emerging politics in order that it may be analysed and critiqued.[11]

While Duggan's analysis is specifically centred in the United States, similar ideas have emerged elsewhere. In Canada it has been argued that in the written and oral submissions on the legislation to expand rights of same-sex partners and to allow same-sex marriage, 'feminist voices are marginalised' and 'conservative and heteronormative discourses on marriage and family are reinforced.'[12] An analysis of legal submissions made as part of the fight for same-sex marriage in Canada demonstrates that they are predicated on the normalisation of whiteness in the gay subject, masking racial privilege.[13] In South Africa it has been argued that lesbian and gay politics that ignore the ways in which class, race and gender intersect with sexuality tend to reproduce rather than redress these hierarchies, producing a homonormativity in the process.[14] Young's chapter in this volume (chapter 6) is concerned with the submersion of classed and gendered aspects of the recognition of same-sex couples in tax provisions. To the extent that homonormativity is about reproducing and rewriting race, class and gender hierarchy in gay rights claims and struggles, these analyses suggest that homonormativity may be emerging in particularly local forms elsewhere. What is important, in my view, is destabilising the progressive narrative of the modern liberal state in achieving 'gay' rights,[15] making visible the ways in which 'gay' is raced, classed and gendered, and highlighting the limitations of the rights.

The idea of homonormativity has been extended to homonationalism in an analysis of the United States as producing collusion between homosexuality and US nationalism; attention to race-sexuality reveals the 'idealization of the US as a properly multicultural heteronormative but nevertheless gay friendly, tolerant, and sexually liberated society'.[16] The argument is that the images and rhetoric that emerged post-September 11 encompassed a reinvigoration of white, heterosexual norms through contrast with portrayals of terrorists as effeminate, emasculated and 'perversely

[11] Ibid, 191 n 9.

[12] CL Young and SB Boyd, 'Losing the Feminist Voice? Debates on the Legal Recognition of Same Sex Partnerships in Canada' (2006) 14 *Feminist Legal Studies* 213, 214.

[13] SJ Lenon, 'Marrying Citizens! Raced Subjects/Re-thinking the Terrain of Equal Marriage Discourse' (2005) 17 *Canadian journal of Women and Law* 405, 408.

[14] N Oswin, 'Producing Homonormativity in Neoliberal South Africa: Recognition, Redistribution and the Equality Project' (2007) 32 *Signs: Journal of Women in Culture and Society* 650, 666.

[15] M Eaton, 'Lesbians, Gays and the Struggle for Equality Rights: Reversing the Progressive Hypothesis' (1994) 17 *Dalhousie Law Journal* 130, 133 (critically analysing the idea of law's steady progress from repression to enlightenment).

[16] JK Puar, 'Mapping US Homonormativities' (2006) 13 *Gender, Place and Culture* 67, 68.

racialized'.[17] At the same time a progressive sexuality was championed as a 'hallmark of US modernity'.[18] Tributes to 'gay heros' contrasted with the Taliban's treatment of Afghani women, and emphasis on the safety of the United States for gays compared favourably to the 'Middle East'.[19] These dynamics produced images of gays and lesbians acceptable within the nation, as part of a patriotic nationality. Rather than a strict heterosexual/homosexual divide, gays and lesbians would be divided through more complex images, raced, gendered, classed and aligned with nationalism, into those who were acceptable and those who were not; some queers were clearly better than others.[20] In the post-September 11 production of stories of national identity, it is the queers who most closely conformed to the images of heroes who were the 'good' queers.

These types of analyses use the idea of nations as imagined political communities[21] told in stories that proliferate at times of national crisis. Nations are *imagined* because no member can ever know all of those who make up the nation, and therefore each carries a fictional image or story of the nation, and are imagined *communities* in the sense that all members of the nation are imagined as part of this fiction.[22] As imagined political communities, nations are the stories that are told about collective political identities.[23] These stories of collective identities produce individual identities that are acceptable and even heroic within the community, and also typically mask various forms of inequality, exclusion and exploitation.[24] The inclusion of some identities occurs at the expense of the exclusion of others, and identifying particular national identities serves to repress other possibilities for both national and individual identities, as well as collective and individual differences within the nation.[25] Stories of national identity may also produce internal and external enemies to the nation, and may shift over time, or spring up in response to major events, such as the September 11 attacks.

[17] Ibid, 67.

[18] Ibid, 69–70.

[19] Ibid.

[20] Ibid, 71.

[21] B Anderson, *Imagined Communities: Reflections of the Origins and Spread of Nationalism* (London, Verso, 1991). The nation is also imagined as a sovereign state, territorially limited, internally united and free of interference from other nation-states.

[22] Ibid.

[23] Ibid, 6; C Stychin, *A Nation by Rights* (Philadelphia, Temple University Press, 1998) 1; H Bhaba, 'Introduction: Narrating the Nation', in H Bhaba (ed), *Nation and Narration* (Routledge, London, 1990), 1; *See* AP Harris, 'Comment: Seductions of Modern Culture' (1996) 8 *Yale Journal of Law and Humanities* 213, 213 (the philosophy of the Enlightenment and the Romantic opposition 'shape not only the stories we tell about our individual identities, but also the stories we tell about collective identities').

[24] Anderson, above n 21, 7.

[25] M Davies, *Delimiting the Law: 'Postmodernism' and the Politics of Law* (Pluto Press, London, 1996) 74.

Questions of the boundaries of nations, and internal and external demarcation, intersect with analyses of domestic law and domestication in lesbian and gay lives. Domestic laws are the laws internal to a sovereign state, including its immigration law. The domestic sphere is typically thought of as the home, or the private sphere, traditionally thought of as a place where the law does not intrude. The domestic sphere can be a place for domination along gender lines. Feminists and other critical scholars have critiqued the public/private distinction, the supposedly natural gendering of the two spheres along a male/female divide, and the idea that the law does not intrude into the home.[26] In critical theory domestication may also mean relegation to the domestic sphere, or more generally bringing one group of people under the power or control of another, or the internalisation of the views of the dominant culture as 'common sense'.[27] Using these analyses gays and lesbians might be said to be domesticated when they conform to heteronormative ideas about relationships, such as engaging in long-term monogamous relationships in which they live or aspire to a middle-class lifestyle, and in which they perform their sexuality only or mainly in the private, domestic realm of the household.[28] Katherine Franke argues that the US Supreme Court decision in *Lawrence v Texas*[29] has domesticated sexual liberty, creating a legal landscape that is likely to render 'different legal treatment to those who express their sexuality in domesticated ways and those who don't—regardless of orientation.'[30]

Using the idea of nations as stories told about national identity, I have argued that the recognition of lesbian and gay relationships in the parliamentary debates on the Civil Union Act 2004 (CUA) in New Zealand shifts the heterosexual/homosexual divide to include those same-sex partners willing to embrace heteronormative models of relationships.[31] The stories of national identity told in these debates are in part stories of the progressive (partial) recognition of human rights in a nation moving to realise the promise of modernity, to offer equal treatment under the law. Both those for and against recognition of same-sex relationships told stories of New Zealanders as tolerant and fair, as forwarding-looking progressives who value stable, long-term, committed relationships, warm, loving communities for children, and strong families and family relation-

[26] See Davies, above n 8, 186–72; S Boyd (ed), *Challenging the Public/Private Divide: Feminism, Law & Public Policy* (Toronto, University of Toronto Press, 1997); M Thornton (ed), *Public and Private: Feminist Legal Debates* (Melbourne, Oxford University Press, 1995).

[27] R Robson, 'Mother: The Legal Domestication of Lesbian Existence' (1992) 7 *Hypatia* 172, 172.

[28] DW Riggs, 'Reassessing the Foster-Care System: Examining the Impact of Heterosexism on Lesbian and Gay Applicants' (2007) 22 *Hypatia* 132, 134.

[29] 123 SCt 2472 (2003).

[30] K Franke, 'The Domesticated Liberty of *Lawrence v Texas*' (2004) 104 *Columbia Law Review* 1399, 1416.

[31] S Seuffert, 'Sexual Citizenship and the *Civil Union Act* 2004' (2006) 37 *Victoria University of Wellington Law Review* 281.

ships. To the extent that lesbian and gay relationships can fit into these moulds, these are stories of the homonormatising of lesbian and gay relationships through (partial) inclusion in the collective identity of the nation. In the process of normalising these relationships, the family is reinscribed as the cornerstone of society, and the position of marriage as the 'gold standard' of relationships is reinforced.[32] Boyd and Baldassi's discussion of 'marriage fundamentalism' in this volume (chapter 7) analyses this phenomenon in Canada.

IMMIGRATION POLICY IN NEW ZEALAND: FROM 'WHITER THAN WHITE' TO TIGHTENING AND WHITENING

Immigration and national identity are closely linked. Immigration is domestic law that determines who may enter the nation, policing the boundaries of the nation. National identity is literally embodied in those who enter the country. Some are easily absorbed into the dominant stories of national identity, while others represent the boundary of that identity.[33] I have identified two trends in New Zealand's immigration law and policy since September 11: its 'tightening and whitening', and the opening of borders to those in same-sex relationships. A brief discussion of immigration and New Zealand's national identity is necessary to my analysis of the convergence of these trends.

New Zealand's immigration policy historically focused on creating a 'better Britain', a homogenous white settler society. This policy has been labelled 'whiter than white' to indicate that it was even more restrictive than Australia's 'white only' policy.[34] The informal and unwritten policy, in which government officials had far-reaching discretion, was implemented through tactics such as informing shipping companies confidentially of the types of people who would not be granted an entry permit upon arrival in the country.[35] Other tactics included 'secrecy, a public avoidance of the issue of discrimination and, if necessary, a denial of its existence'.[36] Even during a shortage of labour from the 1940s to the late 1960s, immigration policy was broadened only reluctantly to include immigrants from northern

[32] Ibid, 283; Young, above n 12, 230–35 (arguing that demands by gay rights groups for marriage rather than registered domestic partnerships reinforced the symbolic importance of marriage as a 'gold standard').

[33] N Seuffert, *Jurisprudence of National Identity* (Aldershot, Ashgate, 2006), 117.

[34] M McKinnon, *Immigrants and Citizens: New Zealanders and Asian Immigration in Historical Context* (Wellington, Victoria University Institute of Policy Studies, 1996), 1, 12, 22; T Brooking and R Rabel, 'Neither British nor Polynesian: A Brief History of New Zealand's Other Immigrants', in S Grief (ed), *Immigration and National Identity in New Zealand* (Palmerston North, Dunmore, 1995), 23.

[35] S Brawley, '"No 'White Policy' in New Zealand": Fact and Fiction in New Zealand's Asian Immigration Record, 1946–1978' (1993) 27 *New Zealand Journal of History* 16, 18–19.

[36] Ibid, 20.

Europe: 'Southern and Eastern Europeans were not considered to offer the same potential [for assimilation], and the possibility of non-European migration was dismissed out of hand.'[37]

New Zealand managed to maintain its unwritten discriminatory immigration policy longer than North America and Australia. In part this was the result of the widely held perception that New Zealand had harmonious relations with Maori and an egalitarian society. In fact, colonisation of indigenous people in New Zealand was perpetrated using many of the tactics employed elsewhere by the British government, and 'relations with Maori' were often fraught as a result. Although New Zealand at times embraced more socialist style politics and policies than some other liberal democracies, these were also raced and gendered, tending to benefit disproportionately white men and nuclear families. Nevertheless, it was difficult for the white international community to believe New Zealand discriminated in immigration along racial lines.[38] As a result New Zealand's settler population developed into a particularly homogenous white society, which underpinned national identities such as 'better Britain'.

This 'whiter than white' policy persisted in different forms, with only minor exceptions when labour was needed, until 1986.[39] It was dropped in favour of policies specifically intended to align immigration with New Zealand's whirlwind implementation of radical neoliberal economic policy, and a corresponding shift in national identity from a caring welfare society to an enterprise society.[40] The new laws and policies resulted in more diversity in immigration, and a group of countries including China, India and South Korea, identified as 'Asia', became the leading source of immigrants. The proportion of immigration approvals granted to 'Asians' between 1991 and 1994 grew dramatically to 54.2 per cent of the total. In the years between the 1986 and 1996 census the number of people from Asian and Southeast Asian countries more than tripled, from 48,855 to 160,683. While the population percentage of Asians also more than tripled from 1.45 per cent in 1986 to 4.45 per cent in 1996, the numbers and percentage were still small.[41]

In the increasing panic post-September 11 the New Zealand government implemented successive changes to immigration criteria, tightening and whitening it over several years. One change came in November of 2002, significantly increasing the English-language requirements for those not

[37] Brooking, above n 34, 38–39.

[38] Brawley, above n 35, 29.

[39] Seuffert, above n 33, 49–70, 117–32.

[40] Hon K Burke, *Review of Immigration Policy 1986* (Wellington, Government Printer, 1986) 15–16, 19–21; McKinnon, above n 34, 42; W Kasper, 'Populate or Languish? Rethinking New Zealand's Immigration Policy' (Auckland, New Zealand Business Roundtable, 1990); for an analysis of New Zealand's shift in national identity see Seuffert, above n 33, 71–84.

[41] Statistics New Zealand, *1996 Census of Populations and Dwellings: Ethnic Groups* (Wellington, 1996) Table 1a.

from English-language backgrounds only.[42] In 2003 there was a switch from the old general skills category, where approval was granted to immigrants who met the required number of points, to a new skilled migrant category, with more emphasis on job offers and criteria that allow more bureaucratic discretion.[43] As a result of these two changes, applications in the general skills/skilled migrant categories declined in the year ending in mid-2004, and the total approved applications fell almost 6,000 short of the target.[44] The United Kingdom replaced India and China as the largest source of migrants,[45] echoing pre-1986 'whiter than white' policies. This trend snowballed between 2003 and 2005, with approvals of residency applications from the United Kingdom increasing from 14 per cent of the total in the year ending June 2003, to 21 per cent in the year ending June 2004, to 31 per cent in the year ending June 2005; the United States began to feature statistically in 2005 with 3%.[46] In the same period approvals from China decreased from 16 to 10 per cent and approvals from India decreased from 16 to 7 per cent.[47] Immigration application approvals from India, China and South Korea combined dropped from 37 to 21 per cent.[48] These figures dramatically illustrate the tightening and whitening of immigration policy in New Zealand.

SAME-SEX IMMIGRATION: A STORY OF PROGRESSIVE MODERNITY?

During the same period in which immigration law and policy has been tightened and whitened, a story of legal recognition within New Zealand, and the relaxing of national boundaries into the country, can be told in relation to sexual minorities, and in particular, same-sex couples. It is sometimes told as a story of progressive modernity. The familiar idea is that liberal states, over time, take steps to recognise, and confer rights on, more and more marginalised groups, making progress towards full equality. It is a story in which legal recognition of same-sex relationships in civil unions in New Zealand, and legal equality with married and de facto couples in most other areas, including immigration, at least on one telling, has been achieved with surprising rapidity subsequent to the challenge to the

[42] New Zealand Department of Labour, *Trends in Residence Approvals* 2002/2003' (Wellington, September 2003) 50–51.

[43] New Zealand Immigration Service, *Operation Manual: Residence* (Wellington, Department of Labour, 2005) ch 84-3, para SM3.15–3.25.

[44] New Zealand Department of Labour, *Migration Trends 2003/2004* (Wellington, Immigration Service, Immigration Research Programme, 2004) 1.

[45] Ibid, 1.

[46] Department of Labour, *Immigration Trends 2004/2005* (Wellington, December 2005) 18.

[47] Ibid, 18.

[48] Ibid, 18.

exclusion of lesbians and gay men from marriage on the grounds of discrimination in 1996. This story has parallels in the United Kingdom and Canada. In Canada, once courts began to recognise discrimination on the basis of sexual orientation under the Canadian Charter of Rights and Freedoms in 1995, the legal system's embrasure of non-normative spousal relationships, and the right to marry, occurred with 'startling rapidity'.[49] The Civil Marriage Act, legalising civil same-sex marriage across Canada, was passed on 20 July 2005.[50] In the United Kingdom, same-sex relationships were recognised with civil partnerships in the Civil Partnership Act 2004, which became effective on 5 December 2005, and immigration was liberalised at the same time. Each of these developments has its own trajectory of human rights struggles, the funnelling and construction of political claims into socially acceptable paths and categories, critiques of assimilation and, in New Zealand and the UK, failure to provide full legal equality.[51] Nevertheless, they represent significant shifts in legal recognition of same-sex relationships.

This move towards legal recognition of relationships is reflected in immigration law in New Zealand. The Human Rights Act 1993 (HRA) recognised sexual orientation as a prohibited ground of discrimination.[52] In 1993 the Immigration Act 1987 (IA) gave 'enormous discretion' to the Minister of Immigration and immigration officers.[53] The policy promulgated under the IA provided that the criteria for immigration of de facto partners in heterosexual relationships with New Zealand citizens or residents included that the couple had been 'living together in a genuine and stable relationship for 2 or more years'.[54] The same criteria applied to those in same-sex relationships with New Zealand citizens or residents, except that the relationships had to be '4 years or more' rather than 2 years or more.[55] It was argued in 1994 that this discrepancy constituted discrimination on the basis of sexual orientation.[56] However, whether the prohibition on discrimination applied to immigration law and policy in 1994 was an open question, in part because the government was exempted from the HRA prohibition until the end of 1999.[57] Not surprisingly, then, in December 1998 the Cabinet decided to amend the Government

[49] Young, above n 12, 216.

[50] Ibid, 216.

[51] See Seuffert, above n 33; R Auchmuty, 'Same-Sex Marriage Revived: Feminist Critique and Legal Strategy' (2004) 14 *Feminism & Psychology* 101.

[52] Human Rights Act 1993 (NZ), s 21(1); see C Chauvel, 'New Zealand's Unlawful Immigration Policy' (1994) 4 *Australasian Gay and Lesbian Law Journal* 73, 75.

[53] B Stewart, 'New Zealand Immigration Law and Gay and Lesbian Couples' (1993) 3 *Australasian Gay and Lesbian Journal* 30, 33.

[54] Department of Labour (NZ), *New Zealand Immigration Instructions* (Wellington, 1991) Ch 7-F-16; Immigration Act 1987 s 2(1), 131.

[55] *New Zealand Immigration Instructions*, above n 54.

[56] Chauvel, above n 52.

[57] Ibid, 79.

Residence Policy to treat same-sex couples the same as de facto couples under family immigration policy, and this change was made in 1999.[58] However, de facto couples were still treated differently to married couples, and heterosexual couples had the choice of marriage while same-sex couples did not.

In 2003, just after the English-language requirement was significantly increased for those immigrating from non-English speaking countries, a 'partnership policy' was introduced that aimed to treat those married and those in an 'interdependent partnership akin to marriage', whether opposite-sex or same-sex couples, on the same basis when applying for residency.[59] With the passage of the CUA and the accompanying Relationships (Statutory References) Act 2005 the IA and Immigration Regulations 1999 were further amended to implement the current 'partnership policy' aligning civil unions with marriages, whether of the same- or opposite-sex couples.[60] This trajectory appears to present a story of progressive modernity. However, as I argue below, aligning the criteria for same-sex couples with the existing criteria for heterosexual couples without amending or reshaping the criteria in any way ensures that homonormatised and domesticated same-sex couples, those properly raced and classed, who have mirrored heteronormatised relationships, will benefit disproportionately from the changes.

SAME-SEX IMMIGRATION: THE NUTS AND BOLTS

Immigration law and policy relevant to entry for same-sex couples and same-sex partners of New Zealand citizens and residents is contained in the IA, the Immigration Regulations 1999 and the New Zealand Immigration Service *Operational Manual*.[61] The IA provides that grants of residence and other permits and visas are matters of discretion for the Minister of Immigration ('the Minister'), and the Minister has broad powers to delegate under the IA to any immigration or visa officer.[62] The Minister

[58] Ministry of Justice (NZ), *Same-Sex Couples and the Law: Backgrounding the Issues* (Wellington, 1999) 19, available at http://www.justice.govt.nz/pubs/reports/1999 (last accessed 1 November 2007).

[59] Immigration Amendment Regulations (No 3) 2003 (NZ), amending Regulation 20 of the Immigration Regulations 1999 (NZ), effective 29 September 2003 to 7 April 2005.

[60] Relationships (Statutory References) Act 2005 (NZ), s 7, Sched 1; s 12, Sched 4.

[61] New Zealand Immigration Service, *Operational Manual* (30 July 2007) available at http://www.immigration.govt.nz/nzis (last accessed 1 November 2007). In 2006 a review of the Immigration Act 1987 was commenced; see Department of Labour, 'Immigration Act Review: Discussion Paper' (April 2006). An Immigration Bill to replace the Immigration Act 1987 was tabled in the House of Representatives in August of 2007. Several of the core elements of the 1987 Act remain, and the criteria and rules for residence and temporary entry, with which this analysis is primarily concerned, are not under review. Department of Labour, 'Immigration Act Review: Discussion Paper' (April 2006) 6.

[62] Immigration Act 1987 (NZ), s 2, 8–10A, 13(A), 131.

certifies policy that is then set out in the *Operational Manual*, which is required to be published and available to the public.[63] However, many of the applicable provisions in the *Operational Manual* require the satisfaction of a visa or immigration officer that the criteria are met; the burden of proving that the criteria are met is on the applicant and the partner.[64] Clearly, the 'enormous discretion' of immigration officers referred to in 1993 still exists.

The 'partnership policy' provides entry for partners of New Zealand citizens and residents, and for partners of principal applicants in other categories. Under this policy couples must provide evidence to satisfy an immigration officer that they have been living together for 12 months or more in a partnership that is genuine and stable.[65] The criteria for immigration are therefore living together for 12 months or more, and a partnership that must be 'genuine and stable'.

'Partnership' is defined as a legal marriage, a civil union (whether opposite or same sex), or a de facto relationship (whether opposite or same sex), and 'partner' is defined as one of the parties to one of these relationships.[66] In New Zealand marriage is between opposite-sex partners only.[67] The term civil union is not defined for purposes of immigration. However, the CUA provides reference to a civil union entered into in accordance with the CUA, and includes relationships entered into overseas recognised by regulations under the CUA.[68] As of this writing, the regulations identify only five overseas relationships recognised as civil unions: Finland's registered partnerships; the United Kingdom's civil partnerships; Germany's life partnerships; New Jersey's domestic partnerships; and Vermont's civil unions.[69] Civil unions therefore include only those relationships entered into under the CUA or relationships legally recognised in one of these other five jurisdictions. Same-sex couples who have legally recognised relationships in other jurisdictions, including those married in jurisdictions such as Canada that allow same-sex marriages, or those whose relationships have been recognised in various ways in India,[70] have to come into New Zealand under the de facto relationship category.

'De facto relationship', which was added to the regulations in 2005, is not defined in the IA or regulations; it is defined in the Interpretation Act 1999 to mean a relationship between two people, whether the same or

[63] Immigration Act 1987 (NZ), s 13A.

[64] New Zealand Immigration Service, above n 61, ch 11, R2.1.15, R2.1.20; ch 69, F2.5c.

[65] Ibid, ch 11, R2.1.10, ch 69, F2.5a.

[66] Ibid, ch 69, F2.5b

[67] *Quilter v Attorney-General* [1998] 1 NZLR 523 (CA). New Zealand does not recognise overseas same-sex marriages.

[68] Civil Union Act 2004 (NZ), s 5.

[69] Civil Unions (Recognised Overseas Relationships) Regulations 2005, SR 2005/125, s 3.

[70] R Vanita, *Love's Rite: Same Sex Marriage in India and the West* (Gordonsville, VA, Palgrave Macmillan, 2005).

opposite sex, who live together as a couple in a relationship in the nature of marriage or civil union.[71] While there does not seem to be any definitive authority on this point, the Interpretation Act 1999 may import the further criteria of 'living together as a couple' and 'in a relationship in the nature of marriage' into the immigration regulation interpretation of partnership. These terms may be interpreted differently from the regulation requirement of a genuine and stable partnership. This result would be unfortunate, and probably discriminatory, as it could result in different criteria and treatment for, for example, same- and opposite-sex couples married in Canada.

A partnership is considered to be genuine and stable it if it has been entered into with the intention of being maintained on a long-term exclusive basis and is likely to endure.[72] *Factors* that have a bearing on whether the two people are living together in a partnership that is *genuine and stable* include the duration of the relationship, the existence, nature and extent of the partners' common residence, the degree of financial dependence or interdependence, the common ownership, use and acquisition of property, the degree of commitment of the partners to a shared life, children, the performance of common household duties by the partners, and the reputation and public aspects of the relationship.[73] *Evidence* that the partners are *living together* may include documents showing shared accommodation such as joint ownership of residential property, joint tenancy agreements and correspondence addressed to both of the partners at the same address.[74] *Evidence* that the partnership is *genuine and stable* may include a marriage certificate, a civil union certificate, birth certificates of children, evidence of communication between the partners, photographs of the parties together, documents indicating public recognition of the partnership and other evidence that the parties are committed to each other emotionally and exclusively.[75] This final type of evidence of exclusive emotional commitment may include evidence of joint decision making and plans together, sharing of parental obligations, sharing of household activities, companionship and spare time, leisure and social activities and presentation to outsiders as a couple.[76]

New Zealand's alignment of immigration criteria for same-sex couples with those of opposite-sex couples makes it one of the most 'gay-friendly'

[71] Interpretation Act 1999 (NZ), s 29A(1).

[72] New Zealand Immigration Service, above n 61, ch 11, R2.1.20; ch 69, F2.10.1. If a partnership is found to be genuine and stable but a couple have not been living together for 12 months or more, the final decision may be deferred and a temporary work visa or permit may be granted. New Zealand Immigration Service, above n 61, ch 11, R2.1.15.5; ch 69, F2.10.1; D Ryken, 'Immigration Rights for Cohabitees in New Zealand' (March 2004) 18 *International Family Law Journal* 1, 3–4.

[73] New Zealand Immigration Service, above n 61, ch 69, F2.20b.

[74] Ibid, ch 69, F2.20.15a.

[75] Ibid, ch 69, F2.20.15c.

[76] Ibid.

countries for immigration. Ad hoc reports from (middle-class, white) New Zealanders with partners immigrating to the country suggest that the criteria are often sensitively and fairly applied. Nevertheless, in the next section I want to trouble this progressive narrative of formal equality using the ideas of homomornativity and domestication that I have discussed.

HOMONORMATIVITY AND DOMESTICATION

The border control function involves making determinations about the embodiment of national identity, producing both national and individual identities in the process. Immigration law and policy criteria, and the implementation of the criteria, determine who will be included in and who will be excluded from a nation. The criteria for inclusion tell stories of New Zealand's aspirations for national identity, for its imagined political community. These stories may be multiple, shifting and even contradictory. Those admitted may be differently positioned in the stories, buttressing certain stories by inclusion or by contrast. Further, the implementation of immigration law and policy produces subjects through regulation: 'to become subject to regulation is also to become subjectivated by it, that is, to be brought into being as a subject precisely through being regulated'.[77] The subject is literally brought into the nation through regulation, producing an identity through the performance of meeting the criteria to the satisfaction of the officials.

In this section I want to make two points about the regulatory process for same-sex immigration in New Zealand. First, I want to consider the dynamics of opening the country's borders to lesbian and gay couples while simultaneously tightening and whitening immigration policy. Second, I want to consider the implications of including same-sex couples in the category of de facto, and aligning that category with the categories of marriage and civil union, so that the criteria applied to same-sex couples are the criteria developed to determine which heterosexual couples ought to be included in the nation.[78] I want to analyse the heteronormativity and homonormativity[79] of the criteria. Heteronormativity includes the norms of heterosexuality as well as the failure to recognise any differences in same-sex relationships. Following on from the discussion earlier in the chapter, homonormativity includes depoliticisation as well as domesticity and privatisation. It includes the ways in which entry into the area of domestic law requires proof of domesticity, or taming, and the relegation of sexual identity and practices to the private realm.

The implications of aligning criteria for immigration of same-sex couples

[77] J Butler, *Undoing Gender* (New York, Routledge, 2004) 41.
[78] See Lenon, above n 13, 408.
[79] See Duggan, above n 1, 179

to existing criteria for heterosexual couples foregrounds sexuality as the only difference that is recognised. Lesbian and gay couples have to prove to the satisfaction of immigration officers that they are just like the types of heterosexual couples who meet the criteria except for their sexuality; 'an intelligible legal subject is produced solely against heterosexuality and hence, is "just gay"'.[80] This binary approach to difference fails to address other possible differences, such as class, gender and race. The result is likely to be that those lesbians and gay men admitted to the country will differ from heterosexual couples admitted only in their sexuality; they will tend to be privileged in race, class and gender, and that privilege will be occluded in part by the focus on sexuality.[81] To the extent that the criteria privilege middle-class white men, then middle-class white gay men will be privileged by this approach to same-sex immigration.[82] As discussed above, New Zealand's historical 'whiter than white' immigration policy has been reinscribed in the recent tightening and whitening of immigration law and policy. The new, more stringent English-language requirements were adopted about the same time as the same-sex immigration criteria were implemented. Under the skilled migrant category both principal and non-principal applicants must meet English-language criteria, and it has been argued that immigration officers adopt a restrictive approach to application of the criteria.[83] The criteria and the approach to application are likely to ensure that same-sex immigration approvals are aligned with the overall trend, discussed above, of favouring those from English-speaking, predominantly white, countries.

As discussed above, the CUA regulations recognise only five types of overseas same-sex relationships as civil unions—those of Finland, the UK, Germany, New Jersey and Vermont. All five of these are developed countries/states that are predominantly white. This means that same-sex couples from other countries, even where they have a legally recognised relationship, will be in the de facto relationship category, and may therefore have to meet different, and potentially more stringent, criteria. Interestingly, in the United Kingdom, legally recognised relationships in 25 overseas countries and US states are recognised as civil partnerships in a non-exhaustive list.[84] With one possible exception, this is also a list of

[80] Lenon, above n 13, 408.

[81] K Crenshaw, 'Mapping the Margins: Intersectionality, Identity Politics and Violence Against Women of Color' (1991) 43 *Stanford Law Review* 1241.

[82] See, eg, N Naffine, *Law and the Sexes: Explorations in Feminist Jurisprudence* (Sydney, Allen & Unwin, 1990); Davies, above n 8, 181–82.

[83] New Zealand Immigration Service, above n 61, ch 86, SM5.5, SM5.10; D Ryken, 'Skilled Migrant Category: Skilled Migrants', in *Immigration Law 2007*, LexisNexis Professional Development (Auckland, June 2007) 1–2.

[84] UK Diplomatic Service Procedures, *Entry Clearance*, Vol 1: *General Instructions, Schedule 20, A List of Recognised Overseas Same Sex Relationships*, includes 24 overseas relationships including Massachusetts, Vermont and California.

developed, predominantly white countries.[85] Further, the website of the UK Gay and Lesbian Immigration Group notes that the most common reason given for refusal in the proposed civil partner category is that the relationship is not genuine, and this is particularly true where the foreign applicant is from a developing country.[86] Unfortunately, this type of information is not available for New Zealand. However, the short New Zealand list of recognised relationships, combined with the possibility of different criteria for de facto relationships, and the UK experience, suggest that this is an area for concern, and that it may well be more difficult for those lesbians and gay men from developing countries to immigrate. Combined with the alignment of criteria for same-sex immigration with that of heterosexuals, which I will discuss next, this analysis suggests that the idea of a 'national heterosexuality' that is sanitised and deracialised (white) may fit here.[87]

The existing criteria embrace heteronormativity, or norms of heterosexuality, and as a result tend to call for the production of homonormatised lesbian and gay identities aligned with heteronormativity. Heteronormativity includes norms about what relationships should look like. These norms may be submerged, and difficult to decontextualise,[88] they 'construct and continually reinforce (even if only in the background) our idea of "the normal"'.[89] The immigration criteria require proof of genuine and stable relationships that are entered into with the intention of continuation on a long-term exclusive basis and are likely to endure.[90] These are criteria that embrace heterosexual norms: 'Living together, having joint finances, and publicly demonstrating an exclusive and committed bond, are criteria derived from dominant notions of what it means to be in a relationship, . . . derived from the idealized model of a heterosexual relationship.'[91] Heteronormative models may also set the standard to which lesbian and gay couples have to perform their relationships, in producing a narrative, and therefore their identities, for immigration officials: 'I . . . found it frustrating that in order to fulfil the requirements of my visa application [to Australia] it was implied that I should produce a

[85] Mexico is the exception.

[86] UK Lesbian and Gay Immigration Group, 'Civil Partnership—Immigration Guide', available at http://www.uklgig.org.uk (last accessed 4 November 2007). The 2006 version of this guide noted that evidence was emerging that civil partnership applications were being denied on the basis that the relationship was not genuine, and that this was particularly the case where the applicant was from a developing country. UK Lesbian and Gay Immigration Group, 'A Guide to Civil Partnership' (last accessed November 2006).

[87] L Berlant and M Warner, 'Sex in Public' (1998) 24 *Critical Inquiry* 547, 549.

[88] Butler, above n 77, 41.

[89] SA Chambers, 'Heteronormativity and the L Word', in K Akass and J McCabe (eds), *Reading the L word: Outing Contemporary Television* (London, IB Tauris, 2006) 84.

[90] New Zealand Immigration Service, above n 55, F2.10.1.

[91] M Holt, '"Marriage-like" or Married? Lesbian and Gay Marriage, Partnership and Migration' (2004) 14 *Feminism & Psychology* 30, 32.

narrative of my relationship with Nigel to show how "marriage-like" it is.'[92]

Lesbian and gay couples who may be in long-term relationships but consciously opt out of heteronormative relationship practices for political reasons, as a result of embracing feminist critiques of heterosexual norms, or for other reasons,[93] may be less likely to gain entry to the country. For example, Sue Wilkinson and Celia Kitzinger have written of their relationship that they had both previously come out of long-term 'marriage-like' relationships and were committed, both personally and politically, to having a relationship with more autonomy, freedom and openness.[94] They found the idea of making an ostentatious ceremony of their private commitment embarrassing, and they did not want to promise each other 'unconditional love, lifelong commitment and sexual monogamy'.[95] They chose not to live together; they had individual mortgages, separate houses, separate finances, were on different electoral roles, paid different utility bills and owned nothing in common.[96] As a result of these choices, they note that they would not have met United Kingdom same-sex immigration requirements of two years' cohabitation or Canadian immigration requirements of one year of cohabiting in a conjugal relationship.[97] Given the way they chose to structure their relationship, they may have had a struggle entering New Zealand even under its current gay-friendly criteria. They would have been unlikely to have evidence to show that they had been living together for 12 months or more in a partnership that was genuine and stable, nor would they be likely to satisfy the criteria that there 'were genuine and compelling reasons for any period of separation'.[98]

Wilkinson and Kitzinger's relationship may have been inspired by their politics, and in that sense they were politicised rather than depoliticised in Duggan's terms. Lesbians and gay men who live their politics in their relationships may therefore be less likely to be admitted under the immigration criteria, and those who are 'depoliticised', not questioning of heteronormative relationship models and happy to adopt them, may be more likely to meet the criteria for immigration. Those who chose to 'make a queer world' by engaging in 'kinds of intimacy that bear no necessary

[92] Holt, above n 90, 33.

[93] Ibid: 'lesbians and gay men have been among those challenging the idea that a commitment to another person necessarily entails sexual exclusivity, living together, or fixed gender roles for each partner'.

[94] C Kitzinger and S Wilkinson, 'The Re-branding of Marriage: Why We Got Married Instead of Registering a Civil Partnership' (2004) 14 *Feminism and Psychology* 127, 129.

[95] Ibid.

[96] Ibid; Ryken, above n 72, 3: 'eyebrows are raised by visa officers when they [joint bank accounts] are not produced'.

[97] Kitzinger and S Wilkinson, above n 94, 130–31. These were immigration criteria in 2004, when Kitzinger and Wilkinson wrote their article.

[98] New Zealand Immigration Service, n 61, ch 69, F2.5a, F2.30.1.

relation to domestic space, to kinship, to the couple form, to property, or to the nation' are less likely to be fit subjects for immigration.[99]

The reputation and public aspects of the relationship are also factors that indicate a genuine and stable relationship. To the extent that lesbians and gay men who live their politics in public are less likely to be accepted in mainstream society, or more likely to disrupt dominant notions of commitment, the reputational and public aspects of their relationships may count against them. The reputational aspects of the relationship may also be judged by the couple's reputation with extended family, and non-normative, political behaviour may also impact here. Those lesbian and gay couples whose families are not accepting of their relationships, who may also be less likely to be 'out' in other contexts, will also be disadvantaged by these criteria.

Lesbians and gay men who are not 'out' for any reason, perhaps because the countries in which they live are homophobic or persecute lesbians and gays, will be disadvantaged by all of the criteria as it will be more difficult to live with partners, own property with partners and establish a reputation or public aspects of the relationship.[100] These people may have to resort to the refugee or asylum processes, which are time-consuming, costly and may have erratic results.[101] Further, the treatment of lesbians and gay men in some countries may fall into a gap between persecution meeting the refugee criteria and difficulty living, or being out, without any specific state persecution. For example, in one refugee appeal the Refugee Status Appeal Authority (RSAA) accepted that the appellant, a 28-year-old Nigerian man, would be shunned by his family and ostracised by his church, that his life would be far from ideal and that there was a climate of intolerance towards non-heterosexual relationships in his home country.[102] Nevertheless, refugee status was denied on the basis that, although homosexual acts are a criminal offence in Nigeria, there was no evidence of prosecutions.[103] If the RSAA assessment of homophobia and the law in Nigeria is correct, lesbian and gay couples living in Nigeria might be likely not be out to family and friends, and not live together and build up the indicia of a

[99] Berlant, above n 83, 558.

[100] For stories of asylum-seekers in the UK, see UK Lesbian and Gay Immigration Group, 'Annual Report 2007', 17-18, available at www.uklgig.org.uk (last accessed 2 November 2007).

[101] See *Re GJ*, Refugee Appeal No 1312/93, Auckland, Refugee Status Appeals Authority New Zealand (30 August 1995); D Tennant, 'The Contribution of the New Zealand Refugee Status Appeals Authority to International Refugee Jurisprudence' (undated manuscript on file with the author). In Australia, see J Millbank and C Dauverge, 'Burdened by Proof: How the Australian Refugee Review Tribunal has Failed Lesbian and Gay Asylum Seekers' (2003) 31 Federal Law Review 299; J Millbank, 'Gender, Sex and Visibility in Refugee Decisions on Sexual Orientation' (2003) 18 *Georgetown Immigration Law Journal* 71.

[102] Refugee Appeal No 75250, Refugee Status Appeals Authority New Zealand (28 January 2005).

[103] Ibid.

genuine and stable relationship required by the immigration criteria, making immigration as partners much more difficult, if not impossible.

The basis of the criteria in the dominant heterosexual paradigm and norms also means that there is no recognition of the difficulties that may be associated with realising that one is a sexual minority. For example, a Fijian Muslim man aged 22 originally came to New Zealand to marry a woman chosen by his family.[104] It appears that about nine months later he fell out with his and his wife's families and made friends with a gay man, with whom he later entered into a relationship.[105] At this time he continued to pursue immigration based on his marriage, and it was not until more than a year later that he told immigration authorities that he was in a same-sex relationship.[106] In considering whether the man was living in a stable and genuine relationship with his new partner, the Residence Review Board (RRB) stated that doubt arose as to whether the relationship was genuine due to the fact that the man continued to state that he was committed to his marriage and to trying to make it work after moving in with his same-sex partner.[107] Not surprisingly, it was submitted on the appellant's behalf that 'at the time he was confused with his life and unsure where he was heading'.[108] There is nothing in the criteria that addresses, or provides guidance to officials to respond to these types of situations. Indeed, the RRB decision confirming the denial of his residence application makes no attempt at all to place the man's actions in the context of homophobia; it appears to hold the fact that the man did not reveal his gay relationship earlier in the process against him.[109]

Finally, the immigration criteria also embrace concepts of domesticity in a number of forms. Most obviously, factors such as the performance of household duties and evidence such as sharing parental obligations, household activities and joint decision-making evoke images of domesticity as home, as the realm gendered female. The fact that these criteria are integral to the determination of a genuine and stable relationship suggests that lesbians and gay men have to prove that they are domesticated along gendered, heterosexual lines.

To the extent that the criteria are focused on economic criteria and ownership of property, those with money and middle-class domestic aspirations are privileged. The factors bearing on whether couples are living together in a genuine and stable partnership include the nature and extent of the common residence, the common ownership, use and acquisition of

104 Residence Appeal No 14690, Residence Review Board (28 February 2006) 2–3.
105 Ibid, 11.
106 Ibid, 9.
107 Ibid, 11.
108 Ibid, 12.
109 Ibid, 12–13.

property, and financial dependence or interdependence. Those who cannot afford to own property must prove joint tenancy agreements.

The heteronormativity of the criteria as a whole overlaps with other aspects of domesticity; lesbians and gay men have to prove that they are 'just like' heterosexuals and that their sexuality is private and does not make any real difference. The assumption is that same-sex couples set up house, own property together, participate in child-raising and family gatherings, jointly communicate, socialise with their families and friends, and generally live their lives just like heterosexuals. The reality that they are doing so in heteronormative, homophobic societies that may not recognise and validate their relationships, or that may treat them as second class, in the context of family reactions that may vary from persecution to disassociation to mild disapproval, and that they may be struggling with their own sexual identities, is all rendered invisible by the criteria and determinations to be made. This is not to say that there are no immigration officials who understand heteronormativity or homophobia, and respond sensitively to the situations of lesbian and gay couples, but rather that the criteria mean that when that happens, those individuals will bring it to the process, rather than having that understanding integrally incorporated into the process.

CONCLUSION

This chapter started with the identification of two recent trends in New Zealand's immigration law and policy: the general tightening and whitening post-September 11, and the opening of the nation's boundaries to lesbian and gay partners. It has suggested that attention to the particularities of sexuality, race, class and gender in the immigration criteria for same-sex partners reveals that these two trends are not as contradictory as they might at first appear. The immigration regulations and policies require the production of subjects at the boundaries of the nation who are properly domesticated, both in the sense of being fit for entry into the domestic nation, and being fit subjects of caring and sharing in domestic relationships. The lesbian and gay couples most likely to gain entry to the country easily will therefore be those homonormatised couples who are willing to adopt heterosexual models for their relationships, who do not politicise their sexuality, and who are properly domesticated. They will tend to be from predominantly white liberal democracies, the very places targeted for immigration more generally post-September 11.

Part IV

PUSHING AT THE CONTOURS OF DOMESTIC RELATIONSHIPS

INTRODUCTION

THE CHAPTERS IN this final section recognise a simple truth: that the design of the homes and environments in which we live can either enable and promote, or conversely inhibit, our choices for how 'caring and sharing' can be distributed through a gamut of domestic arrangements. As is acknowledged in Smart's chapter which began this volume, there is a plethora of possibilities in patterns of domestic relations which reach beyond conventional households based on marriage, sexual partnerships or parenthood. In particular there has been a recent interest in the potential of households of friends, often in response to a wish to access the resource of housing as well as to develop patterns of a shared sociability as an alternative to living alone. Added to this, there is the increased recognition that our wishes and needs in relation to housing, how we formulate our ideas of home and household, and the extent to which we seek interdependent patterns of/for caring and sharing, should be viewed within a lifecycle perspective which recognises that, at certain stages in our lives, we may welcome choices in living arrangements beyond those predicated in traditional family and household patterns.

These two final chapters, then, push the contours of domestic relations outwards to reach beyond conventional patterns, and accounts, of households and homes. What is evidenced in both chapters is the complexity of trying to find ways to frame and examine the many issues involved in developing alternatives to conventional domestic patterns. Running through both chapters are three dimensions: the architecture of the built environment; the architecture of legal forms and practices; and the often difficult social issues associated with choosing to share aspects of our domestic living arrangements with others. What is also clear from both chapters is that we need to be careful with any presumption that extending aspects of caring and sharing beyond conventional patterns is necessarily, or too easily thought of, as 'progressive'. The increasing popularity of gated communities reminds us that 'sharing', and the purchase of 'caring', can be an exclusive and exclusionary enactment of privilege, to the radical detriment of those who cannot afford to enter such communities, or whose social characteristics make them unwelcome. Even the language we use when examining the terrain, and beginning to map it, is fraught with difficulty. 'Intentional communities'; 'co-operative' housing schemes; CoHousing, etc, are mobile terms often used interchangeably. However, whilst they connote similar objectives, the terms can be associated with often very distinctive projects, in which the nuances of difference may be crucial but not always immediately visible.

In these chapters we begin an exercise in mapping from two different entry points. In the first chapter, Bottomley examines co-operative housing schemes developed in England in the late 19th and early 20th centuries in order to 'tease out' the patterns, and problems, associated with developing alternatives to conventional household and housing patterns. She distinguishes between schemes focused on 'co-operative housekeeping', and co-operative housing schemes concerned with providing access to good-quality housing (and associated amenities), based on a 'mutual' governance model. In both, she finds evidence of progressive potentials, as well as locating key, and recurring, problems and challenges. It is her argument that, by examining this history, we can become more clear-sighted about the range of aspirations and foci which are folded into contemporary accounts of the arrangement of, and potential in, alternative forms. In the second chapter, Scott-Hunt examines the developing CoHousing movement in the UK through an analysis of the legal documentation used to construct a legal form for their incorporation, as well as providing a framework for matters of governance, and provision for such issues as individuals entering and exiting a scheme. Her chapter highlights a pattern of individuals coming together knowing 'how' they would like to share elements of their domestic lives, and then needing to seek and develop legal forms suitable to their circumstances. She illustrates this by examining two rather different groupings: the first a grouping of middle-class and relatively wealthy families developing a rural site of individuated homes sharing facilities, and the second a grouping of older single women seeking to develop an urban scheme. In the second case, lack of financial resources, as well as a commitment to share the scheme with women who would otherwise be housed in social housing, creates a very different spectrum of issues and concerns from the first scenario. However, both cases illustrate not only the shared perceived benefits in a more communal mode, or setting, for domestic relations, but also the extent to which, whilst legal forms can be stretched to meet their requirements, there remains problems in setting up such schemes when considering financial arrangements, as well as finding a good balance between, or pathways for dealing with, the inevitable tensions which arise within and between scheme members and the 'collective' interest.

Ending this collection with Scott-Hunt's chapter is particularly valuable in that her focus on older women reminds us, again, that 'caring and sharing' needs to be considered within the different contexts thrown into relief by a 'lifecycle' approach to domestic relations. Designing patterns, in law and the built environment, which maximise the choices available to us when considering 'caring and sharing' requires that we push against the conventions of a more limited account of domestic relationships. Feminist scholarship has long argued that the limitations of a conventional family model, and an overly crude division between public and private lives, has been detrimental to developing the potential of other forms of living arrangements which could, at least, extend our choices, and, at best, develop more inclusive, fluid and adaptable domestic patterns. These chapters indicate some of the potential, as well as the murky and mundane issues involved, in thinking the domestic differently.

9

'They shall be simple in their homes . . .': The Many Dimensions of the Idea and Practices of Co-operative Housing[1]

ANNE BOTTOMLEY

INTRODUCTION

THERE IS A 19th-century hymn, once popular within the British co-operative movement, which begins with the uplifting line: 'These things shall be!'[2] The five verses which follow outline the ethos of the 'New Jerusalem', making clear that building it takes place in the home, as much as in public life and in international relations. The line 'They shall be simple in their homes', which introduces the third verse, exemplifies not only an understanding of the interrelationship between the domestic and public spheres, but also how much could be conveyed in the use of that small and mundane word 'simple'. From a widespread concern to turn away from the divisive and labour-intensive pursuit, and display, of excessive consumption, through to Edward Carpenter's more esoteric and spiritual

[1] This chapter is dedicated to the memory of Lotte Kent (born Vienna 1917, died Letchworth 2006). An active member of the co-operative movement, she had a special interest in co-operative housing and was a founding member of a North London co-operative housing scheme. My thanks to my father, Trevor Bottomley, who spent his working life in the co-operative movement, and continues to be actively engaged in debates on the history, contemporary profile and potential of co-operation. I am indebted to him for his enthusiasm in helping me with research for this project, and for his companionship in accompanying me on site visits.

[2] The words were written by John Addington Symons, a friend of Edward Carpenter, see below n 14. Aspects of the vision he outlines in his hymn, some of which is, as with many other 19th-century 'progressive' texts, deeply (and interestingly) problematic when encountered with the hindsight of the 21st century.

pathway for a 'simple life', the lodestone of 'simplicity' in domestic lives is touched again and again in the 19th century, as an organising principle in the building of a more just society, as well as in the search for a more fulfilling life(style).

A commitment to 'simplicity' did not just connote a style in décor, design or choices made in the everyday of domestic detail, it was also connected, on the one hand, to questions concerned with the balance between material comforts and spiritual insights, and, on the other hand, to questions focused on how 'caring' (for) and 'sharing' (with) each other was structured within and through the design of 'homes'. In other words, and returning to the hymn, these questions of domestic ordering were understood to be political questions: the public and the private spheres were implicated in each other, inextricably linked together, and to be addressed together, in building the 'New Jerusalem'.

In 1872 Edward Vansittart Neale, the well-respected first secretary of the British Co-operative Union, wrote an article in *Co-operative News*[3] advocating the development of a form of co-operative housing which he called 'associative housing'. Neale's article, designed as an appeal to a co-operative movement, increasingly focused on consumer co-operatives, to extend the virtues of mutuality and self-help into housing schemes, outlined two dimensions to the development of 'associative housing'. Firstly, in relation to the built environment, individuated domestic units would be clustered around a focal point of shared communal facilities, thus providing an infrastructure for a degree of 'co-operative housekeeping'. Secondly, in relation to the legal and fiscal framework, the schemes would be co-operative enterprises: prospective tenants would be required to become members of the housing co-operative through investment (the purchase of a share) in the enterprise, ownership of the land would be vested in the co-operative, and all profits would be held (and distributed) within the co-operative. However, recognising that it would be virtually impossible for prospective 'associative housing schemes' to be dependent on member investment alone, the purpose of Neale's article was to encourage consumer co-operatives to help initiate such schemes in their own locales by investing in them, developing a form of supportive partnership designed to 'kick-start' housing schemes, as well as extending the principles of co-operation through what we might now think of as a form of ethical investment (on a very limited return).

Neale's article is interesting in that he outlines two dimensions to co-operative (or 'associative') housing: on the one hand, a pattern of building to allow for sharing and caring (in)between households, and, on the other, a governance form founded upon self-help though mutuality. Neale was advocating (what I think of as) a 'combined' co-operative model,

[3] EV Neale, 'Associated Homes' (1872) 2(4) *Co-operative News* 37.

a synergy of two complementary dimensions feeding from and into a mutual ethos. Both dimensions carried important references to a 'simple life' approach: both in designs to enable sharing, and thereby minimising, domestic labour, and in promoting co-operation between households ceasing to compete with each other but rather combining for self-improvement, 'associative housing' was one model (among a number promoted in the same period)[4] for developing what we might now think of as 'alternative lifestyles'. However, his vision for the potential of co-operative housing did not form a blueprint for subsequent developments. Both dimensions proved problematic within the co-operative movement – many members of the movement did not share his enthusiasm for designs promoting collective housekeeping, and, in developing a scheme which promoted partnerships between scheme members and those who could provide (inward) investment capital, he explicitly recognised the centrality of the issue of 'funding' schemes and, but only implicitly, the potential conflict of interests between investors and investor/members. The 19th-century British co-operative movement did not, in any major way, commit itself to, or promote, Neale's vision of 'associative housing'. However, by the early years of the next century, a different but related trajectory, the garden city movement, provided a vector for developing co-operative housing schemes which returned to, and built on, the virtues of being 'simple in their homes'.

Why return to this period, and seek to recover one aspect of the history of co-operative housing, for inclusion in this collection? My purpose is twofold. Firstly, there is clearly a contemporary interest in the potential for developing alternative models for our domestic lives; models which either eschew, or refuse to be limited to, 'homes' predicated solely on traditional familial forms.[5] Thus, one aspect of 'changing contours' is, necessarily, to consider developments which move beyond (or in between) the orthodoxies of home and family. Parallels can, I think, be drawn between the aspiration, in previous centuries, to build and follow a 'simple life', and the contemporary focus on (economic, environmental and social) sustainability. From this perspective, what has interested me in returning to this historical material, is the way in which it evidences and parallels so many other aspects, issues and problems which befuddle and confuse our expectations of, and explorations into, contemporary co-operative housing. The term contemporary 'co-operative housing' is, at this point, deployed, purposely,

[4] See L Pearson, *The Architectural and Social History of Co-operative Living* (London, Macmillan, 1988).

[5] See, eg, S Scott-Hunt, 'Intentional Communities and Care-giving: Co-Housing Possibilities', ch 10 in this volume. The reference to 'again' is simply to acknowledge that this trope has (as this chapter evidences) a long history of regular 'returns' to an interest in developing alternative domesticities. See, eg, B Taylor, *Eve and The New Jerusalem* (Cambridge, Harvard University Press, 1983), and D Hardy, *Alternative Communities in Nineteenth Century England* (London, Longman, 1979).

rather loosely. I have been interested in how it moves between being used to describe forms of shared ownership, forms of governance in housing and approaches to forms of lifestyle, all of which connote some aspect of mutuality and/or self-help in constructing and inhabiting domestic space, but which are also characterised, at the very same time, by wide divergences between them—in what they stand for (shared ownership or something other than 'being owners'), in what they choose to share, in how they are experienced (lived in), in who they care for, and in whether they tend to bend inwards towards the privileges of exclusivity, or reach outwards and stretch themselves to strive for a more inclusive ethos. So, secondly, my aim in this chapter is to begin to lay a foundation for an examination of these many dimensions (both as ideas and as practices) by teasing them out from an investigation into earlier trends and patterns, rather than by directly addressing them. However, in order to engage with this material, it is necesary to begin with some background in relation to both the co-operative and the garden city movements.

THE CO-OPERATIVE MOVEMENT IN THE 19TH CENTURY

For historians of the co-operative movement 'co-operation' connotes 'mutual self-help'; the coming together of a group of individuals who choose to pool their resources in order to, collectively and individually, better their access to, and use of, those resources. To be 'co-operative' is to share and develop a mutuality of interest.

During the early 19th century, localised co-operative initiatives (artisans forming production co-operatives, consumer co-operatives, building societies, etc) began to develop into a federated system in order to support each other and to promote the development of other co-operative enterprises. From 1831 to 1835 annual Co-operative Congresses were held under the auspices of Robert Owen and his followers, but it is was the holding of the 1869 Congress, established specifically within and for the co-operative movement (and the subsequent establishment of the Co-operative Union in 1873), from which the development of the modern movement can be dated.[6]

Amongst the early leaders of this movement, the key figures who dominated the development of what was otherwise very much a product of the traditions of working-class association (already well honed through the running of friendly societies, early trade union activities and Chartism),

[6] The Co-operative Union was renamed Co-operatives UK in 2002. Moving into a more formalised framework for federation required the adoption of a clearer definition of the principles entailed in the practices of co-operative enterprises: referred to as the 'Rochdale Principles', after the first consumer society, they remain, although modified, touchstones within the co-operative movement.

represented a wide range of influences feeding into the principles and practices of co-operation. Firstly, the heritage and influence of Robert Owen, and his adoption as a founding theorist for the movement,[7] was significant in a number of ways. The political agenda inherited from Owen was one which argued that radical, transformative, socioeconomic change could be achieved through individuals organising collectively in ways which would eventually lead to a major restructuring of both the economic order of the free market, and the political order which represented and upheld existent economic and social inequalities. In a phrase used frequently in the 19th century this offered, it was argued, 'a peaceful path to revolution'.[8] Owen also provided a link back to utopian ideals about community living, and the history of a number of attempts in the first half of the 19th century, both in the UK and in the USA (in particular), to develop Owenite colonies.[9] However, what this also carried was the sharp memory of the failure of the Owenite communities, not only as economic projects but also in terms of trying to design and run 'complete' communities of a new social and economic order. It has been suggested that this memory served as a warning to the co-operative movement to avoid such experiments and to remain rooted in more specific mutual projects within host, ie existent, communities.[10]

Whilst Owen remained an inspirational figure, by the 1860s more pragmatic influences and needs dominated the agenda. The movement could not survive and flourish without a framework for mutual support between co-operative enterprises, and the certainty of a legislative structure within which to be able to amalgamate and trade. Three lawyers, Thomas Hughes,[11] Edward Vansittart Neale and John Ludlow (all Christian Socialists), became crucial in this period. All three were active in drafting (and promoting amendments to) the statutory framework through which co-operative enterprises were able to incorporate in law: The Industrial and Provident Societies legislation. Ludlow became a Registrar of Friendly Societies, a role and function established under this legislation, and Hughes and Neale became key organisers within the movement (Hughes as President of the first Congress, and Neale as the first Secretary of the Co-

[7] G Holyoak, *The History of Co-operation* (London, Fisher Unwin, 1906).

[8] This political agenda, already in tension with the Chartist programme for enfranchisement, later became the target for both Fabian and Marxist critiques—leading both to dismiss 'utopian socialism', and to distance themselves from many aspects and practices of the co-operative movement. However, the co-operative movement, in both its origins and its later development, did not wholly adopt this political agenda. It was only one thread of influence.

[9] See, eg, Taylor, above n 5, and Harvey, above n 5.

[10] My father, Trevor Bottomley, has come to this conclusion after extensively examining the history of the movement—and I am persuaded that it is a strong argument. For a survey of Owenite communities, see JFC Harrison, *Robert Owen and the Owenite Communities in Britain and America* (Oxford University Press, 1969).

[11] Once a pupil at Rugby School, the author of *Tom Brown's School Days* later established a co-operative community in the United States, which he called 'Rugby'.

operative Union). Recognising the importance of these three is significant: it reminds us that one thread within the movement was the benevolent concern within progressive sections of the upper middle classes, often associated with radical Liberalism, to be actively involved in pragmatic schemes for the promotion of social justice.

As consumer co-operative societies became increasingly successful, they were encouraged to establish schemes to alleviate the appalling housing conditions endured by many of their members. Rochdale, for instance, built houses for rent. Rochdale also established a successful mutual building society to enable members to save (and borrow) in order to purchase housing: the origin of the Nationwide. But the mainstream movement did not produce schemes for developing co-operative principles in land holding for domestic dwellings—a means by which people could co-operate in collectively owning and managing settlements of housing within which they resided.[12]

To some in the movement, including Neale, applying the principles of co-operation to housing schemes seemed an obvious and important extension of co-operation into domestic living arrangements. Especially as, by the late 19th century, the chronic housing conditions experienced by the majority of urban industrial workers had become an increasing focus for concern. The appalling conditions within which they lived, with no control over rents and no security of tenure, as well as the vast profits made by developers and landlords, formed the context within which a number of initiatives were taken by individuals and organisations to try and alleviate a scenario in which market forces determined the pattern of development.[13] Hence, the housing conditions of the urban working classes set an agenda for seeking radical alternatives to the operation of the market. When combined with an interest in 'the simple life', traceable in part to Robert Owen, what developed was an ethos which sought to find an alternative to a social order based on individuals and families being in competition with each other (working not merely to survive, but to accumulate assets), exploited and encouraged by a market economy, which was not only socially divisive but also economically inefficient. This approach had inspired Owenite communities (as it had resonated in many other utopian projects), and, rooted strongly within the English traditions of Christian

[12] See J Birchall, *Building Communities the Co-operative Way* (London, Routledge, 1988) 90–94.

[13] Within working-class movements, mutual building societies was one initiative developed to improve access to housing through home ownership but was, obviously, limited to the better-paid sections of the working population in secure employment. Other schemes, eg Fergus O'Connor's Chartist villages, focused on a 'return to the land', in the form of renting agricultural small-holdings (one, O'Connorsville, is now part of salubrious Herons Cross, Hertfordshire). One factor behind both initiatives was the incentive to move families into accommodation which, by virtue of tenure and valuation for purposes of rates, enfranchished the men. See Hardy, above n 5.

socialism, the ideal of simplicity was further revived as a central theme of middle-class radicalism in the late 19th century, allied to the aesthetical politics of William Morris and manifested in a range of texts, initiatives, movements and organisations.[14]

These two tropes, a concern with urban housing conditions and the range of ideas and practices associated with 'the simple life', form the immediate backdrop to the publication of Ebenezer Howard's influential book, *Tomorrow: A Peaceful Path to Real Reform*, published in 1898, and subsequently remarketed in 1902, with some amendments, as *Garden Cities of Tomorrow*. It was the 'garden city movement' and the building of garden cities, villages and suburbs[15] that provided, to those interested in the potential for co-operative living, a form and a place within which to develop their ideas in practice. Further, as the title to the 1898 book makes clear, Howard was signalling that his scheme offered a 'peaceful path' to 'real reform', a means by which to begin the establishment of a new order.[16]

GARDEN CITIES

Howard devised the 'garden city' as a model which would provide an alternative to the cramped living conditions of contemporary cities. He believed that, by establishing *one* garden city to exemplify a different approach to urban living, others would follow suit and opt into this new lifestyle by creating further schemes, thus literally abandoning the old ways of the unplanned, market-created, urban infernos. It was a radical vision premised not only on good design principles, but also on the principle that the land on which his cities were to be built would be held for the benefit of the

[14] See, eg, S Rowbotham, *Edward Carpenter: A Life of Liberty and Love* (London, Verso, 2008), and F MacCarthy, *William Morris: A Life for our Times* (London, Faber and Faber, 1994). In 1937, George Orwell, writing of a visit to Letchworth Garden City, parodied the extremes of the 'simple life' movement as one which drew together 'every fruit juice drinker, nudist, sandal wearer, sex-maniac, Quaker, nature cure quack, pacifist and feminist in England'. G Orwell, *The Road to Wigan Pier* (London, Penguin, 1962) 152–53.

[15] Although always referred to as 'the garden city movement' (because Howard wanted to build urban environments combining residence, employment and civic amenities to replace existent cities), the design features he promoted (a planned and pleasantly verdant built environment) were taken up by others to build suburbs (eg Hampstead Garden Suburb, London) and villages (eg Burnage Garden Village, Manchester).

[16] Howard's vision was challenged by both the English Marxists and the Fabians, who argued that only a radical change in the ownership of land, through land nationalisation, would prove sufficient to provide a means to 'real reform'. Howard, against any form of dependency on state agencies, preferred to promote a 'peaceful path' through exemplifying the potential of combining self-help with the 'benevolent' economic investment and support of those sections of the upper middle classes who recognised that social justice demanded change (and that sufficient change might avoid a less peaceful path to 'real reform'!). See further M Miller, *Letchworth: The First Garden City* (Chichester, Phillimore, 2002) and R Beevers, *The Garden City Utopia: A Critical Biography of Ebenezer Howard* (London, Macmillan, 1988).

community. He believed both these aspects to be fundamental in promoting a socially cohesive environment. In contemporary terms, what Howard sought to achieve was an architectural form, both in terms of the built environment and in the legal structure, which would facilitate the development of social capital.

Two garden cities, both in Hertfordshire, Letchworth (1903), and then Welwyn (1919), were built under his auspices. However, finding and implementing a suitable legal structure proved problematic—he had envisaged a form of trust (for the benefit of the community), into which the land upon which the city was built would eventually by conveyed. However, the initial process for financing garden cities was, necessarily, through a company form which involved investors (albeit investors who initially agreed to be limited to a minimal return) in order to finance the purchase of land, and provide the initial development costs. Ownership of the land was thus vested in the company. All building within the garden city, whether commercial or domestic, was to be held as leases to ensure that the land was kept as an estate, and Howard designed a leasehold arrangement which, he thought, would allow for sufficient capital to be accrued in order to compensate the investors when the land eventually was transferred to the trust. In practice, not only did it prove very difficult to accrue money in this way, but the company form also opened the process to the potential of incoming investors resisting a limitation on their return, and potential increases in capital value once the city was functioning made the project vulnerable to a future financial 'take over'.[17] Indeed, when Howard thought that Letchworth was sufficiently established to begin to think about developing the trust, he was persuaded by the company lawyer that the trust which he had envisaged as the future form the garden city would take, was not only too difficult to construct in law, but that it would be even more difficult to gain the agreement of the shareholders to the transfer of the estate. The trust idea was therefore abandoned—leaving the garden city, predictably, open to market forces. Finding ways through which to protect social capital against the pressures of economic interests became a major struggle for both of the garden city developments.[18] Attempting to protect, and occasionally rework, Howard's ideals, especially

[17] George Bernard Shaw, a supporter and investor in the project (as well as in many of the housing schemes associated with the garden city movement), frequently warned Howard of this likelihood. See, eg, Miller, above n 16, 19.

[18] The company was threatened by a takeover in 1960 and only saved (after a protracted campaign) by a private Act of Parliament in 1962, which incorporated it, somewhat unusually, as a public corporation. This was later replaced, again by an Act of Parliament, by The Letchworth Garden City Heritage Foundation, a charity incorporated as an Industrial and Provident Society. Following the New Towns Act 1946, Welwyn applied for 'New Town' status as a means by which, they thought, to protect themselves from a private takeover, as well as to be able to access government funding. This move effectively nationalised their assets, which were consequently privatised by the Treasury as part of the winding down of the 'New Towns' programme after 1981.

in the face of problems arising from the need for investment, but also in the difficulty in developing suitable legal forms, is paralleled in the co-operative housing schemes which, enthusiastically supported by Howard, developed in the garden cities.

CO-OPERATIVE HOUSING IN GARDEN CITIES

Once the infrastructure for Letchworth was in place, Howard turned to the potential for co-operative housing. Two separate but related strands informed his approach. The first, under the significant influence of Raymond Unwin,[19] was to consider the potential in 'co-operative dwellings', ie buildings in which individuated units would share common domestic facilities. 'Co-operative housekeeping', or 'socialised domestic work', had become an increasingly popular idea amongst sections of the radical middle classes in the late 19th century.[20] The second, again a concern shared between Howard and Unwin, was to find a means by which to finance and build good-quality working-class housing, designed (both architecturally and legally) to encourage the development of a (responsible) community ethos.

The first strand, the development of co-operative housekeeping schemes, is the one which remains most visible: traces can be readily found in the built environment of contemporary Letchworth and, perhaps in part because it seems so much more architecturally interesting and so much more overtly challenging in terms of an alternative lifestyle, it is this strand that is more remembered, recorded, and celebrated. However, as we shall see, the second strand, the means by which good-quality housing was provided for a section of the working class, is equally interesting although much less visible within the built landscape as 'radical' in design, and much less remembered, recorded and celebrated. Both strands are brought together within the context of Howard's vision of a 'garden city' as a place within which to pursue the potential for a different form of living: a simple life premised within enhancing the value of community.

HOMESGARTH: A 'CO-OPERATIVE HOUSING SCHEME'

The best-documented example of co-operative housing in Letchworth is the Homesgarth[21] scheme opened in 1910 by Letchworth Co-operative

[19] A radical architect and early town planner: his career forms a fascinating trope combining garden cities, co-operative housing and the aesthetics of the simple life. See M Miller, *Raymond Unwin: Garden Cities and Town Planning* (Leicester, Leicester University Press, 1992).

[20] This is extensively covered in Pearson, above n 4.

[21] Photographs of Homesgarth, now called Sollershot Hall, can be seen on the Letchworth Garden City website, Letchworthgc.com; see also Letchworthgardencity.net. See further

Houses Ltd, a company formed two years earlier. Howard was a Board member, actively promoting the project through writings and speeches. He lived in Homesgarth from 1911 until 1921, when he moved into more conventional housing in Welwyn Garden City.

Homesgarth was designed by Clapham Lander, an architect closely associated with both the garden city movement and designs for co-operative living. Having presented a paper on co-operative housing at the first garden city conference, held in Bournville in 1901,[22] Lander and Howard planned Homesgarth as a model, an example for others to follow. What did they mean when they presented this scheme as 'co-operative housing'? Both the design of the building[23] and the company prospectus make clear that what was envisaged was a form of what has been more precisely called 'co-operative housekeeping'.

'Co-operative housekeeping' was based on a pattern of individual dwellings with shared facilities (communal rooms and leisure facilities), and the provision of centralised services to the individual units. Such a scheme blended the potential for a community spirit of like-minded people (sharing the pleasures of eating in a shared dining hall, smoking or reading in shared sitting-rooms, or playing tennis or bowls on the greens) with the functional value of not having to organise or deal with cooking, or cleaning, in individual domestic units. In other words, it also dealt with the 'servant problem', crucially for those who could not really afford good domestic service, any more than they could afford to have the facilities offered in what was, in many ways, an astute blend of the benefits of college living, Oxbridge style, and a club. Offering, in effect, serviced apartments for the middle classes, Homesgarth added a further twist: the occupants entered into this arrangement, initially at least, with a certain commitment to it as *the* best, most progressive way, to organise domestic lives. Thus the co-operative element was not limited to a functional account of the benefits of such a lifestyle, but was seen as exemplifying one way, an efficient and economical way, to live 'the simple life'.

Pearson, above n 4, and I Borden, 'New Ways of Housekeeping: Social Space and Co-operative Living in the Garden City Movement' (Fall 1999) 1(3) *Journal of Architectural and Planning Research* 242. (And download his 2004 inaugural lecture 'Machines of Possibility', which includes references to his work on co-operative housing, from his webpage, accessed via www.bartlett.ucl.ac.uk.) Material relating to the early development of Homesgarth (prospectus, maps, photographs, etc) is held in the Letchworth Garden City Foundation Museum.

[22] Copies of his lecture can be accessed through the library website of the London School of Economics, via www.lse.ac.uk/library/.

[23] The scheme was designed as a quadrangle facing inwards onto a court. Three sides were to be terraced houses linked by a covered walkway, the fourth side communal rooms below (dining-room, smoking-room, library, etc), with the housekeeper's room and servants' living quarters above. Only two sides were actually built—one of dwellings and one of the communal facilities, the others were to have been added when finances allowed. The grounds were extensive and included tennis courts, a kitchen garden and orchards.

However, the limitations of it as a model for co-operative housing are, and were, all too apparent. The most obvious factor was that it addressed the needs and aspirations of a middle-class clientele who could afford to live there, something of which many of the supporters of the scheme were crucially aware, particularly as they were often the very same people who were committed to improving conditions in working-class housing. Howard argued that the Homesgarth model could be adapted for different client groups, but the only proposal for a working-class co-operative housekeeping scheme in Letchworth which got as far as being designed 'on plan', and a company formed to promote it, was never followed through.[24] Had it continued it would have had to address the increasing evidence that working-class tenants found few attractions in co-operative housekeeping, prizing individual dwellings with separate facilities, having too often experienced indignity, discomfort and inconvenience in the provision of communal ones.[25]

However, both versions of 'co-operative housekeeping' could still be said to share aspects of a design for a simpler life: some rationalisation of housework, and a recognition that, whether undertaken by female servants attached to individual households, or wives, sisters and daughters, the solitary drudgery of unremitting domestic labour was not only economically inefficient, but also more than often detrimental to the aspirations of women who sought more than a life of domestic servitude.[26]

Combining the theme of 'lack of efficiency' (a call for a more rational and scientific system) with a potentially emancipatory approach to women's role in relation to domestic work had been a feature of utopian thinking since Owen, and had been reinvigorated by contemporary writers and campaigners, including Florence Perkins Gilman and HG Wells.[27] Despite the middle-class imperative to find an answer to the 'servant problem', and their often patronising designs for working-class settlements which did not address what potential occupants might actually want, there are progressive threads which run through these schemes: a commitment to sharing resources which carries the value of co-operating together, as well as a challenge to the presumption that domestic labour needs to be organised around, and carried out by, women in individual households.

[24] The scheme was promoted by Ellen Pearsall. It is suggested by Pearson that the reason she failed to continue with the scheme was the illness and death of her husband, see Pearson, above n 4, 162–64.

[25] Whereas Homesgarth presumed that domestic labour would be provided by servants, the Pearsall scheme focused on shared facilities for housewives, eg a laundry, or the pooling of their resources, eg sharing childcare. (Homesgarth had no provisions for childcare at all, tenancies only being available to those having no children living with them!)

[26] Howard thought that the experience of domestic service in co-operative housekeeping schemes would be much better than working in individual houses, and that, through good training and under the auspices of a professional housekeeper, servants would be able to take pride in their work and feel more valued.

[27] Pearson, above n 4, provides extensive coverage.

But all co-operative housekeeping schemes were limited by the crucial factor of finding ways to fund them. Howard had hoped that Homesgarth would be financed through a combination of resident investment plus investment provided by philanthropic supporters who would be willing to accept a limited return. However, finding investors proved difficult, and few who lived there actually invested. As Homesgarth struggled to survive economically, the social capital element of a shared community spirit became downplayed, for both potential investors and potential occupants, and increasingly the scheme was presented, and thereby experienced, as a convenient means by which to provide for serviced units rather than as a radically different way of living. Further, the division between investors and inhabitants meant that there was always the potential for conflict over the use of resources and income.

The company granted short-term leases to the occupants. Rental as the form of tenure would not have been an issue for the middle-class inhabitants; it was the predominant tenure form for their class in this period. However, the combination of having external investors, with a legal model which gave occupants no more than a tenancy, left the project open to an economic model replacing an investment in social capital. Eventually the initial investors, sympathetic to the social experiment and willing to be limited in their return, were replaced by investors whose sole focus was on the economics of the project. Homesgarth was first remodelled as a club with associated dwellings and some services available, then finally, soon after the Second World War, all the shared facilities and services were withdrawn (the communal rooms being remodelled as domestic dwellings).[28]

As with his scheme for financing Letchworth Garden City, it could be argued that Howard had not really thought through how to protect the more radical co-operative element in his projected fiscal/governance arrangements. He probably had hoped that the rental income would be sufficient, eventually, to keep investors happy, and that investors sympathetic to the project would be willing to remain limited in their return on their investment. What he did not do, and does not seems to have considered, was to investigate the possibility, following Neale's scheme for 'associative housing', of a fiscal/governance arrangement which would underpin the co-operative element of the enterprise. He had certainly hoped that the tenants would themselves invest, but this was not actively promoted and the tenants remained as no more than tenants. And, as the scheme began to advertise itself more in terms of the benefits of its services than as a community of like-minded people, it could only further reconfigure the arrangement as one of convenience rather than commitment, to

[28] Sollershot Hall no longer has the extensive communal grounds, and a block of modern flats has been built near to the original buildings. It is now a pleasant small development of owner-occupiers (mostly on long leases), with an active residents' association who manage the scheme.

be judged by its economic return rather than by its ideal. But, whilst recognising some of the factors that made it vulnerable, we should also recognise those aspects that made it originally attractive in terms of seeking alternative ways of living and helped it to survive, albeit in a modified form, for 40 years. Three significant factors in Howard's scheme still hold purchase today: finding ways of enhancing a community lifestyle balanced with individual privacy; organising domestic labour and services so that these are not focused on individuated housekeeping; and accessing resources and facilities that could not otherwise be afforded. What changes is the nature of the 'needs' and 'resources' which come into play as (potentially) elements which make aspects of 'co-operative housekeeping' (still) attractive.

MEADOW WAY GREEN: CO-OPERATIVE HOUSING FOR WOMEN

Co-operative housekeeping also offered a style of living that could be attractive to those with a limited range of domestic arrangements available to them. During the latter part of the 19th century, housing for single professional women entering the labour market was problematic. Seeking an alternative to a drab existence in lodgings or hostels, co-operative housekeeping for single women offered not only the benefits of the provision of domestic services, but also companionship and a respectable domestic lifestyle.[29]

A few years after the opening of Homesgarth, two women, Miss Pym and Miss Dewe, partners since they had met at school, approached Howard with a proposal for a co-operative housekeeping scheme for single women in Letchworth.[30] Both women had capital (and private incomes), and were willing to put this to use in developing a scheme, but they required further economic investment. In 1911, Howard had formed the Howard Cottage Society to provide (and promote) working-class housing through making use of government grants that had become available for such provision. The plan was to build the scheme under the auspices of the Society, thereby accessing such a grant. Misses Pym and Dewe would provide initial capital

[29] Pearson, above n 4, again provides a comprehensive account.

[30] Pearson reports (based on interviews, undertaken in 1983, with people who knew the two women) that on a trip to Germany they visited a co-operative housekeeping scheme for women which had given them the idea (above n 4, 10). Interestingly, no mention is made of the 1909 development of Waterlow Court, in Hampstead Garden Suburb. An initiative of Henrietta Barnett, it was built under the auspices of the Improved Industrial Dwellings Company, founded by Sidney Waterlow in 1863. Ballie Scott's design provided a quadrangle of cottages for single professional women, with shared dining facilities and housekeeping services. Given extensive press coverage, it housed a number of feminists and suffragists. It remained co-operative housing for women until 1954, when men were allowed into the scheme, and, after it had been sold to a private company, communal meals were stopped in the 1960s. The cottages are now owner-occupied: peaceful, pretty and very affluent!

(and a guarantee to the Society should the units prove hard to let) and, in return, the two women would determine the design of the property and select the tenants. The plan to access public funds failed, on the grounds that the rents would be too high for working-class tenants, but the Howard Cottage Society went ahead and provided the additional funding for the project, whilst making sure that, should it fail, it could be converted into separate dwellings.

The first units were opened in 1914, a second phase in 1916 and in 1925 a final phase completed the project.[31] The scheme had been a success. An open quadrangle had been built, with a dining-room forming the central section of the north side. Importantly, the two women were amongst the first tenants, continuing to live at 7 Meadow Way Green until 1946, when Miss Pym died. Long-term residence was common in Meadow Way Green, which proved to be extremely popular—partly because it is conveniently situated near the town centre, but also because of the pattern of co-operative housekeeping designed by Misses Pym and Dewe (in which tenants took the 'housekeeper role' in turns), and, in particular, the provision of a daily communal meal. In 1944, the two women lost control over deciding who should live in the scheme, which was taken over by the Howard Cottage Society. The daily communal meal was retained until 1976.[32] Meadow Way Green eventually became open to male residents, and the communal rooms were converted to provide further living accommodation. It is now run by the housing association which replaced the Howard Cottage Society.

Meadow Way Green survived for 30 years in its original form, and, for just over 60 years, continued to provide a communal focus through the provision of a shared daily meal. This level of success must partly be attributed, at least initially, to the economic investment made by the two women, as well as to their commitment to the style of living evidenced by their decision to live there themselves. Through their economic investment, and in turning to the Howard Cottage Society as their partner, they avoided the fate of similar schemes originally developed by philanthropic investment companies, but later taken over by companies with purely commercial interests.[33] Hence, Meadow Way Green survives under the auspices of a housing association, rather than having been transformed into units of owner-occupation.

However, what could not be maintained through this model was a commitment to a particular type of resident, or a particular type of lifestyle. Misses Pym and Dewe, whilst in residence and with the right to

[31] Photographs of the scheme can be seen on the Letchworth Garden City website, see above n 21.

[32] I was at school in Letchworth, and my memory is that it ended when the cook died and the Society argued that it was no longer a necessary function to provide meals.

[33] As happened with Waterlow Court, see above n 30.

select tenants, could ensure that the tenants selected, and the way in which the tenants lived within the scheme, met the standard of co-operative living that they envisaged. (In all the other schemes for women in this period, which I know of, the promoters of the schemes were not designing a lifestyle for themselves, as much as one that they thought suitable for other women.)[34] But equally, as with so many communal arrangements, it is clear that the 'leaders' of the scheme set the tone and detail of the domestic arrangements, rather than all the residents. Community values can, in practice, depend upon a level of conformity, working most efficiently when those who are allowed to reside in the scheme have been selected as 'suitable'.

However, Meadow Way Green can be used as an example of a shared community of interests: women who preferred to live with an element of communality, rather than in the totally individuated units which would otherwise have been their lot. As women in paid employment, to 'come home' to a shared meal which had been prepared for them was an attractive option; not only in providing companionship with similar women, but also in providing some domestic labour. Again, in part, this provided a solution to the 'servant problem', but, again, and recalling Gilman,[35] we can see the progressive element in sharing a limited resource which functioned to support women as they entered the labour market. Providing an infrastructure that gave emotional, social and economic support to working women was welcomed by the inhabitants of Meadow Way Green, and it is easy to imagine a similar arrangement still being attractive to many contemporary women.

Whilst Meadow Way Green survives to the advantage of housing association tenants, it does so under the housing association's general remit rather than in having any obligation to maintain the original design of a co-operative housekeeping scheme for women. When the crucial decisions were made to allow men to become tenants and to bring the communal meal to an end, the wishes of the residents were not paramount. In this sense co-operative housekeeping schemes, with their focus on a mode of living, rather than on constructing them as co-operative enterprises with a focus on shared 'ownership' and 'control' of the developments, were always bound to be precarious in terms of accountability to those defined as 'residents', rather than 'members' of the enterprise.

Whilst Homesgarth's co-operative housekeeping scheme became vulnerable not only because of its muted commitment to a co-operative ethos, but also because of its financial vulnerability through external investment,

[34] Residence in Waterlow Court, however popular, was constrained by a lengthy list of rules which one cannot imagine Henrietta Barnett having been willing to subject herself to! These were not rules designed by the residents, but rather rules laid down as conditions of their residency. See further Pearson, above n 4.

[35] See above n 27.

Meadow Way Green's co-operative ethos became vulnerable through its establishment within the frame of the Howard Cottage Society. Today, the aspirations of people who might wish to build co-operative housekeeping schemes, but lack the economic resources to finance them themselves, replicate the issues faced by Misses Pym and Dewe. To what extent is it possible to try and access funding, and take on a legal and governance form which allows access to funding, without compromising the co-operative ethos of the enterprise? And, as co-operative housekeeping schemes address only one aspect of co-operative living, only one aspect of Neale's 'associative housing', they do not address the extent to which a co-operative ethos could be successfully sustained within a different legal form. They are not, in my terms, a 'combined' co-operative model.

EASTHOLM AND WESTHOLM: CO-PARTNERSHIP TENANCIES

In 1905 and 1910, a far less well-documented scheme had been developed in Letchworth which linked more directly with the co-operative movement, and with a concern to develop housing schemes for the working classes. Eastholm, and later Westholm, are small schemes of cottages built around a shared green. Pleasantly situated, their architecture does not suggest any radical impetus behind their development.[36] The Letchworth city guide describes them as being built under the auspices of 'The Letchworth Co-Partnership Tenants Society', and as designed by Raymond Unwin, but makes no further remark upon them. Little has been written on the co-partnership tenant movement: perhaps, in part, because such schemes leave few overt traces, in their architectural form, of the radical project which inspired them.[37]

The Letchworth Society had been formed as a branch of Co-partnership Tenants Ltd, a group established by a radical Liberal MP, Henry Vivian, who became its first chairman. When Vivian gave a paper at the 1906 Garden City Association Conference, entitled 'Co-Partnership in Housing', he had already established a track record for his form of co-operative housing through the establishment, in 1901, of Ealing Tenants Ltd, an Industrial and Provident Society, which built Brentham Garden Suburb, London. He subsequently influenced the establishment of co-partnership housing schemes in Letchworth and, from 1907, in Hampstead Garden Suburb and (as we shall see) elsewhere.

Vivian was building on a thread within the co-operative movement which is associated with the term 'co-partnership'. This thread, somewhat

[36] Photographs of the scheme can be found on the Letchworth Garden City website, see above n 21.

[37] Some coverage is given in J Birchall, *Building Communities the Co-operative Way* (London, Routledge, 1988) 94–97.

unevenly woven into the cloth of the co-operative movement, had been marginalised as the century progressed, and produced a tension within a movement which increasingly thrived from a focus on consumer enterprises. Co-partnership derives, although again only in part, from an Owenite argument that radical social progress could be made by more equitably sharing the profits derived from the production of wealth, between the holders of the means of production, and those who put their labour into wealth-producing enterprises. This approach particularly appealed to artisans who, when formed into production co-operatives, argued that the co-operative movement was failing to equitably reward them for the value their labour produced, to the benefit of consumer co-operatives. They also argued that a focus on developing the movement through consumer co-operatives failed to engage with the full radical potential of the Owenite 'plan' to restructure society through wealth transfer.[38] Co-partnership, in this sense, did not operate only on an horizontal axis of mutuality through self-help, but also on a vertical one: what was important was that projects be established which were aimed at moving wealth (including wealth represented in land) from being consolidated within a small section of society, into a broader pattern of more equitable distribution. Co-partnership schemes, in encouraging an equitable sharing of capital and profit, provided a challenge to those who held capital and profit to distribute it more equitably as a means by which 'peaceful revolution' could be achieved.[39]

'Co-partnership' co-operators were more open to the idea of developing the co-operative movement into projects, such as co-operative housing schemes, than the mainstream of the movement, which was increasingly focused on consumer co-operatives. At the 1884 Co-operative Congress Henry Vansittart Neale (son of Edward) called for the development of co-operative housing schemes along co-partnership lines, and in 1888 he formed Tenant Co-operators Ltd. His scheme was focused on providing working-class co-operative housing by combining initial funding from local co-operative consumer societies, with investments made by the prospective tenants through the purchasing of a 'share' in the co-operative housing enterprise. However, Neale's focus on the need to provide housing meant that his scheme was, in practice, designed to promote local consumer co-operatives investment into housing, with an 'encouragement' to prospective tenants to become involved through purchasing a share. The level of investment they were encouraged to purchase was low enough so as not to exclude a wide range of prospective tenants (who both needed housing, and were members of the local consumer societies). Both the low level of investment, and being 'encouraged' rather than 'required' to buy a share,

[38] Holyoak was a strong advocate of co-partnership; hence the emphasis he gives in his history to Robert Owen's influence on the co-operative movement (see above n 5).

[39] As with the use of the term 'co-operative', tracing the use of the term 'co-partnership' reveals shifts in the ways in which it is used and understood.

fatally weakened the potential for a close relationship between 'investment' and 'inhabitation', and a commitment by the tenants to the enterprise as 'theirs'. Neale was caught between wanting to provide housing, and wanting to provide a new form of co-operative housing in which tenants would be controlling members of the enterprise.

Tenant Co-operators Ltd were instrumental in the building of a number of schemes in London, but none of these schemes succeeded in transforming tenants into members, ie in becoming the owners and controllers of their own scheme. Tenants remained, rather stubbornly, tenants, and wanted to treat the co-operative as landlords. Few tenants invested, and even fewer became active members. Most wanted good housing and little more, whoever provided it and through what form. Sustained by a small group of volunteers, Neale's vision and organisation continued to encourage the development of co-operative housing by local consumer societies—but his co-partnership model did not evolve into a partnership between existent consumer co-operatives and emergent housing co-operatives. Neither 'wealth transfer' nor 'shared profit' between these groups were sustainable, nor were the tenants sufficiently economically strong, or politically educated, to actively participate in the partnership. At best, decent housing at a decent rent was what could be provided. Further, it became very clear from these schemes that what the tenants wanted was 'houses' rather than 'flats', and that they were not interested in communal facilities. Both aspects of his father's scheme for 'associated housing' proved problematic within the context of the mainstream co-operative movement and its membership.

Vivian's scheme differed from Neale's in that it was predicated on linking inhabitation to investment, and in requiring a relatively high level of capital investment in order to buy a share. Rather than being concerned with promoting the provision of working-class housing, his more focused interest was in providing a framework for mutual self-help amongst economically stronger, and more politically educated, 'self-improving' artisans. Brentham, for instance, was initially developed by and around a group of local artisans already organised as a production co-partnership in trades related to building. And whilst Vivian recognised the need for inward investment, he turned not to existing co-operative societies, but forged a co-partnership link with the philanthropic traditions of investment in housing limited to a 5 per cent return. This linkage not only satisfied a co-partnership model, but also drew into his organisation a number of middle-class philanthropists and activists (including Unwin), who lent their services and support, and provided him with sufficient income to develop a central organisation, with offices and a full-time staff.

Vivian's model combined mutual self-help with the traditions of philanthropic investment into housing, in a project focused on partnership between investors and inhabitants. By insisting that inhabitants became investors (therefore having influence, as investors, in matters of governance), and by using a co-operative form to 'dress' ownership and occupation, he proactively encouraged self-help and mutuality. Prospective tenants, purchasing shares in the housing scheme became able, in Vivian's words, 'to own collectively and to rent themselves'.

Brentham Garden Suburb was not only the first, but also the largest co-partnership scheme.[40] Like Hampstead Garden Suburb, it was designed as 'a suburb' of housing, and community and recreational facilities. However, whilst linked by design features, most especially the commitment to build an environment planned to enhance the quality of life for individuals and to promote social capital, Brentham, unlike Hampstead, was built entirely through a co-partnership model. Hampstead, conversely, was the product of the philanthropic endeavours of Henrietta Barnett, who supported the development of co-partnership housing schemes *within* the garden suburb, just as Howard was keen to promote them as providers of housing schemes within Letchworth.

Brentham was an extraordinary achievement (60.5 acres of 620 housing units plus community and recreational facilities), but it did not achieve the full potential of Vivian's plan. Even early on, maintaining the link between investment and inhabitation proved to be problematic, and some were allowed to become tenants without taking out a share and becoming members. Even more problematically, the estate was never able to raise sufficient capital through income to pay back, or buy out, the philanthropic investors, whose shares in the estate increasingly passed into the hands of investors with a greater interest in an economic return, than a social commitment to preserving the co-partnership ideal. In 1940 the majority of shares were purchased by a private company—the only original investor who would not sell his shares was George Bernard Shaw. Thereafter, long leases were offered for purchase, on very favourable terms, and most of these leases were then enfranchised after 1967. Brentham had become a comfortable suburb of privately owned houses.[41] There is a particular irony in this: when the plans for Brentham were first being discussed, a number of the original group suggested that they should build houses for their individual purchase, a not surprising suggestion given that this was the socioeconomic class which was moving into owner-occupation, seeking respectability as well as security, as part of a self-improving ethos. Vivian countered this with strong arguments about the benefits of a co-partnership arrangement. I do not know what arguments he used, but I can suggest some factors which might have been pertinent to the discussion. In general, concerns with security of tenure were often given as a reason for turning to

[40] See further A Reid, *Brentham: A History of the Pioneer Garden Suburb* (London, Brentham Historical Society, 2000).

[41] The clubhouse and associated facilities were privatised in 1947 into a private club, but the Brentham Institute still survives as a community facility, run as a trust.

owner-occupation, but under a co-partnership scheme this would not be an issue. Having 'something to pass on' has also often been cited as a factor inclining people towards owner-occupation; but under many co-partnership schemes, including Brentham, provision was made for descendants to become members. Benefiting from a potential increase in the capital value arising from ownership was probably not seen as a particularly important factor at this point; many were more concerned by the potential of debt than attracted by the potential of capital represented in the home.

Further, Brentham was being planned at the same time as Howard's books were published, and the 'garden cities' idea had become the subject of widespread interest. Central to his design for 'garden cities' was a layout and infrastructure which promoted a community ethos, through the provision of leisure, recreational and educational facilities. Provision of such facilities required finance; one means by which this could be accomplished was through a co-partnership model. Individuated private property holders could not, easily, either finance or administer the provision of such extensive facilities for community use. A focus on developing housing for private ownership would, necessarily, detract from providing community facilities. The members of Ealing Tenants Ltd benefited from recreational and educational facilities which would otherwise have been far beyond their ability to access through their individual means. Again, but in a different form to Homesgarth, access to a limited and expensive resource was made possible through co-operation. What the members of Ealing Tenants Ltd wanted, and what the garden city model provided for, was individual homes serviced by shared recreational and educational facilities. They did not want co-operative housekeeping, but they did want a communal and community ethos built through the sharing of facilities of a different scale. In this sense, Neale's vision of 'associative housing' was built not through communal housekeeping, but through community recreation and education.

Co-tenants in developments such as Brentham benefited from 'garden city' housing and layouts which drew upon a rich tradition of 'village' iconography, verdant streets and 'vernacular' cottages with good-sized gardens. These evocations of a simpler, and fuller, life, not only provided a template for good design, but also lent an immediate respectability to the project. By establishing a strong connection with the garden city movement, the co-partnership housing movement (following Vivian) found a 'form', an 'ethos', through which to express the benefits of co-partnership. Many of the smaller, but still substantial, co-partnership schemes not only took on the design features of the 'garden city model' (often helped by Unwin), but also incorporated 'garden' into their titles. Thus, in Leicester, Anchor Tenants Ltd built Humberstone Garden Village in 1902, and Manchester Tenants Ltd built Burnage Garden Village in 1906.[42]

[42] Both schemes still survive as co-partnership entities. Humberstone, of approximately 90 houses, is now referred to as a 'Garden Suburb', because of the encroachment of the city. It has

In the early years of the twentieth century the combination of co-partnership with a 'garden' model seemed to be thriving. However, from Brentham, through Humberstone and Burnage, and back to Westholm and Eastholm in Letchworth, the model of co-partnership was actually stretched to cover a range of very different scenarios. Brentham, partly because of its scale, was difficult to protect as an ongoing entity: the interests of economic investors, and a mid-20th century shift towards owner-occupation, resulted in its privatisation.[43] Westholm and Eastholm, and a number of other similar developments in Letchworth, Hampstead and elsewhere, were really closer to a tenancy model rather than a co-tenancy one. Looking back we might now see them as an early form of 'housing association', and indeed, when not privatised, that was what many of them became. Two things really mark this type of co-tenancy: that they were mostly concerned with the provision of housing per se, and that they never developed a close association between 'investment' and 'inhabitation'.[44] Early schemes depended upon philanthropic investment, and later schemes tried to access public funding: both detracted from the principle of collective tenant 'ownership' of the estate through membership of the co-operative (taken up by the purchase of a share), as well as having to face the simple fact that rental income could rarely buy out external investors.[45] Co-partnership schemes always have, at root, a potential and very basic conflict between 'partners' if they do not manage to actually transfer wealth from 'one partner' to another. Those that survive managed to negotiate this transfer: through a combination of more consistently benevolent 'sponsorship' (rather than active investment), and a more proactive concern amongst the tenants to achieve the aim of independence.[46]

Tenants were more likely to understand, and be committed to, the overall aim of co-partnership if they were already well versed in the principles and

lost some of its original facilities (tennis court, bowling green, etc), but still has a 'Hall' and an active and committed community, many of whom are descendants of the original members. Burnage, of approximately 130 houses, calls itself 'The Garden Village' and retains its original facilities of tennis courts, bowling green and 'Village Hall'. It also has an active and committed community, but not linked back so closely to its original members. Eight other co-partnership schemes of this period still survive in England—all are smaller. The factors that enabled these co-tenancies to continue need more examination, and form a focus for my work at present.

[43] See details of the demise of the co-partnership scheme in Reid, above n 39.

[44] Also factors such as scale and where sited ('garden city' environments already provided recreational and educational facilities for inhabitants), impacted on community design features—sometimes reducing them to little more than a shared green or open recreational area.

[45] Arguably Howard was, 'informally', using a co-partnership model when he established Homesgarth, and Meadow Way Green did succeed in one form of wealth transfer between 'partners': from Misses Pym and Dewe into assets held by the Howard Cottage Society.

[46] A scheme in Bournville survives, having benefited from the continued support of the Bournville Village Trust. Manchester Tenants Ltd seems to have been helped by 'sponsorship' from a benevolent local co-operative, which has not acted to access assets invested in the scheme. The archive held by Anchor Tenants Ltd records their concern, and the efforts they took, to free themselves from external investors.

practices of both co-partnership and co-operation. Humberstone, for instance, was established by a group of artisans who had already formed themselves into a boot and shoe production co-partnership. Although they had split away from a co-operative factory, they maintained strong links with the co-operative movement: helped by Vivian in developing their scheme (and Unwin provided the layout for them), they also turned to Neale for advice, and originally (but unsuccessfully) looked to the local co-operative for economic support. Well practised in developing and running mutual organisations, their project was made stronger, not only by their links to, and experience of, both co-partnership and co-operative organisation, but also by the scale of their scheme and the close ties between all their members.[47]

At the beginning of the 20th century both the 'garden city' model and the development of co-partnership tenancies were thought by their advocates to offer a blueprint for modern housing development.[48] The First World War, and the subsequent need for an extensive and economical plan for the provision of housing, brought an end to both of these visions.[49] Increasingly state provision of housing and, somewhat later, the boom in building for owner-occupation, 'squeezed' out what some have since called a 'middle way' of mutualism.[50] The co-partnership movement in housing did not expand after 1914–18. 'Garden city planning' was transmuted into a set of design features, including such issues as density of housing and the provision of localised services, for 'New Towns' developed and financed by the state.[51] Howard's vision of 'community ownership' of assets was lost as the state became the provider of services and infrastructure, and as the population strove to enter the new democracy of owner-occupation. When in the 1980s Margaret Thatcher's government entered into a partnership with members of the co-operative movement to reinvigorate 'co-operative housing' schemes, she did so clearly stating that she saw it as a way to bring people into owner-occupation, and, indeed, when they were encouraged to

[47] Anchor Tenants Ltd very directly referenced their allegiance to the philosophy of a 'simple life', by taking as their motto a quote from Ruskin: 'Not greater wealth, but simple pleasures.'

[48] See Miller, above n 16, and Birchall, above n 37. By 1912 14 schemes had been built under the auspices of Vivian's organisation (6,595 homes for 30–35,000 people)—I can find no record (as yet) of the total number of schemes developed in this period.

[49] However, co-operative housing had been successfully exported overseas, carried within the governance of the Empire by a small but significant number of colonial officers who had been involved in, or influenced by, the co-operative movement. They remain, for instance, a vibrant part of the provision of housing in India—where contemporary litigation, as well as statutes, continues to provide a jurisprudence for their development and use. See A Lewin, *Housing Co-operatives in Developing Countries* (London, Wiley, 1981). On different patterns of co-operative housing and their potential in terms of broader concerns with development or regeneration schemes, see further I Skelton, 'Supporting Identity and Needs: The Many Faces of Co-op Housing' (2002), available at http://www.irrt.org.uk and material on the www.ica.coop/al-housing website.

[50] See, eg, J Birchall (ed), *The New Mutualism in Public Policy* (London, Routledge, 2001).

demutualise after 1980, the majority of these schemes did just that. 'Members' became 'owner-occupiers', with considerable windfalls, leaving only a residual role for the co-operative in holding and managing any common parts existent after the dismembering of the scheme.

CONCLUSION

Within more recent years there has been another revival of interest in co-operative housing. Changes in a volatile housing market suggest the potential for a reconfiguration of housing supply and tenure—arising not only from the need to build more housing, but also addressing the vexed question of meeting the aspiration to 'owner-occupation' when so many potential owners have been priced out of the market. A plethora of schemes, between government and agencies building and financing 'homes', subsidies for 'key workers' and finance packages which combine loans and mortgages, have developed alongside mixed-tenure packages (a proportion 'owned' and a proportion 'rented'), and even schemes which 'sell' the house but not the land. All have been tried, but with mixed success.

Meanwhile the Labour government still waivers on the question of whether it should become more involved, again, in the provision of social housing. Whilst increasingly recognising the disastrous consequences of the loss of council housing through the 'right to buy' (in terms of the overall provision of social housing stock), the results of the privatisation of swaths of council housing is still being played through. For many advocates of co-operative housing this is both a time of potential, and of danger. 'Privatisation' has moved some 'once public' housing stock into 'tenant's co-operatives', but it has been the 'difficult to let' or 'difficult to manage' estates which have been targeted—estates which have the greatest social and economic problems. Despite brave words, imported from the United States, that this process can 'empower' tenants, the evidence too often suggests that they have little purchase on 'empowerment', being left to struggle with intractable problems with few resources and little infrastructure to support them.[52]

Conversely, small groups of activists are embracing a version of the co-operative model (often a blend between a 'sharing' lifestyle, and wanting to avoid individuated ownership); but, when finding themselves without adequate resources to make it feasible, seek means by which to access government funding without losing their co-operative ethos. Funding issues become even more critical when such groups are concerned not to limit

[51] See, eg, P Hall and C Ward, *Sociable Cities: The Legacy of Ebenezer Howard* (London, Wiley, 1998).

[52] See D Rodgers, 'Housing Co-operatives and Social Exclusion', in Birchall, above n 50, Skelton, above n 49, and the 2004 Research Report 'Community Land Trusts and Mutual

access to their projects to only those who can find the means to invest in them. Again, as with the co-partnership model, tensions in mixing a mutual self-help ethos with the need to source economic investment, and a concern to make housing options available to those without economic resources, weakens the potential of a co-operative model for ownership and governance of the enterprise.

For those who have the economic resources to mount schemes providing the lifestyle of sharing which they seek, forms of 'co-ownership' that allow them to own individuated units within a scheme of shared facilities have developed. These schemes evoke a form of co-operative housekeeping, including access to shared resources which might otherwise be unavailable to them, within a modified form of individuated ownership requiring economic investment from each participant, and a high level of 'similarity' between participants in order to work. Such schemes benefit those who partake in them, allowing them to buy into a lifestyle of co-operation, but involve no element of wealth transfer between groups and no potential for access by the less economically well off.

A survey of the range of contemporary 'co-operative housing' reveals a disjuncture between those focused on 'tenant provision' and those focused on 'co-living' arrangements. The difference between the two is huge—both in economic and class terms, and in aspirations. The former is too often a scheme imposed without either the economic, social or political infrastructure to maintain it. The latter too often a lifestyle choice sustained by social ties, economic bargaining power and a shared commitment to finding a legal form through which to provide a suitable structure for governance. The first does not involve any necessary commitment to closely 'sharing' facilities or lifestyle, and the latter is predicated on it. Neale's vision of 'associative housing', a combined model for co-operative living, is as difficult to sustain now as it was then.

One other factor plays through this contemporary picture: a concern with the environment and with 'sustainable communities'.[53] Many 'intentional communities' have placed themselves firmly within an ethos of environmental and social sustainability. It is as if, to this extent, the garden city movement has been redrawn into an eco-friendly movement, providing a form, focus and ethos (a 'vector' or 'channel') for more community-focused housing schemes.

An aspiration to build truly sustainable communities reconfigures the ethical concern to be 'simple in their homes'. In looking back to earlier attempts to build co-operative housing, we can draw lessons for the potential, as well as the limitations, in co-operative living arrangements, in all its many dimensions. Factors relating to economics and governance, the strengths of common interest and purpose, the problems of conformity and exclusion, and the differences between those who view co-operation as a lifestyle choice and those who view it as background to a successful community, remain ongoing issues that we have to be sensitive to. Using co-operative enterprises to access limited resources will always be a motive. For some it will operate so as to privilege their needs and wishes over others in the community, and for many, especially those who more readily understand individuated ownership of wealth rather than the principle of stewardship, the ideal of full mutuality of interests will prove too indistinct and fuzzy. In the early twenty-first century, as we turn again to the potential for thinking differently about how we organise our domestic living arrangements, recovering the many dimensions of the idea and practices of co-operative housing, as evidenced at the turn of the last century, provides an invaluable resource.

10

Intentional Communities and Care-giving: Co-Housing Possibilities

SUSAN SCOTT HUNT

INTRODUCTION

THE TERM 'COHOUSING' covers a great variety of 'intentional' community developments that involve members of a group sharing residential and social needs. If there is a spectrum of intentional communities stretching between the informal, 'utopian', often ideologically defined 'commune' at one end, and the affluent, exclusive 'gated community' at the other, then, in its 'effort to resolve competing desires for inclusivity of community and exclusivity of privacy',[1] CoHousing seeks to occupy a middle ground. CoHousing communities allow members to share motivation and purpose, as well as deciding whether to cluster around similar socioeconomic, eg age-related, characteristics or shared interests. Often linked to what might be called a 'lifestyle ideology', such as environmentalism,[2] CoHousing can be a particularly attractive option for those who do not fit, or do not want to fit, into a domestic lifestyle based upon the heterosexual family unit. And, whilst 'caring and sharing' are merely incidental to the legal and physical configuration of CoHousing communities, in another sense, they are its main organisational impetus. Focused on patterns which develop 'caring and sharing' within the intentional community, CoHousing is associated with a commitment to 'domestic relationships' in the wider sense of relationships between people in a 'residential community', an integrated neighbourhood.

The definition proposed by Mark Field (a leading authority on Co-

[1] M Fenster, 'Community by Covenant, Process and Design: CoHousing and the Contemporary Common Interest Community' (1999) *Journal of Land Use & Environmental Law* 1.

[2] The websites of both the UK and the USA CoHousing movements, www.cohousing.org.uk and www.cohousing.org, respectively, include details of a number of environmentally responsible features of CoHousing communities.

Housing in the United Kingdom), in his book, *Thinking about CoHousing*,[3] focuses on the sharing of living space and, by clear implication, on caring for people with whom living space is shared, as essential characteristics of CoHousing:

> A CoHousing 'organisation' is taken to mean an autonomous association of households united in their aspirations to meet shared residential and social needs within a jointly-owned and democratically-controlled 'intentional neighbourhood'.[4]

As in other parts of the world, the main reasons for the growing CoHousing 'movement' in the UK arise from the perception that established forms of housing development and redevelopment fail to provide a desired balance between, on the one hand, independence, privacy and flexible financial security, and, on the other hand, social connection, social contact and the financial advantages of combining housing capital. With origins in Denmark[5] and the Netherlands, currently by far the largest and most varied number of CoHousing communities are found in the United States. CoHousing communities in the UK, whilst able to claim as historically important ideological predecessors the late-Victorian garden cities and model towns, and to show a close relation to the well-established public or semi-public co-operative housing form,[6] are small but increasing in number. Over the last decade, CoHousing communities have begun to be developed and established in the UK more frequently and, it appears, with more permanency and sustainability; and yet they remain positioned on the margins of housing, rather than being recognised for their potential as a mainstream option.[7] Further, it could be argued that CoHousing communities can make a social contribution beyond the interests of their members that merits support and encouragement on public policy grounds. Does, for instance, CoHousing in the UK, carry a significant potential to address issues of housing provision contributing to the well-being and care of elderly people, as has been the case in the Netherlands and Scandinavian countries?[8]

[3] M Field, *Thinking about CoHousing* (London, Diggers & Dreamers, 2004).

[4] Ibid, 198.

[5] The term 'CoHousing' is an approximate translation from the Danish *Bofaellesskaber*. See C Scotthanson and K Scotthanson, *The Cohousing Handbook; Building a Place for Community* (Gabriola Island, Canada, New Society Publishers, 2005) 3.

[6] See S Bottomley, '"They shall be simple in their homes . . .": The Many Dimensions of the Idea and Practices of Co-operative Housing', ch 9 in this volume.

[7] For a full comparison of CoHousing models in California and in the UK, arguing that CoHousing in the UK should be encouraged because it provides greater sustainability than other UK housing forms, see J Williams, 'Sun, Surf and Sustainable Housing—CoHousing, the California Experience' (2005) 10 *International Planning Studies* 145.

[8] M Brenton, *We're in Charge* (London, Policy Press, 1998); JS Choi, 'Evaluation of Community Planning and Life of Senior CoHousing Projects in Northern European Countries' (2004) 12 *European Planning Studies* 1189.

To begin to examine these issues, we need, firstly, to have an 'image' of the typical design features that characterise CoHousing schemes. Whether newly built or adapted from an existing building, CoHousing schemes are physically characterised by a combination of private family or individual accommodation, with shared communal areas and facilities. Often the shared facilities are centrally positioned, although in adapted buildings this is less likely to be the case. Sometimes the whole of the land upon which the CoHousing scheme is situated is shared, whilst in other schemes limited undeveloped land parcels form part of the private accommodation units. Where possible, kitchens, sitting-rooms and porches or balconies of private areas are positioned so as to look out on to shared spaces, and pedestrian walkways linking private and shared areas are intentionally configured so as to increase both visibility and the frequency of social interaction. And, generally, parking areas on non-urban CoHousing schemes are on the periphery.

The extent and variety of the shared facilities of CoHousing communities depend on a number of factors, including space, cost and the priorities of the people living there, often dictated by age, interests and so forth. Shared communal cooking faculties are frequent, though it is by no means a mandatory characteristic that CoHousing communities share meals regularly.[9] Childcare, entertainment areas, laundries, business equipment and premises, woodworking and craft-making areas are sometimes provided. The linking of the buildings in CoHousing communities frequently provides an opportunity to maximise shared systems in order to reduce costs, to decrease environmental impact or to increase the quality of service. Thus, several new-built or renovated schemes have shared heating systems, water systems, gardens and intranet facilities.[10]

The size of CoHousing communities varies, but is deliberately limited in physical size and total population to the extent that is thought necessary[11] to foster and support a sense of community and shared enterprise. Finding this balance is the key aspect of what has been called a 'CoHousing dynamic'.[12]

Thus we can begin to 'read' from the built environment the features that support, promote and sustain the integrated 'caring and sharing' environment which characterises CoHousing. However, within English common law, as developed and supplemented by statute, there is no specific legal model designed for use by CoHousing schemes. It has been a matter of

[9] Scotthanson and Scotthanson, above n 6, 4; Field, above n 3, 9. The Community Project of East Sussex, for instance, has a Friday 'pot-luck' supper.

[10] The Springhill cohousing community near Stroud has a number of 'eco-features', although some which had been planned were abandoned for reasons of cost. 'Britain's first new-build cohousing scheme' *The Independent*, 9 January, 2007.

[11] Most UK CoHousing projects are of between 10 and 30 units.

[12] Field, above n 3, 13.

working with, and sometimes between, existing legal forms for property holding and management—teasing out those aspects that are useful, and trying to militate against the potential impact of aspects that are less useful. Through examining the, often very creative, blending and adapting of legal categories and principles within the documentation establishing such schemes, and providing governance structures for them, we are able not only to map the range and potential of the available legal frames, but also to trace in their usage the continuing problem of addressing the difficult balance between the interests of individual (or familial) members, and the interests of the scheme as a 'collective'.

With such issues in mind, the purpose of this chapter is to begin to explore the potential for the growth (and use) of a CoHousing model in the UK, by examining the legal frames operative specifically in England and Wales which can be utilised to promote property relations that enable 'sharing'. Section I outlines the most frequently used legal frameworks for CoHousing, and section II moves on to examine how these frames have been operationalised in relation to two very different CoHousing communities: the first a community of 'families' of various configurations, and the second a 'family' of older women who wish to live singly or in pairs within the CoHousing site. Section III maps the potential in other legal forms to establish and run CoHousing communities, with an emphasis on the recent 'commonhold' legislation, the modernisation of charity law and the introduction of the 'community interest company.' By way of conclusion, I shall then return to the question of the extent to which a CoHousing model may carry general social benefits, in particular in relation to an aging population, within the context of differences between living a lifestyle predicated on dependence, and a lifestyle designed to maximise interdependence.

I

Organisational Framework

What distinguishes CoHousing in terms of a conceptual and organisational framework is that it is conceived, initiated and, entirely or predominantly, *controlled* by those who reside in it.[13] While other types of group housing or, perhaps more accurately 'home grouping', involve aspects of group initiation and control, for CoHousing the combination of a high degree of privacy and ownership rights over residential units, with a, generally, equally shared decision-making responsibility for, and control over, the

[13] D Fromm, *Collaborative Communities: CoHousing, Central Living and Other Forms of New Housing with Shared Facilities* (New York, Van Nostrad Reinhold, 1991).

function of common areas that rests exclusively, or substantially, with the neighbourhood's households, is essential. Unsurprisingly then, the extent of a consensus-based process of community decision-making and dispute resolution, as well as controls on membership and restrictions on alienation of interests in the private units, are the other main hallmarks of the legal architecture of CoHousing. What is required is a legal and organisational framework able to achieve the typical aims of CoHousing communities in relation to both the provision of key rights and obligations in relation to the individual participants, as well as recognising and supporting the interests of the group.

In my experience, there is a bundle of core legal issues that will always need to be addressed, which include:

- a means by which to allow for 'owner-occupation' rights over the interior of residential units, combined with shared rights over the common parts;
- A mechanism for sale, disposal and the encumbrance of equitable interests in the residential units that is consistent with the aims of the CoHousing community; and
- residents' equal commitment to, and participatory control of, the management of common areas and facilities.

Stages of Organisational Framework

The legal needs of the initial (founding) group are different in a few important respects from those of the established group into which they hope to evolve. Key legal and practical issues in the initiation and development stage of a CoHousing community include the need to form a separate recognisable identity that can command credibility within the market for real property, act quickly, borrow money, and present a persuasive and coherent voice to relevant governmental agencies, such as planning authorities. The financial risk and the financial security needs of individuals or 'families' in the group should to be addressed from the outset, and balanced against the needs and interests of the group acting as an entity. When, however, the project is built, or the refurbishment complete, the legal and organisational priorities generally shift into those concerned with governance, and the mutual rights and obligations both between and amongst participants, and between participants and the group. Thus, for instance, a key CoHousing organisational feature in the up-and-running stage will be a workable mechanism for controlling membership, whilst keeping restrictions on transferring (property) interests in housing tenure to the absolute minimum.

The Entity and Form of Ownership

In the initial stages of a CoHousing development, a number of factors will influence the extent of the need to form a group of people into a recognisable entity that can be tailored to achieve a specific shared ambition.[14] The essential choice will be whether or not to opt for an entity providing legal personality. Whilst such a decision may not need to be made before any meaningful steps can be taken to form a group, or to identify the group's priorities and objectives, the advantages of gaining legal personality through the formation of a company, whether limited by shares or guarantee, are very significant. It is noticeable that, of the small number of successful and viable CoHousing schemes recently established in the UK, all have, either initially or subsequently, adopted a company form.[15] The reasons are easily identifiable. A company structure is well recognised by those established entities within the housing market (eg lenders and governmental agencies, building contractors and professional advisors) with which the initiating group will need to deal. The company is a form that can accommodate differing and often flexible levels of individual financial commitment and, importantly, it carries limited liability. Further, the process of formal registration is usually unproblematic, involving the filing of the company's Memorandum of Association with Companies House and the payment of appropriate fees. There are two forms of company which can be deployed: a company limited by shares, and one limited by guarantee. Although, as discussed below, there has been a traditional preference for the use of the latter, the former offers many advantages.

Companies Limited by Shares, or by Guarantee

Shareholder-directors, who may have equal or unequal numbers of shares, control a company limited by shares. It is possible for all shareholders to be directors, but it is also possible to have an executive committee to whom the directors delegate responsibility for various matters. Other potential advantages to choosing a company limited by shares include the ease with which share ownership can be acquired and transferred, not only to individuals as either investors or future residents, or both, but also to other groups or entities, such as investing development partners (whether other limited liability companies, or governmental or quasi-governmental agencies). The cost of transfer of shares is generally much lower than the cost of transferring leaseholds, and is potentially tax advantageous.[16] Also, shares

[14] Brenton, above n 8, 69.

[15] Field, above n 3, 105.

[16] This will certainly be the case in regard to Capital Gains Tax, but Stamp Duty is payable on all share transactions and does not have the advantage of the nil rate band.

may have an investment potential in that a CoHousing company can increase in value. Of course, whether, and to what extent, transferability and the potential for value increase are important will depend upon the characteristics, and objectives, of a particular CoHousing group. For example, when the acquisition of a site for the project is not a key objective—because, for instance, the site is owned by existing participants—the members of a potential resident group might find it most advantageous to purchase shares in the company to the value of the planned residential units. And if securing the site is not the principal object of the initial stage, formation of a company limited by shares may attract and facilitate 'outside' investment partners whose capital can assist in developing the site.

A significant factor in practically all schemes which may impact on the desirability of forming a company limited by shares is the frequently varying financial resources of participants and their respective liquidity. When individuals in an initiating group are of significantly unequal financial worth, the exposure to risk of the wealthiest is greater because a wealthy director can be more conveniently sued for the actions of other, less financially wealthy, directors or the group. An additional concern with using this legal frame can be the unfamiliarity of potential residents with the notion of purchasing a property interest in the form of a shareholding, rather than in the form of a lease.[17] And, whilst many banks, building societies and other lenders do lend on property using shares as security, this is not the most familiar practice in relation to property purchase and may result in an increase in the cost of borrowing. Indeed, some potential lenders insist that shares be subject to a right of conversion into leasehold. Therefore, in circumstances in which it is necessary for some members to borrow money in order to enter the scheme, a company limited by shares is usually best avoided in favour of one limited by guarantee, or the utilisation of a simple leasehold arrangement. However, it is possible to allow for a conversion of shares into a conventional lease later, although this involves the agreement of all members of the eventual group.[18]

As they wish to access public funding in order to develop a scheme, as well as often being concerned that potential members should not be excluded simply because they lack the economic resources to invest in the scheme, some CoHousing projects decide to opt for mixed tenure. A development partnership with, for instance, a registered social landlord, such as an existing housing co-operative, is likely to be predicated on agreeing to a mixed scheme which includes the provision of low-rent units. A company, whether limited by shares or by guarantee, provides a convenient legal

[17] C Pickering, E Parry, K, Jinkins and A Jolliffe, *A Different Way of Living: CoHousing for Older Women* (London, The Housing Corporation, 2004).

[18] Ibid, 15.

structure for a mixed-tenure scheme that uses investment from a separate entity partner, such as a housing association or, conceivably, a private developer. Utilising the company limited by share model can, in these circumstances, be particularly useful. The partner might, for example, join as a member by buying shares equal to the whole value of particular housing units, and then act as owner-landlord of the rented accommodation within the scheme. It is also possible, when the financial muscle of the initiating group is sufficient and confidence in the market for rented accommodation within the scheme is high, for the CoHousing company to buy out the shares representing the units not subscribed for by resident members, and thus become a 'landlord' offering the units for rent.[19]

A further advantage of a company limited by shares is the potential to create differentiated classes of non-voting and voting shares, and non-equity and equity shares. An outside institutional investor may be willing to hold non-voting equity shares, whereas residents of rented accommodation may hold non-equity voting shares. Further, the convenience of differentiated types of share ownership allows for 'staircasing', ie the buying of shares by individuals to the value of equity required, an arrangement that is suitable for people in shared ownership homes.

Despite all these many advantages, there has been a preference amongst UK-based CoHousers for the 'company limited by guarantee', rather than the company limited by share. It has been suggested that this arises from the compatibility of the former with the 'egalitarian' principles that have strongly influenced the development of most CoHousing schemes, and that the benefits of the form make it a 'benchmark against which other legal frameworks could be evaluated'.[20] This company form is established for 'community benefit', drawing close parallels between it and principles of mutuality. Directors of a company limited by guarantee can derive no personal financial benefit, and their liability is limited to the (usually) nominal value of shares, although they remain responsible for the 'formal effects of the company'.[21] The company must agree and adopt a Memorandum and Articles of Association which, in combination with the contracts and agreements mutually entered into between and amongst the members of the group and the company, define the responsibilities of members in relation to the scheme. Importantly these documents not only set out a general statement of the initiating members' aims and objectives, but also describe the legal basis of the group entity's formal ownership of common facilities and create a structure for decision-making.[22]

19 Income accruing from the rented units could be used to offset ongoing maintenance costs on the common parts of the site, or as an amalgamation to the development funds of the project or, indeed, as distributable profit between the shareholders.

20 Field, above n 3, 105 and 112.

21 Ibid, 105.

22 Where versions of certain model rules of a model Memorandum and Articles of Association accepted by a relevant authority are used, the registration fee may be reduced.

II

Having outlined the major aspects of choice in relation to the use of the company form for CoHousing, this section examines its operational value in relation to two, rather different, schemes, both of which illustrate the preference for using the company limited by guarantee.

The Community Project, East Sussex

What is now 'The Community Project' in Laughton, East Sussex, began in the early 1990s amongst a small number of 'thirty-something' middle-class friends in north London. They started to think about how a greater sense of community could be sustained and how, for some, a better context in which to raise children could be found, by pooling home equity and sharing responsibilities, yet without sacrificing either a high degree of autonomy in their lives (as individuals, couples or families),[23] or long-term individual financial security tied to housing equity.

The project took form in 1997 with the purchase of a cluster of disused hospital buildings, set in over 20 acres of countryside. Some residential units have been crafted out of the existing buildings; some are newly built dwellings that have been constructed with sensitivity to the environment. The houses contain between three and five bedrooms, and there are also a few flats, some of which are designated as rental accommodation. Most residences are arranged in terraces around open courtyards, looking out onto a road leading to a large common house and miscellaneous outbuildings. There are shared, environmentally sound, sources of heating and water, as well as gardens, woods, a pond, fields and a paddock for horses.

Set up as a company limited by guarantee, the initial funding for the project came from private loans, of various amounts, and from a nucleus group who used their savings, or mortgaged, or sold, their London homes. The members of this group entered into a deed that set out a detailed scheme for sharing risk, calculating interest and providing formulae for loans and interest thereon, to be set against the acquisition costs of individual units, as determined by independent valuation. This arrangement was underpinned by an alternative dispute-resolution mechanism, involving the use of an expert valuer. All leaseholders became directors and all residents, including non-leaseholders, members, with prospective residents given associate membership. The Memorandum and Articles of Association adopted by the Community Project are standard documents,[24] with the

[23] Drawn from conversations, over several years, with Linda Glenn a founder member of The Community Project.

[24] The documents were drafted by Malcolm Lynch Solicitors and ICOM (the Industrial Common Ownership Movement Limited), Leeds, England.

Memorandum broadly defining the company's objects, and limiting liability to £1. Objects include the power to

> acquire and provide housing and communal facilities for the benefit of the Company's members through the provision of individual dwelling units on a purchased leasehold basis and the maintenance and management of common areas and facilities.

Other than in this clause, there is virtually no clue as to the CoHousing nature of the association; there are standard powers to carry on any advantageous trade or business, to purchase any type of property, to borrow, mortgage, lend, invest, etc, and the company can enter into a variety of partnership arrangements.

The lease is used as the means for defining owner-occupation rights over the interior of the residential units, and shared rights over the common parts (and does so by setting covenants between the occupier and the company). Essentially, as in a standard lease, the inside surfaces of the units and the window glass is part of the lease, and the structure and utilities conduits (those 'not solely for the purpose of one unit'), as well as the surrounding land, roads, entrances and facilities, are owned by the company. The company, as landlord, is owed ground rent, and has the right to levy a service charge, linked to an indexed measure of inflation, as well as holding rights in relation to access, the serving of repair notices and the approval of alterations. The leaseholder has rights to peaceable enjoyment, reinstatement out of insurance proceeds and the benefit of the proper maintenance of the reserved (common) parts. The company covenants to supply heat and water from communal facilities.

The lease contains provisions that control sale, disposal and encumbrance of legal and equitable interests in the residential units, and the company covenants not to grant leases of units other than in substantially similar terms—a standard term. To this is added a detailed schedule restricting dealings: when a leaseholder wishes to sell, he or she activates the mechanism for independent valuation of the unit to be sold, based on an 'agreed consideration' of the lease, at a price that takes into account the open market value, but 'disregarding the effect on valuation of the existence of the community comprising the occupiers of the units', and ignoring the restriction on assignment as well as any incumbrances created by the occupier. The company then has a three-month period, from receipt of the independent valuation, to find a 'nominee' buyer, who is approved as 'suitable', in being willing to subscribe to the principles of, and participate in, the community. Under the terms, the company has a right to nominate up to three nominee buyers. However, should the company fail to find a suitable nominee within the period, the leaseholder is free to find her/his own buyer, provided that the agreed price does not exceed the independent valuation.

There is no prohibition on sub-letting, but sub-lessees must be approved by the company and the length of a sub-lease is limited to a period of five years within any ten-year period. When a lease is devolved by way of intestacy or will, the company cannot refuse membership to the person to whom it is devolved, provided he or she agrees to a direct covenant to 'pay rent and perform and observe the covenants of [the] lease'. In the case of repossession by a mortgagee who exercises the mortgagee's power of sale, the company has the right to approve membership of a buyer but cannot 'unreasonably or capriciously refuse membership to a prospective assignee from such Mortgagee who is shown likely to be a respectable and responsible tenant'.

The residents' equal commitment to, and participatory control of, the management of common areas and facilities is provided mainly through the Articles of Association. All members (leaseholders, whether joint or single, and renting residents) have an equal vote, and are all entitled to notice of meetings. There are provisions for loss of membership—when a member resigns, dies, ceases to be eligible to be a company director by reason of bankruptcy or otherwise, ceases to meet the qualification of leaseholder or resident, or is expelled.[25]

The community makes an effort to minimise meetings, and to make the provisions for notification and convening as uncomplicated as possible. However, the governing principle for decision-making is a 'consensus' model for the mundane, ongoing business of the community, and generally meetings must therefore

> endeavour to arrive at a decision by consensus, by which is meant that all those present and entitled to vote (in person or by proxy) are in agreement with the proposal or agree not to maintain an objection to it.

If consensus fails, the first step is to defer the meeting and to try again later for a consensus, but if this again fails the matter is then put to the vote and decided by a simple majority. However, in respect of particular types of decisions, provisions for 'special' and 'elective' resolutions require a super-majority (three-quarters), and a unanimous vote, respectively.[26] There are provisions for quorums, and voting is usually by show of hand but may be secret in some circumstances. Some business is delegated to temporary committees, or individuals, but the Board of Directors is coextensive with the membership and there is a permanent, or occasionally temporary, chairperson.

Making decisions by consensus is 'fundamental to the way [the Com-

[25] Expulsion is initially by consensus, and thereafter by majority.

[26] 'Special resolutions' cover alterations to the Memorandum and Articles, winding up, and other matters mandated by statute, whereas 'elective resolutions' include those dispensing with annual general meetings, laying of accounts and reports and appointment of auditors.

munity Project] operates'[27] but it can be difficult and frustrating. In the words of two representatives of the Community Project:

> It is not easy for more than thirty adults to make decisions together. Meetings can be very lengthy when everyone wants their say and it can be difficult to resolve opposing views. Everyone at one time or another has had to let go of dearly held opinions for the sake of finding some consensus with the wider group. While we strive to avoid a sense of institutionalisation, inevitably, members may need to give up certain individual freedoms—for example, with no private land on the site, people need to negotiate before undertaking anything major in the garden areas. Compromise and negotiation remain the name of the game, although we are determined to improve our use of consensus decision-making to remove the tendency for current procedures to leave people feeling frustrated or sidelined. We remain committed to 'decision by consensus' despite knowing that we need to make it work better. This is because we know from other communities that other forms of democracy using majority voting means people can become marginalized and excluded and this undermines group functioning.[28]

Older Women's CoHousing, London

This group is currently in the development phase, and hopes to purchase a site in north London.[29] They plan a mix of 25 single- and shared-ownership[30] units, combined with low-rent units for those eligible for social housing, clustered around a common-room, guest accommodation and some shared facilities. The long-term ambition of the group is to create a number of such CoHousing communities throughout London.

Two features which distinguish OWCH from more mainstream CoHousing groups are that their project is limited to women over 50,[31] and that it is geared to accommodate a social housing element. As such, it has provoked some interest amongst academics, and has been the subject of study over several years by sociologists and housing experts supported by the Housing Corporation.[32]

Like the Community Project, OWCH has incorporated as a company limited by guarantee[33] and ownership will be by means of conventional

27 Field, above n 3, 32.

28 Ibid, 33.

29 See the OWCH website: www.owch.org.

30 Which can include part tenancies shared between the resident and the company.

31 The requirement limiting membership to women does not contravene the Equality Act 2006 because a private non-profit body is permitted to discriminate on the grounds of gender.

32 Pickering et al, above n 17.

33 The company, which will be called a CoHousing 'Society', may consider conversion to a co-operative at some point following full occupancy, but a major factor in making this decision will be whether such a move will impose an over-burdensome regulatory regime.

leases,[34] but, as they will operate in partnership with an existing housing association,[35] that association will become a member and hold the lease of the rented flats.

Extensive work has been undertaken on a package of legal documents for OWCH as a case study: these include a membership agreement, a purchase agreement and a standard lease. Eventually, there will also be a development agreement,[36] agreements between the housing association landlord and member tenants of rented units, as well as a standard company Memorandum and Articles. To raise sufficient finance, members will pay a deposit to the CoHousing company, funds will be advanced by the housing association and a commercial loan will be sought. Most of the lease is standard, dealing with such things as ground rent, service charges and access for repairs. However, clauses that are notable in defining the CoHousing aspects of the project include a lessee's covenant to remain a member of the CoHousing company, with resignation or expulsion requiring that the unit be automatically offered back to the lessor. In other words, an expelled member, for example, is treated as having proposed to sell under the mechanism set out in the lease. Encumbrance is allowed, with notice to the company, but sub-letting is restricted to someone who has previously become a member by signing the membership agreement. The lessor covenants to consult the lessee on changes in the landlord's management policies and performance.

The restrictions on alienation adopt a different mechanism from that used in the Community Project lease, but the effect is much the same. OWCH leaseholders are required to offer to assign the lease of the unit back to the company, or as the company directs.[37] The offer must be at a 'fair market price', to be stated by the leaseholder, who is also to propose terms of the contract of assignment. The Society then can agree, or dispute, the price and the terms, and make counter-offers. There is a strict timetable for this negotiation process, and rules dealing with the sending of communications and the effect of non-response. There is provision for the nomination of a qualified arbitrator to decide disputes on price and terms, and when there is no agreement on the appointment of an arbitrator, there will be an outside appointment. If the CoHousing society cannot afford to

[34] A lifetime interest scheme was considered but rejected, as OWCH was seeking charitable status, at least in the short term, and because of regulatory concerns.

[35] The website of Housing for Women is: www.h4w.org.uk. They are a RSI and so eligible for a social housing grant.

[36] The development agreement will provide for the sale of units to the CoHousing company by the developer, within a set period backed up by loss of deposits and a penalty for failure to purchase, with a right held by the developer to sell unclaimed units on the open market.

[37] Although the requirement limiting membership to women does not contravene the Equality Act 2006 (above n 31), subsequent dealings by member-leaseholders could indirectly discriminate by limiting transfer. For this reason, the resale provision requires transfer back to the Society, which can then resell under the exemption.

buy back the lease, they must allow it to be sold on the open market 'with removal of the special CoHousing term'. This clause ensures a degree of certainty and security to leaseholders and if, eventually, the CoHousing company is unable to find members, and thus cannot continue to exist, it can convert into an ordinary leaseholders' company.

The OWCH membership agreement is a separate document between each member and the 'Society', and it is in the membership agreement that the CoHousing nature of the project is most obviously expressed. Members undertake to 'promote a combined private and communal life as an intentional community based on specific principles of CoHousing communities'. In addition, principles for the interpretation of all the agreements between the members and the society (ie the lease as well) include not only the principle that an occupant must be a member, but also that

> the successful working of a CoHousing community demands mutual acceptance of responsibilities, obligations and duties that go beyond the ordinary requirements of behaviour as a good neighbour in ordinary residential accommodation.

All members are directors, but there is a management committee that appears to have quite extensive powers to create further rules, regulations and 'policies'. Members promise to attend general meetings, or seek permission for absence, to undertake a fair share of the administrative and other work involved in running the organisation, and to carry out obligations in respect of the common facilities (such as are reasonably required by the management committee). Certain matters, including changes in the terms of the membership agreement, require a vote of three-quarters of members.[38] Altogether, the framework requires considerable 'participation' by members, and members have to accept that failure to observe the terms of the membership agreement can lead to expulsion, with expulsion leading to a presumed offer to sell the lease.

III

The risk for CoHousers of not incorporating is individual exposure to liability for the group's actions. This factor may largely account for the current predominance of the company form within the UK. Legal vehicles other than the company form, however, have aspects that could make a contribution to the aims of CoHousing in particular circumstances. These include the familiar housing co-operative and the less familiar co-ownership society;[39] the housing association governed by the Housing Corporation; the partnership; and the registered charity, including the charitable trust. To

[38] There is no detailed consensus-making system described in the project documentation.

[39] Co-ownership societies have a membership structure that is consistent with the membership framework for CoHousing, and can distribute homes to members as profit of the society.

these have recently been added the commonhold association, and the common interest company (CIC). A full discussion of the relevance of each of the forms to CoHousing is beyond the scope of this chapter, but a few aspects of some forms will briefly be considered, particularly in relation to the social purposes of CoHousing vehicles.

Co-operatives, especially, are well-established vehicles with a recognised mutual support purpose and model rules that set minimum numbers of subscribers, and combine rental housing with a form of limited-equity home ownership. Model rules for a 'CoHousing co-operative' have been created and registered,[40] but they contemplate only a mixed-tenure scheme. Further, the co-operative is, in practice, an umbrella-like structure lacking the degree of direct initiation, design and control by residents through a participatory democracy, combined with the degree of private ownership of dwellings by which CoHousing is characterised.

Partnerships are only likely to be relevant either tangentially, or in the start-up stage as a convenient vehicle for managing initial financial contributions, identifying and researching potential sites, and sharing risks in the very first stages of formation of a CoHousing group. A partnership will not be useful as a permanent form of CoHousing, both because it lacks limited liability and because it does not offer, as the company form does, a flexible means for accommodating changing membership. However, a partnership to combine with another legal entity can frequently benefit a CoHousing group if its purposes and that of the other entity sufficiently coincide, and especially when it is intended to provide mixed-tenure residence as a means of part-funding the scheme.

Like the partnership form, the charitable organisation may have a supporting role to play in CoHousing, but is unsuitable as an entity itself.[41] Charitable organisations in housing may adopt a number of differing entity forms: they may be trusts, or community land trusts[42] or CICs, and housing associations may themselves gain charitable status. Although the Charities Act 2006 has greatly expanded and 'modernised' charity law in a way that might, on a broad construction, include at least some aspects of some Co-Housing schemes, the ability of a CoHousing to meet the requirement that the activities of a body having charitable status be exclusively 'for the benefit of the public' is problematic.[43] Arguably some aspects of the activ-

[40] Above n 3, 106. Model rules were created by Catalyst Collective, a body supporting co-operatives.

[41] Further, the trustees of a charity cannot themselves benefit from the scheme, which would preclude residents from being trustees.

[42] See the website of the Community Land Trust: www.communitylandtrust.org.uk. See also 'Community Land Trusts—The Legal Perspective' a paper presented by Catherine Hand of Trowers & Hamlins, Solicitors, and 'CLT: Affordable Homes in Sustainable Communities', a CLT policy paper. Both are available through the website.

[43] Following a consultation process, the Charity Commissioners reworked the public benefit requirement, removing any presumption of public benefit and continuing to preclude recognition as charitable provisions essentially intended for a closed group, unless they are provided

ities of some CoHousing communities, actual or proposed, are now somewhat more likely to be able to take advantage of the expanded list of charitable 'heads', especially, for example, in so far as environmental activities are concerned, as the 'advancement of environmental protection or improvement' is a specific new 'head' of charity under the 2006 Act. Environmentally sustainable design has been a significant feature of new-build CoHousing, and existing CoHousing communities are quite frequently involved in activities of an educational,[44] and therefore 'charitable', nature in 'spreading the word' about CoHousing theory, design and practice to others, including nascent CoHousing groups. Finally, a very broad interpretation of the broader view of charitable status contained in the Act might, in the case of mixed-tenure projects created in partnership with a registered social landlord, conceivably allow the recognition of CoHousing on the grounds that it advances 'citizenship or community development', another one of the new categories listed in the Act.

The Potential Usefulness of Commonhold and CIC forms

The Commonhold and Leasehold Reform Act 2002 created a new form of landholding designed to assist owners of 'interdependent' residential (or commercial) units that are physically adjacent, contiguous or enclosed within a larger structure and therefore likely to share common parts. The major policy concern behind the Act was to provide an alternative, in such circumstances, to the limitations of leasehold tenure, and the legislation allows for the registration of what were once leaseholders of each unit, as freehold owners of both the unit, and of the common parts held as 'commonhold'. Whilst, for many reasons, there has been very limited uptake in using the commonhold form in the scenarios it was designed to obviate, and, although it may not immediately provide all the necessary and desirable features for a CoHousing scheme, the commonhold form is undoubtedly interesting, and may have a significant relevance to the development of CoHousing.

The organisational mechanism for commonhold association is similar to that which has become the dominant form of modern British CoHousing: the owners of individual units are automatically members of a commonhold association, which is incorporated and registered as a company limited by guarantee. Only leasehold unit owners can be members, and the liability of members for the debts of the company is limited to £1.

by reason of characteristics of members of that group which make them particularly needed, such as poverty or disability.

44 The Vivarium project, which hopes to model itself on Danish and Dutch CoHousing for older people and will be located near Fife in Scotland, has applied for charitable status. See www.paperclip.org.uk.

However, the commonhold form does not preclude a mixed-tenure scheme, as it allows for sub-leases in individual units of less than 21 years, or, indeed, possibly, out of the freehold of the common parts. In addition, a 'web of rights and duties'[45] between commonholders must be contained within, and prescribed by, a commonhold 'community statement', which is a mandatory model document under the legislation and accompanying regulations.[46] However, it is this feature which may impede the usefulness of the commonhold as an entirely sufficient legal package for prospective CoHousing communities, in that it seems to allow less room for creativity and response to the particular character of a CoHousing scheme. The contents of the model statement includes matters that a CoHousing scheme organised as a company would be likely to include in its Memorandum of Association: allocation of rights and duties; definitions of permitted uses; financial arrangements for meeting expenses, reserving funds for maintenance; insurance of the common parts; and arrangements for resolution of disputes between and amongst the unit holders and the commonhold association.[47] But a much greater degree of social association and interdependence than is represented by the commonhold model statement is desirable in CoHousing.

The legislation does appear to allow for 'local rules' setting out additional requirements applicable to a particular scheme.[48] These, as well as the terms of the general model, appear to be underpinned by a provision to the effect that '[a] duty conferred [by the statement] on a unit holder shall not require any other formality'. In other words, they shall not be required to be comprised in a deed of transfer.[49] Further, transferees of the unit holders take subject to all existing rights and duties. Thus far, so good; the commonhold appears to be a sufficient vehicle. However, a further and possibly serious impediment is presented by a prohibition on restriction of transfer: the statement reads that the rules 'may not provide for the transfer or loss of an interest in land on the occurrence or non-occurrence of a specified event'. The purpose of this provision is to prevent precisely the danger of forfeiture for breach of covenant that was so objectionable in its application to long-leasholders. The difficulty is that it may also fetter the ability of CoHousing entities to enforce rules that restrict the sale of leases to persons not vetted by, or acceptable to, the community.

Arguably, the emerging practice of having a tailormade set of legal documents, underpinned by the company entity, may more closely achieve the particular local concerns of CoHousing communities in the UK. On the

[45] JA Mackenzie and M Philips *Textbook on Land Law* (11th ed, Oxford University Press, 2006).

[46] See CR 2004 Regs 13 and 14, Schedules 1 and 2.

[47] Alternative dispute resolution is encouraged by the legislation.

[48] Above n 45, 260.

[49] S 31(7).

other hand, it has to be recognised that this practice has not yet been seriously tested in the courts. Thus, there would appear to be one clear advantage to trying to fashion a commonhold arrangement for the purposes of a CoHousing scheme: the enforcement provisions contained in section 37 of the Commonhold and Leasehold Reform Act, which sets out specific descriptions of enforceable rights and duties (including liabilities for compensation for breaches of duties, and for contributions to cost of common parts maintenance) obviates the problem of tackling enforcement issues through affecting free-fashioned rules and by-laws in a CoHousing entity operating as a company limited by guarantee. Moreover, whilst company-form CoHousing provisions can contain clauses requiring arbitration,[50] the commonhold statutory framework sets up, as a requirement, participation in an ombudsman scheme.

Another recent introduction which merits attention is the CIC, a new form of company created by Part Two of the Companies (Audit, Investigations and Community Enterprise) Act 2004.[51] Designed to recognise the needs of non-charitable, but nonetheless 'socially beneficial', enterprises formed by shareholding, in this respect it is an appropriate new form for organisations that have purposes that lie somewhere between a business and charity. There are already a growing number[52] of diverse enterprises that have adopted the model, and are engaged in a variety of activities 'using business solutions to achieve public good'.[53] They include mutual organisations, such as co-operatives and companies limited by guarantee or shares, and groupings dedicated to the furtherance of such causes as fair trade, an improved environment, social justice, community transport, childcare, and a whole host of unique commercial community-based efforts including, for example, the running of a village shop selling local produce. To be accepted for registration as a CIC, an organisation must satisfy the regulator that its purpose 'could be regarded by a reasonable person as being in the community or wider public interest and to confirm that access to the benefits it provides will not be confined to an unduly restricted group'.[54]

Organisationally, the CIC is subject to 'light-touch' regulation (compared with other company forms or charities[55]), by an independent regulator.[56] CICs are obliged to involve stakeholders in decision-making, but are mainly

[50] This is so for the Community Project documents.

[51] The Act received Royal Assent on 28 October 2004 and, following approval of the regulations, it has been possible to register CICs since 1 July 2005.

[52] There are over 300 CICs now and the number is increasing rapidly. See www.socialenterprise.org.uk, the website of the Social Enterprise Council.

[53] The CIC website is www.cicregulator.gov.uk .

[54] Ibid.

[55] A CIC cannot have charitable status.

[56] An annual report explaining how the activities of the CIC have benefited the community is required.

run by boards of directors, who can be paid reasonable remuneration. Although there can be distribution of profits and assets to member-shareholders, they are strictly limited, with profits being mainly reinvested for the purposes of the company, and assets subject to a statutory 'asset lock'. Although CICs do not share the tax concessions enjoyed by charities, there are fiscal advantages for some CICs through relief for investors.[57]

The potential usefulness of the CIC for CoHousing is clearly not in relation to the holding of the property interests. However, within particular CoHousing contexts, and taking into account the interests and priorities of its membership, the form could be imaginatively and advantageously employed for adjunct activities, such as provision of childcare, educational and cultural programmes, environmental conservation projects, the provision of a shop for the community and surrounding area, or for other purposes that would be considered by a 'reasonable person' to be in the interest of both the community and the wider public.

CONCLUSION

There is currently huge energy and a growing momentum in CoHousing in the UK. In comparison with the situation in North America, Denmark and the Netherlands, however, the movement is only just beginning to accelerate, and is generally still widely viewed as rather unorthodox. In defining their outward legal status and their internal legal relationships, UK's CoHousers appear to have adopted a pattern of creative adaptation of the company limited by guarantee, and are not attempting to create new legal forms specifically designed for purpose.[58]

The growth of CoHousing in the UK, especially in England and Wales, has happened at an interesting, and perhaps propitious, moment in the development and 'reform' of certain aspects of housing and non-business 'organisations' law: the recent introduction of commonhold; the modernisation and expansion of charity law; and the wider recognition of enterprises that have a 'community' benefit in the invention of the CIC, are all potentially useful. On the other hand, it could be argued that these legislative developments, whilst useful as adjuncts to the arrangements, activities and interests of CoHousing communities, are not really catalysts for the

[57] Community Interest Tax relief is 5 per cent tax relief to those investing in a Community Development Finance Institution that provides funds to CICs, and CICs are also eligible for the usual company tax reliefs.

[58] In this respect they appear to follow developments in North America CoHousing. In North America, units will typically be owned via a condominium or subdivision, with adjacent land owned through a co-operative, or a land trust, being used partly as a undeveloped environmentally protected buffer, and partly for the provision of common facilities. Even small parcels of undeveloped common, CoHousing, land can sometimes attract subsides if it can be shown that it contributes to conservation.

further growth of CoHousing. The ingenuity of UK CoHousing communities in adopting the company limited by guarantee to their purposes, sometimes in combination or in collaborative partnership with existing social housing entities, is much to be admired and holds promise for further expansion in CoHousing.

It will be interesting to see how quickly and variously CoHousing develops in the UK in the next decade. The website of the UK CoHousing Community[59] lists eight fully established communities, and 13 as planned or starting. Geographically, they spread from the Scottish Highlands to the English south coast. And, albeit slowly, government departments and financial institutions are becoming more interested and actively involved.

Is expansion and (economic) public support of the sector in the wider public interest, as CoHousers claim? Private-sector housing development has often had a negative environmental and social impact. However, a frequent criticism of Cohousing is that those able to participate in the movement are largely limited to middle-income owners of existing property, although, as seen in the ongoing efforts of OWCH, this is not uniformly the case. Inclusion of an element of 'affordable' housing appears to be an aim that many CoHousers view as desirable, if not always feasible. Similarly, the environmentally sensitive innovations of some existing and planned CoHousing communities, whilst widely enough adopted to be seen to be central to the 'ethos' of UK CoHousing efforts, are not essential to the form. So, the claim that CoHousing is sufficiently in the public interest on these accounts is not particularly persuasive.

The case that CoHousing in the UK might have claim to public funding and support on the grounds that it is capable of addressing issues of social cohesion and isolation, especially in such groups as the elderly in an ageing population, is, in my opinion, rather stronger. High urban property values, land scarcity and high living costs increasingly force ageing members of society to see their housing equity as a retirement resource, which nonetheless can trap them in neighbourhoods that lack cohesion and structures for mutual social support.[60]

In respect of projects such as OWCH, modelled on the considerable experience of Danish and Dutch CoHousing for older people,[61] there is a powerful argument that CoHousing can, by combating isolation, greatly increase the general health, well-being and longevity of residents, thus reducing the cost to the public of social care as well as addressing issues arising from the pain, anxiety, loneliness and sorrow of isolated individuals. The website of UK CoHousing Network reports a recent CoHousing

[59] www.CoHousing.org.uk.

[60] See A Bottomley, 'Managing Complexity: Multi-generational Housing Arrangements', accessed through www.enhr2007rotterdam.

[61] Brenton, above n 8. See also, K Croucher, L Hicks and K Jackson, *Housing With Care for Later Life; A Literature Review* (York, Joseph Rowntree Foundation, 2006), 21–22.

venture of this kind, in West Yorkshire, providing more evidence of a focused interest in CoHousing addressed to this purpose. Styled the 'Lifetime Community Project', the West Yorkshire group addresses those who seek 'a co-operative and self-responsible life style for their later years', and aims to provide support for members allowing them 'to grow older together' and to 'age in place', 'safely and enjoyably'.

The rise in the proportion of the elderly, especially women, will, in most Western European countries, be this century's defining demographic trend, and should therefore influence the direction of politics, helping to strengthen the case for greater political and public encouragement for CoHousing.[62]

A perceived decline in 'local social capital' in part motivates the current Labour government's interest in supporting more sustainable housing models.[63] CoHousing can clearly make a contribution to stronger communities through its core values relating to control, accountability, provision of individual financial security and, especially, through its model of deliberative, consensus-based and democratic participation. As Fenster has argued, from the viewpoint of the North American CoHousing movement, '[t]o the extent that original residents initiate and participate in a CoHousing project's development, [their] identification with the community is likely to be greater'.[64] At the same time, CoHousing carries the potential to make a contribution towards addressing a failure of modern Western society (including in law) to conceptualise, acknowledge and celebrate a 'good' form of adult dependency,[65] in which people consciously construct shared spaces within which mutual 'caring and sharing' is fostered.

[62] F Carncross, 'Forever Young: a Survey of Retirement' [2004] *The Economist* March 27.

[63] Williams, above n 7.

[64] Fenster, above n 1, 19.

[65] H Lim and J Roche, 'Feminism and Children's Rights', in J Bridgeman and D Monk (eds), *Feminist Perspectives on Child Law* (London, Cavendish Publishing, 2000).

Bibliography

AM Ambert, *Cohabitation and Marriage: How are they Related?* (Ottawa, Vanier Institute of the Family, 2005).

B Anderson, *Imagined Communities: Reflections of the Origins and Spread of Nationalism* (London, Verso, 1991).

R Auchmuty, 'Same-sex Marriage Revived: Feminist Critique and legal Strategy' (2004) 14 *Feminism & Psychology* 101.

N Bamforth, 'Same-sex Partnerships and Arguments of Justice', in R Wintemute and M Andenas (eds), *Legal Recognition of Same-sex Partnerships: A Study of National, European and International Law* (Oxford, Hart Publishing, 2001).

N Barker, 'Sex and the Civil Partnership Act: The Future of (Non)Conjugality?' (2006) 14 *Feminist Legal Studies* 241.

A Barlow, 'Regulation of Cohabitation, Changing Family Policies and Social Attitudes: A Discussion of Britain within Europe' (2004) 26 *Law and Policy* 57.

——, 'Cohabitation Law Reform—Messages from Research' (2006) 14 *Feminist Legal Studies* 167.

A Barlow, S Duncan, G James and A Park, *Cohabitation, Marriage and the Law: Social Change and Legal Reform in the 21st Century* (Oxford, Hart Publishing, 2005).

C Barton and G Douglas, *Law and Parenthood* (London, Butterworths, 1995).

R Beevers, *The Garden City Utopia: A Critical Biography of Ebenezer Howard* (London, Macmillan, 1988).

L Berlant and M Warner, 'Sex in Public' (1998) 24 *Critical Inquiry* 547.

E Berscheid and LA Peplau, 'The Emerging Science of Relationships', in HH Kelley et al (eds), *Close Relationships* (New York, WH Freeman and Co, 1983).

H Bhaba, 'Introduction: Narrating the Nation', in H Bhaba (ed), *Nation and Narration* (Routledge, London, 1990).

J Birchall, *Building Communities the Co-operative Way* (London, Routledge, 1988).

J Birchall (ed), *The New Mutualism in Public Policy* (London, Routledge, 2001).

K Boele-Woelki et al, *Matrimonial Property Law from a Comparative Law Perspective* (*Huwelijksvermogensrecht in rechtsvergelijkend perspectief*) (2000), *Stichting ter Bevordering der Notariële Wetenschap,* in the Series Ars Notariatus C111 (Deventer, Kluwer, 2000), English translation available at http://www.reading.ac.uk/nmsruntime/saveasdialog.asp?lID=7018&sID=34870.

K Boele-Woelki and A Fuchs (eds), *Legal Recognition of Same-Sex Couples in Europe,* (Antwerp, Intersentia, 2003).

I Borden, 'New Ways of Housekeeping: Social Space and Co-operative Living in the Garden City Movement' (Fall 1999) 1 *Journal of Architectural and Planning Research* 242.

A Bottomley, 'From Mrs. Burns to Mrs. Oxley: Do Co-habiting Women (Still) Need Marriage Law?' (2006) 14 *Feminist Legal Studies* 181.

A Bottomley and S Wong, 'Shared Households: A New Paradigm for Reform of Domestic Property Relations', in A Diduck and K O'Donovan (eds), *Feminist Perspectives on Family Law* (Abingdon, Routledge-Cavendish, 2006).

SB Boyd, 'Family, Law and Sexuality: Feminist Engagements' (1999) 8 *Social and Legal Studies* 369 .

SB Boyd (ed), *Challenging the Public/Private Divide: Feminism, Law & Public Policy* (Toronto, University of Toronto Press, 1997).

SB Boyd and C Young, 'Feminism, Law, and Public Policy: Family Feuds and Taxing Times' (2004) 42 *Osgoode Hall Law Journal* 545.

S Brawley, '"No 'White Policy' in New Zealand": Fact and Fiction in New Zealand's Asian Immigration record, 1946–1978' (April 1993) 27 *New Zealand Journal of History* 16.

M Brenton, *We're in Charge* (London, The Policy Press, 1998).

J Bridgeman and D Monk (eds), *Feminist Perspectives on Child Law* (London, Cavendish Publishing, 2000).

T Brooking and R Rabel, 'Neither British Nor Polynesian: A Brief History of New Zealand's Other Immigrants', in S Grief (ed), *Immigration and National Identity in New Zealand* (Palmerston North, Dunmore, 1995).

LA Buckley, 'Matrimonial Property and Irish Law: A Case for Community? (2002) 53(1) *NILQ* 76.

Hon K Burke, 'Review of Immigration Policy 1986' (Wellington, Government Printer, 1986).

K Busby, 'Common Law Partnerships and Marital Property: Time for a Change?' (2004) 23 *Jurisfemme: News from the National Association of Women and the Law* 2.

J Butler, 'Merely Cultural' (1997/1998) 227 *New Left Review* 33.

——, *Undoing Gender* (New York, Routledge, 2004).

Canada, Department of Finance, Budget Papers, Supplementary Information (February 25, 1992).

——, *Tax Expenditures: Notes to the Estimates/Projections, 2004* (Ottawa, 2004).

——, *Tax Expenditures and Evaluations, 2005* (Ottawa, 2005).

Canada, Department of Finance, 'Legislative Proposals and Explanatory Notes Concerning Specified Investment Flow-through Trusts and Partnerships', available at http://www.fin.gc.ca/drleg/ITA-l_ftt1206e.html .

A Carling, S Duncan and R Edwards (eds), *Analysing Families, Morality and Rationality in Policy and Practice (*London and New York, Routledge, 2002) .

J Carsten, *After Kinship* (Cambridge, Cambridge University Press, 2004).

SA Chambers, 'Heteronormativity and the L Word', in K Akass and J McCabe (eds), *Reading the L Word: Outing Contemporary Television* (London, IB Tauris, 2006).

C Chauvel, 'New Zealand's Unlawful Immigration Policy' (1994) 4 *Australasian Gay and Lesbian Law Journal* 73.

JS Choi, 'Evaluation of Community Planning and Life of Senior CoHousing Projects in Northern European Countries' (2004) 12 *European Planning Studies* 1189.

P Clarke, 'The Family Home: Intention and Agreement' (1992) 22 *Family Law* 22.

H Conway and P Girard, '"No Place like Home": The Search for a Legal Framework for Cohabitants and the Family Home in Canada and Britain' (2004–2005) 30 *Queen's Law Journal* 715.

E Cooke, 'Miller/McFarlane: Law in Search of Discrimination' (2007) 19 *Child and Family Law Quarterly* 98.

E Cooke and A Barlow, 'Community of Property: Some Final Reflections', paper presented to the University of Staffordshire conference, February 2007.

E Cooke, A Barlow and T Callus, *Community of Property: A Regime for England and Wales?* (Bristol, Policy Press, 2006).

D Cooper, *Challenging Diversity, Rethinking Equality and the Value of Difference* (Cambridge, Cambridge University Press, 2004).

B Cossman, 'Family Feuds: Neo-liberal and Neo-conservative Visions of the Reprivatization Project', in B Cossman and J Fudge (eds), *Privatization, Law, and the Challenge to Feminism* (Toronto, University of Toronto Press, 2002).

B Cossman and J Fudge (eds), *Privatization, Law, and the Challenge to Feminism* (Toronto, University of Toronto Press, 2002).

B Cossman and B Ryder, 'What Is Marriage Like? The Irrelevance of Conjugality' (2001) 18 *Canadian Journal of Family Law* 269.

K Crenshaw, 'Mapping the Margins: Intersectionality, Identity Politics and Violence Against Women of Color' (1991) 43 *Stanford Law Review* 1241.

S Cretney, *Elements of Family Law* (London, Sweet & Maxwell, 1987).

——, 'Community of property imposed by judicial decision' (2003) 119 *LQR* 349.

——, *Family Law in the Twentieth Century* (Oxford, Oxford University Press, 2003).

K Croucher, L Hicks and K Jackson, *Housing With Care for Later Life; A literature review* (York, Joseph Rowntree Foundation, 2006).

M Davies, *Asking the Law Question* (Sydney, Law Book Co, 1994).
——, *Delimiting the Law: 'Postmodernism' and the Politics of Law* (Pluto Press, London, 1996).
Department of Trade and Industry, *Final Regulatory Impact Assessment (RIA): Civil Partnership* (London DTI, 2004).
Department of Social Security, *Children Come First, The Government's Proposals on the Maintenance of Children* Cm 1264 (London, HMSO, 1990).
J Dewar, 'The Normal Chaos of Family Law' (1998) 61 *Modern Law Review* 467.
A Diduck, 'Fairness and Justice for All? The House of Lords in *White* v *White* [2000] 2 FLR 981' (2001) 9 *Feminist Legal Studies* 173.
——, 'Rights, Fairness and the Financial Consequences of Partnering and Separating', unpublished paper, 2008.
——, *Law's Families* (London, Butterworths; Cambridge, Cambridge University Press, 2003).
——, 'Shifting Familiarity' (2005) 58 *Current Legal Problems* 235 .
A Diduck and F Kaganas, *Family Law, Gender and the State* (2nd edn, Oxford, Hart Publishing, 2006).
A Diduck and K O'Donovan, 'Feminism and Families: *Plus Ça Change?*', in A Diduck and K O'Donovan (eds), *Feminist Perspectives on Family Law* (Abingdon, Routledge-Cavendish, 2006) .
A Diduck and H Orton, 'Equality and Support for Spouses' (1994) 57 *Modern Law Review* 681.
G Douglas, J Pearce, and H Woodward, *A Failure of Trust: Resolving Property Disputes on Cohabitation Breakdown* (Cardiff, Wales, Cardiff Law School, 2007).
G Douglas and A Perry, 'How Parents Cope Financially on Separation and Divorce—Implications for the Future of Ancillary Relief' (2001) 13 *Child and Family Law Quarterly* 67.
L Duggan, 'The New Homonormativity: The Sexual Politics of Neo-liberalism', in R Castronovo and DD Nelson (eds), *Materializing Democracy: Toward a Revitalized Cultural Politics* (Durham, Duke University Press, 2002).
S Duncan, A Barlow and G James, 'Why Don't They Marry? Cohabitation, Commitment and DIY Marriage' (2005) 17(3) *Child and Family Law Quarterly* 383 .
GA Dunne, 'A Passion for "Sameness"? Sexuality and Gender Accountability', in EB Silva and C Smart (eds), *The New Family?* (London, Sage, 1999) .
M Eaton, 'Lesbians, Gays and the Struggle for Equality Rights: Reversing the Progressive Hypothesis' (1994) 17 *Dalhousie Law Journal* 130.
J Eekelaar, 'Asset Distribution on Divorce—Time and Property' (2003) 33 *Family Law Journal* 828.
——, 'Property and Financial Sharing on Divorce—Sharing and Compensating' (2006) 36 *Family Law Journal* 753 .
J Eekelaar and M Maclean, 'Marriage and the Moral Bases of Personal Relationships' (2004) 31 *Journal of Law and Society* 510 .
ESRC, *ESRC Society Today—Welfare and Single Parenthood in the UK Fact Sheet* (2005).
European Commission, *Green Paper on Matrimonial Property Regimes,* COM (2006) 400.
M Fenster, 'Community by Covenant, Process and Design: CoHousing and the Contemporary Common Interest Community' (1999) *Journal of Land Use & Environmental Law* 1.
L Ferguson, 'Family, Social Inequalities and the Persuasive Force of Interpersonal Obligation' (2008) 22 *International Journal of Law Policy and the Family* 61.
M Field, *Thinking about CoHousing* (London, Diggers & Dreamers, 2004).
J Finch, *Family Obligations and Social Change* (Cambridge, Polity, 1989).
J Finch and J Mason, *Negotiating Family Responsibilities* (London, Tavistock/Routledge, 1993).
——, *Passing On: Kinship and Inheritance in England* (London, Routledge, 2000).
R Fine, `Europe and Antisemitism: Whither Postnationalism?', University of Warwick, unpublished paper, 2008.
MA Fineman, *The Autonomy Myth: A Theory of Dependency* (New York, The New Press, 2004).
M Foucault, *The History of Sexuality*, vol 1 (London, Allen Lane, 1979) .
K Franke, 'The Domesticated Liberty of *Lawrence v Texas*' (2004) 104 *Columbia Law Review* 1399.
N Fraser, 'Social Justice in the Age of Identity Politics: Redistribution, Recognition and Partici-

pation', in N Fraser and A Honeth (eds), *Redistribution or Recognition? A Political-Philosophical Exchange* (London, New York, Verso, 2003).
——, 'Reframing Justice in a Globalizing World' (2005a) 36 *New Left Review* 69.
——, 'Mapping the Feminist Imagination: From Redistribution to Recognition to Representation' (2005b) 12 *Constellations* 295.
D Fromm, *Collaborative Communities: CoHousing, Central Living and Other Forms of New Housing with Shared Facilities* (New York, Van Nostrad Reinhold, 1991).
S Gardner, 'Rethinking Family Property' (1993) 109 *Law Quarterly Review* 263.
S Gavigan, 'Equal Families, Equal Parents, Equal Spouses, Equal Marriage: The Case of the Missing Patriarch' (2006) 33 *Supreme Court Law Review* (2d) 317.
CS Gibson, *Dissolving Wedlock* (London, Routledge, 1994).
BG Glasyer and AL Strauss, *The Discovery of Grounded Theory* (Chicago, Aldine de Gruyter, 1967).
N Glover and P Todd, 'The Myth of Common Intention' (1996) 16 *Legal Studies* 325.
R Graycar and J Millbank, 'The Bride Wore Pink ... to the Property (Relationships) Legislation Amendment Act 1999: Relationships Law Reform in New South Wales' (2000) 17 *Canadian Journal of Family Law* 227.
P Hall and C Ward, *Sociable Cities: The Legacy of Ebenezer Howard* (London, Wiley, 1998).
D Hardy, *Alternative Communities in Nineteenth Century England* (London, Longman, 1979).
AP Harris, 'Comment: Seductions of Modern Culture' (1996) 8 *Yale Journal of Law and Humanities* 213.
S Harris-Short, 'Family Law and the Human Rights Act 1998: Judicial Restraint or Revolution?' (2005) 17(3) *Child and Family Law Quarterly* 329.
JFC Harrison, *Robert Owen and the Owenite Communities in Britain and America* (Oxford, Oxford University Press, 1969).
J Haskey, 'Cohabitation in Great Britain: Past, Present and Future Trends—and Attitudes' (2002) 103 *Popular Trends* 4.
——, 'Living Arrangements in Contemporary Britain: Having a Partner who Usually Lives Elsewhere and Living Apart Together (LAT)' (2005) 122 *Population Trends* 35.
J Haskey and J Lewis, 'Living Apart-together in Britain: Context and Meaning' (2006) 2 *International Journal of Law in Context* 37.
J Herring, 'Why Financial Orders on Divorce Should be Unfair' (2005) 19 *International Journal of Law, Policy and the Family* 218.
M Holt, '"Marriage-like" or Married? Lesbian and Gay Marriage, Partnership and Migration' (2004) 14 *Feminism & Psychology* 30.
G Holyoak, *The History of Co-operation* (London, Fisher Unwin, 1906).
Housing, Family and Social Statistics Division, 'Women in Canada: Work Chapter Updates' (Ottawa: Statistics Canada, 2004) available at http://www.statcan.ca/english/freepub/89F0133 XIE/89F01 33XIE2003000.pdf .
E Howard, *Tomorrow: A Peaceful Path to Real Reform* (London, Swann Sonnerschein, 1898).
——, *Garden Cities of Tomorrow* (London, Swann Sonnerschein, 1902).
K Hull, *Same-Sex Marriage: The Cultural Politics of Love and Law* (Cambridge, Cambridge University Press, 2006).
S Irwin, 'Interdependencies, Values and the Reshaping of Difference: Gender and Generation at the Birth of Twentieth Century Modernity' (2003) 54 *British Journal of Sociology* 565 .
A Jagose, *Queer Theory* (Dunedin, University of Otago Press, 1996).
L Jamieson, 'Intimacy Transformed? A Critical Look at the "Pure Relationship"' (1999) 33 *Sociology* 477.
L Jamieson, M Anderson, D McCrone, F Bechhofer, R Stewart and Y Li, 'Cohabitation and Commitment: Partnership Plans of Young Men and Women' (2002) 50 *Sociological Review* 356 .
S Jeffreys, 'The Need to Abolish Marriage' (2004) 14 *Feminism and Psychology* 327.
O Kahn-Freund, 'Inconsistencies and Injustices in the Law of Husband and Wife' (1952) 15 *Modern Law Review* 133.
W Kasper, 'Populate or Languish? Rethinking New Zealand's Immigration Policy' (Auckland, New Zealand Business Roundtable, 1990).
HH Kelley, 'Love and Commitment', in HH Kelley et al (eds), *Close Relationships* (New York, WH Freeman and Co, 1983).

C Kitzinger and S Wilkinson, 'The Re-branding of Marriage: Why We Got Married Instead of Registering a Civil Partnership' (2004) 14 *Feminism and Psychology* 127.
W Lafferty, *Sustainable Communities in Europe* (London, Earthscan, 2001).
Law Commission, *Financial Provision in Matrimonial Proceedings* (Law Com No 25, 1969).
——, *Family Property Law Working Paper No 42* (London, HMSO, 1971).
——, *First Report on Family Property: A New Approach* (Law Com No 52, 1973).
——, *Third Report on Family Property: The Matrimonial Home Co-ownership and Occupation Rights and Household Goods*, Law Com No 86 (London, HMSO, 1978).
——, *Sharing Homes: A Discussion Paper* (Law Com No 278, Cm 5666, 2002).
——, *Cohabitation: The Financial Consequences of Relationships Breakdown* (Law Com Consultation Paper No 179, 2006).
——, *Cohabitation: The Financial Consequences of Relationship Breakdown* (Law Com No 307, Cm 7182, 2007).
——, *Cohabitation: The Financial Consequences of Relationship Breakdown Law Com No 307 Executive Summary* (London, Law Commission, 2007).
Law Commission of Canada, *Beyond Conjugality: Recognizing and Supporting Close Personal and Adult Relationships* (Ottawa, 2001).
Law Society, *Cohabitation: The Case for Clear Law* (2002).
J Law, *After Method: Mess in Social Science Research* (London, Routledge, 2004).
SJ Lenon, 'Marrying Citizens! Raced Subjects/Re-thinking the Terrain of Equal Marriage Discourse' (2005) 17 *Canadian journal of Women and Law* 405.
H Lessard, 'Charter Gridlock: Equality Formalism and Marriage Fundamentalism' (2006) 33 *Supreme Court Law Review* (2d) 291.
A Lewin, *Housing Co-operatives in Developing Countries* (London, Wiley, 1981).
E Lewin, *Recognizing Ourselves: Ceremonies of Lesbian and Gay Commitment* (New York, Columbia University Press, 1998).
J Lewis, *The End of Marriage? Individualism and Intimate Relationships* (Cheltenham, Edward Elgar, 2001).
——, 'Perceptions of Risk in Intimate Relationships: The Implications for Social Provision' (2005) 35 *Journal of Social Policy* 39.
H Lim and J Roche, 'Feminism and Children's Rights', in J Bridgeman and D Monk (eds), *Feminist Perspectives on Child Law* (London, Cavendish Publishing, 2000).
F MacCarthy, *William Morris: A Life for Our Times* (London, Faber and Faber, 1994).
T MacCharles, 'It's Not the Same as Being Married' [20 Dec 2002] *Toronto Star* A1.
JA Mackenzie and M Philips, *Textbook on Land Law* (11th ed, Oxford, Oxford University Press, 2006).
K Makin, 'Common-law Property Rights Denied' [20 Dec 2002] *Globe and Mail* A1.
M Maloney, 'What is the Appropriate Tax Unit for the 1990s and Beyond?', in A Maslove (ed), *Issues in the Taxation of Individuals* (Toronto, University of Toronto Press and the Ontario Fair Tax Commission, 1994).
D Martiny, 'A Matrimonial Property System for the European Union?', paper presented to the UK–German Judicial Family Law Conference, 8–11 September 2004, Cardiff.
J Mason, 'Tangible Affinities and the Real Life Fascination of Kinship' (2008) 42 *Sociology* 29.
M McKinnon, *Immigrants and Citizens: New Zealanders and Asian Immigration in Historical Context* (Wellington, Victoria University Institute of Policy Studies, 1996).
J Miles, 'Principles or Pragmatism in Ancillary Relief; The Virtues of Flirting with Academic Theories and Other Jurisdictions.' (2005) 19 *IJLF* 242.
J Millbank, 'Gender, Sex and Visibility in Refugee Decisions on Sexual Orientation' (2003) 18 *Georgetown Immigration Law Journa*l 71.
J Millbank and C Dauverge, 'Burdened by Proof: How the Australian Refugee Review Tribunal has Failed Lesbian and Gay Asylum Seekers' (2003) 31 Federal Law Review 299.
J Milllbank and K Sant, 'A Bride in Her Everyday Clothes: Same Sex Relationship Recognition in NSW' (2000) 22 *Sydney Law Review* 181.
J Millbank and W Morgan, 'Let Them Eat Cake and Ice Cream: Wanting Something "More" from the Relationship Recognition Menu', in R Wintemute and M Andenas (eds), *Legal Recognition of Same-sex Partnerships: A Study of National, European and International Law* (Oxford, Hart Publishing, 2001).
M Miller, *Raymond Unwin: Garden Cities and Town Planning* (Leicester, Leicester University Press, 1992).

——, *Letchworth:The First Garden City* (Chichester, Phillimore, 2002).

M Minow and ML Shanley, 'Relational Rights and Responsibilities: Revisioning the Family in Liberal Political Theory and Law' (1996) 11 *Hypatia* 4 .

D Morgan, *Family Connections* (Cambridge, Polity Press, 1996).

MJ Mossman and M MacLean, 'Family Law and Social Assistance Programs: Rethinking Equality', in P Evans and G Wekerle (eds), *Women and the Canadian Welfare State* (Toronto, University of Toronto Press, 1997) .

N Naffine, *Law and the Sexes: Explorations in Feminist Jurisprudence* (Sydney, Allen & Unwin, 1990).

National Statistics, *Living in Britain: The 2002 General Household Survey* (London, TSO, 2004).

——, *Birth Statistics: Review of the Registrar General on Births and Patterns of Family Building in England and Wales, 2002*. Series FM1, no 31 (London, TSO, 2004).

New Zealand Ministry of Justice, 'Same-Sex Couples and the Law: Backgrounding the Issues' (Wellington, 1999).

New Zealand Department of Labour, 'New Zealand Immigration Instructions' (Wellington, 1991).

——, 'Trends in Residence Approvals 2002/2003' (Wellington, September 2003).

——, 'Migration Trends 2003/2004' (Wellington, Immigration Service, Immigration Research Programme, 2004).

——, 'Immigration Trends 2004/2005' (Wellington, December 2005).

——, 'Immigration Act Review: Discussion Paper' (April 2006).

New Zealand Immigration Service, 'Operation Manual: Residence' (Wellington, Department of Labour, 2005).

——, *Operational Manual* (30 July 2007).

M Nussbaum, 'Capabilities as Fundamental Entitlements: Sen and Social Justice', paper delivered at the London School of Economics, 13 March 2002.

Ontario Fair Tax Commission, Women and Tax Working Group, *Women and Taxation* (Toronto: Ontario Fair Tax Commission, 1992).

M Orton, 'Common law? Learn the Rules' [6 April 2003] *Ottawa Citizen* D1.

G Orwell, *The Road to Wigan Pier* (London, Penguin, 1962).

A Oswald, 'The Housing Market and Europe's Unemployment', Warwick University, 1999 available at http://www2.warwick.ac.uk/fac/soc/economics/staff/faculty/oswald/homesnt.pdf.

N Oswin, 'Producing Homonormativity in Neoliberal South Africa: Recognition, Redistribution and the Equality Project' (2007) 32 *Signs: Journal of Women in Culture and Society* 650.

J Pahl, 'Individualisation in Couple Finances: Who Pays for the Children?' (2005) 4(4) *Social Policy and Society* 381.

R Pahl and L Spencer, 'Personal Communities: Not Simply Families of "Fate" or "Choice"' (2004) 52 *Current Sociology* 199.

L Pearson, *The Architectural and Social History of Co-operative Living* (London, Macmillan, 1988).

LA Peplau, 'Roles and Gender', in HH Kelley, E Berscheid, A Christensen, JH Harvey, TL Huston, G Levinger, E McClintock, LA Peplau and DR Peterson (eds), *Close Relationships* (New York, WH Freeman and Co, 1983).

L Philipps, 'Tax Law and Social Reproduction: The Gender of Fiscal Policy in an Age of Privatization', in B Cossman and J Fudge (eds), *Privatization, Law and the Challenge to Feminism* (Toronto, University of Toronto Press, 2002).

C Pickering, E Parry, K Jinkins, K and A Jolliffe, *A Different Way of Living: CoHousing for Older Women* (London, The Housing Corporation, 2004).

C Powell and M Van Vugt, 'Genuine Giving or Selfish Sacrifice? The Role of Commitment and Cost Level upon Willingness to Sacrifice' (2003) 33 *European Journal of Social Psychology* 403.

JK Puar, 'Mapping US Homonormativities' (2006) 13 *Gender, Place and Culture* 67.

H Reece, *Divorcing Responsibly* (Oxford, Hart Publishing, 2003).

A Reid, *Brentham: A History of the Pioneer Garden Suburb* (London, Brentham Historical Society, 2000).

M Richards, 'Genes, Genealogies and Paternity: Making Babies in the Twenty-first Century', in JR Spencer and A du Bois-Pedain (eds), *Freedom and Responsibility in Reproductive Choice* (Oxford, Hart Publishing, 2006).

DW Riggs, 'Reassessing the Foster-Care System: Examining the Impact of Heterosexism on Lesbian and Gay Applicants' (2007) 22 *Hypatia* 132.

R Robson, 'Mother: The Legal Domestication of Lesbian Existence' (1992) 7 *Hypatia* 172.

——, 'Assimilation, Marriage and Lesbian Liberation' (2002) 75 *Temple Law Review* 709.

D Rodgers, 'Housing Co-operatives and Social Exclusion', in J Birchall (ed), *The New Mutualism in Public Policy* (London, Routledge, 2001).

C Rogerson and R Thompson, 'Spousal Support Advisory Guidelines: A Draft Proposal' (Toronto, University of Toronto, 2005) available at http://canada.justice.gc.ca/eng/dept-min/pub/ss-pae/proj/ssag-idpa.pdf .

N Rose, *Inventing Our Selves: Psychology, Power, and Personhood* (Cambridge, Cambridge University Press, 1996).

S Rowbotham, *Edward Carpenter: A Life of Liberty and Love* (London, Verso, 2008).

Royal Commission on the Status of Women in Canada, *Report* (Ottawa: Information Canada, 1970).

D Ryken, 'Immigration Rights for Cohabitees in New Zealand' (March 2004) 18 *International Family Law Journal* 1.

——, 'Skilled Migrant Category: Skilled Migrants', in *Immigration Law 2007*, LexisNexis Professional Development (Auckland, June 2007).

J Scherpe, 'Matrimonial Causes for Concern: A Comparative Analysis of Miller v Miller; McFarlane v McFarlane' (2007) 18 *King's Law Journal* 348.

C Scotthanson and K Scotthanson, *The Cohousing Handbook; Building a Place for Community* (Gabriola Island, Canada, New Society Publishers, 2005).

S Seuffert, 'Sexual Citizenship and the *Civil Union Act* 2004' (2006) 37 *Victoria University of Wellington Law Review* 281.

——, *Jurisprudence of National Identity* (Aldershot, Ashgate, 2006).

S Sheldon, 'Reproductive Technologies and the Legal Determination of Fatherhood' (2005) 13 *Feminist Legal Studies* 349.

B Shipman and C Smart, '"It's Made a Huge Difference": Recognition, Rights and the Personal Significance of Civil Partnership' (2007) 22 *Sociological Research Online*, January 2007.

KB Silbaugh, 'The Practice of Marriage' (2005) 20 *Wisconsin Women's Law Journal* 189.

I Skelton, 'Supporting Identity and Needs: The Many Faces of Co-op Housing' (2002), available through http://www.irrt.org.uk.

L Spencer and R Pahl, *Rethinking Friendship: Hidden Solidarities Today* (Oxford, Princeton University Press, 2006).

C Smart, *The Ties That Bind: Law, Marriage and the Reproduction of Patriarchal Relations* (London, Routledge and Kegan Paul, 1984).

C Smart, 'There Is Of Course the Distinction Dictated by Nature: Law and the Problem of Paternity', in M Stanworth (ed), *Reproductive Technologies* (Cambridge, Polity Press, 1997).

C Smart, 'Stories of Family Life: Cohabitation, Marriage and Social Change' (2000) 17 *Canadian Journal of Family Law* 20.

C Smart, *Personal Life: New Directions in Sociological Thinking* (Cambridge, Polity Press, 2007).

C Smart, 'Same Sex Couples and Marriage: Negotiating Relational Landscapes with Families and Friends' (2007) 55 *Sociological Review* 687.

C Smart and B Neale, *Family Fragments?* (Cambridge, Polity Press, 1999).

Statistics Canada, 'Analysing Family Income' available at http://www12.statcan.ca/english/census01/products/analytic/companion/inc/canada.cfm#4 .

——, 'Analysing Family Income', (3 March 2004) available at http://www.12.statcan.ca/english/census01/products/analytic/companion/inc/canada.cfm#14 .

——, *Changing Conjugal Life in Canada* (Ottawa, Statistics Canada, Housing, Family and Social Statistics Division, 2002, Catalogue No 89-576-XIE).

——, 'Divorces', *The Daily* (4 May 2004) available at http://www.statcan.ca/Daily/English/040504/d040504a.htm.

——, *Earnings of Canadians: Making a Living in the New Economy* (Ottawa, Statistics Canada, 2003).

——, *Family Portrait: Continuity and Change in Canadian Families and Households in 2006: Findings* (Ottawa, Statistics Canada, 2007).
Statistics New Zealand, '1996 Census of Populations and Dwellings: Ethnic Groups' (Wellington, 1996).
B Stewart, 'New Zealand Immigration Law and Gay and Lesbian Couples' (1993) 3 *Australasian Gay and Lesbian Journal* 30.
C Stychin, *A Nation by Rights* (Philadelphia, Temple University Press, 1998).
——, *Governing Sexuality* (Oxford, Hart Publishing, 2003).
——, 'Couplings: Civil partnership in the United Kingdom' (2005) 8 *NY City Law Review* 543.
——, 'Family Friendly? Rights, Responsibilities and Relationship Recognition', in A Diduck and K O'Donovan (eds), *Feminist Perspectives on Family Law* (London, Routledge-Cavendish, 2006) .
B Taylor, *Eve and The New Jerusalem* (Cambridge, Harvard University Press, 1983).
D Tennant, 'The Contribution of the New Zealand Refugee Status Appeals Authority to International Refugee Jurisprudence' (undated manuscript).
M Thornton (ed), *Public and Private: Feminist Legal Debates* (Melbourne, Oxford University Press, 1995).
J Tibbetts, 'Common Law not Equal to Marriage: Unmarried Couples Denied Right to 50/50 Asset Split' [20 Dec 2002] *National Post* A1.
DAR Thompson, 'Annotation *Walsh v Nova Scotia*' (2002) 32 RFL (5th) 81.
J Tronto, *Moral Boundaries* (London, Routledge, 1993).
UK Lesbian and Gay Immigration Group, 'Civil Partnership—Immigration Guide', available at http://www.uklgig.org.uk.
——, 'Annual Report 2007' 17–18, available at www.uklgig.org.uk.
R Vanita, *Love's Rite: Same Sex Marriage in India and the West* (Gordonsville, VA, Palgrave Macmillan, 2005).
E Vansittart Neale, 'Associated Homes', (1872) 2(4) *Co-operative News* 37.
C Vogler, 'Cohabiting Couples: Rethinking Money in the Household at the Beginning of the Twenty First Century' (2005) 53 *Sociological Review* 1.
C Vogler and J Pahl, 'Money, Power and Inequality within Marriage' (1994) *Sociological Review* 263.
M Warner, 'Introduction: Fear of a Queer Planet' (1991) 29 *Social Text* 3.
J Weeks, 'Elective Families: Lesbian and Gay Life Experiments', in A Carling, S Duncan and R Edwards (eds), *Analysing Families, Morality and Rationality in Policy and Practice* (London and New York, Routledge, 2002) .
J Weeks, B Heaphy and C Donovan, *Same Sex Intimacies: Families of Choice and Other Life Experiments* (London, Routledge, 2001).
K Weston, *Families We Choose: Lesbians, Gays, Kinship* (2nd edn, New York, Columbia University Press, 1997).
C Wiggins, 'Women's Work: Challenging and Changing the World', research paper prepared for the 2003 Canadian Labour Congress Women's Conference, May 2003, available at http://canadianlabour.ca/index.php/Women/548 .
J Williams, 'Sun, Surf and Sustainable Housing—CoHousing, the California Experience' (2005) 10 *International Planning Studies* 145.
G Wilson, 'Financial Provision in Civil Partnerships' (2007) 37 *Family Law Journal* 31.
S Wong, 'Constructive Trusts over the Family Home: Lessons to be Learned From Other Commonwealth Jurisdictions?' (1998) 18 *Legal Studies* 369.
——, 'Property Regimes for Home-sharers: The Civil Partnership Bill and Some Antipodean Models' (2004) 26 *Journal of Social Welfare and Family Law* 362.
——, 'The Human Rights Act 1998 and the Shared Home: Issues for Cohabitants' (2005) 27 *Journal of Social Welfare and Family Law* 265.
——, 'Response to the Law Commission Consultation Paper No 179 "Cohabitation: The Financial Consequences of Relationship Breakdown"' (2006), unpublished paper.
——, 'The Shared Home: A Rational Solution Through Statutory Reform?', in H Lim and A Bottomley (eds), *Feminist Perspectives on Land Law* (Abingdon, Routledge-Cavendish, 2007).
C Young, *What's Sex Got To Do With It? Tax and the Family* (Ottawa, Law Commission of Canada, 2000).

CFL Young, 'Taxing Times for Lesbians and Gay Men: Equality at What Cost?' (1994) 17 *Dalhousie Law Journal* 534.

——, 'Spousal Status, Pension Benefits and Tax: *Rosenberg v Canada (Attorney-General)*' (1998) 6 *Canadian Labour and Employment Law Journal* 435.

C Young and SB Boyd, 'Losing the Feminist Voice? Debates on the Legal Recognition of Same Sex Partnerships in Canada' (2006) 14 *Feminist Legal Studies* 213.

Index